WORDS MATTER

D0170815

WORDS MATTER

Writing to
Make a Difference

Edited by

Amanda Dahling

and

Mary Kay Blakely

UNIVERSITY OF MISSOURI PRESS

Columbia

ISBN: 978-0-8262-2089-9
Library of Congress Control Number: 2015960027

♾™ This paper meets the requirements of the
American National Standard for Permanence of Paper
for Printed Library Materials, Z39.48, 1984.

Typeface: Minion Pro

For permissions, see pp. 347–348

CONTENTS

FOREWORD
The Journey of Writing

Amanda Dahling

Writers are not born great. There is no writing gene or innate knowledge of the skills that lead to talented and impressive prose. Nor is there one clear path to achieving such skills. Writers are cultivated through passion for the work and fertilized by each and every mistake, misprint, and misinterpretation. With years of practice, influence, and mediocrity, they make their way through the cruel and painstaking task of becoming worthy. Worthy of reader approval, a good grade, publication, praise, awards, and trust among audiences and sources alike. Becoming a great writer is a journey, and no one starts at the finish line.

The writers in this book have written in varied forms throughout their careers, backpacking their way through this journey with varied inspirations, paths, and resources, and now they find themselves at different destinations. Along the way, their paths led them for a time to the University of Missouri School of Journalism, where they equipped themselves with tools for the road. Although their differences are vast, it is obvious that they have shared not only their time at Mizzou but also a common writer experience, an ever-changing one that requires creativity, ingenuity, and hard work just to keep up. Regardless of the paths each writer chooses, the media are fraught with new styles, new ways to tell a story, and a continual influx of new talent. Exciting? Definitely. Daunting? Assuredly.

This book is arranged in three broad categories: profiles, first-person journalism, and personal memoirs. Following each piece, the contributors discuss what they've learned about writing, journalism, getting published, and making a name for oneself.

Becoming a writer or being a writer who is looking for a change can be really scary, but there is a community out there, and no one has to travel alone. Read great pieces. Read average pieces. Read everything. And read some more. There's a lot of scenery to be relished on a writer's journey, along with a lot of pit stops and out-of-the-way tourist attractions. Take the detours. It's in those moments that you might pick up a story that forever changes how you write or how you view the world. That job that isn't exactly what you're looking for might offer the chance of a lifetime. Take in the scenery, and find inspiration in those who have traveled the path before you.

Inspiration is a funny thing, because we're often inspired by the untouchable. Big names, whose paths and careers seem like a fairy tale, a dream we can never hope to reach. But when you move beyond those easy targets, you find something even better than mere inspiration: possibility. This book is filled with amazing writers, the names of whom you may or may not know, including Pulitzer Prize winners, authors, professors, freelancers, and more. What makes this collection so special is its relatability. You are these writers, and these writers are you. They're not pushing grandiose ideas about writing and journalism, instead they offer their own experiences, so that you might smile, cringe, laugh along, and, most important, set out to share your own.

This book might be labeled an educational textbook on writing, and it offers plenty to learn, for writers old and new. But make no mistake, it's not a tome. It's neither a boring nor a brazen lecture on journalism, where it's been and where it's going. Rather it's a companion on your journey. These writers are your new road-trip buddies, here to ride shotgun and direct you off the beaten path to one where the scenery is far more mesmerizing.

Through their journalistic contributions here and their words of wisdom about their trade, these writers share what they've learned along the way. Maybe their journeys will offer a road map for yours. 🪷

ACKNOWLEDGMENTS

M.K. Blakely

This book grew from a vague idea after many long-distance conversations with former students, who often tracked me down to get answers to a few questions, mainly whether "this writing thing" was worth all the time and stress. Then they'd send links to their stories and articles, and it was clear why they were writers: They all had something important to say. At the outset, none of us imagined it would take six years and endless correspondence before we'd have a book we could actually hold in our hands. Due dates were constantly renegotiated to accommodate multiple other obligations, as you can imagine: One or another was on a job deadline or getting married or having a baby or draining communication batteries on the other side of the globe. But the commitment of the 26 writers between these covers never flagged, along with countless other talented journalists, editors, and advisors who labored with us. There were times it was hard to believe we'd reach the finish line, or that there even *was* a finish line. We finally did, with a lot of help from our friends.Most graduates of the Journalism School call themselves the "Mizzou Mafia." I get what they mean, extreme loyalty and allegiance and all that. Like veterans of the same boot camp, they're mightily committed to their work and each other. But as I've said again and again, the name is unfortunate. (I've spent too many years living in New York City, where "Mizzou Mafia" prompts images of feet being planted in cement. They laugh, as if I'm so yesterday… and I suppose I am.) Their generosity, candor and wit—with each other and with me—were the currents we traveled since this work began. I'm truly going to miss them.

Colleagues and friends at the J-School provided incredible support, particularly professors Steve Weinberg, Jan Colbert, Jennifer Rowe, Jacqui Banaszynski, Michael Grinfeld, John Fennell, Berkley Hudson, Don Ranly, Danita Allen, Heather Lamb, Katherine Reed, Greg Bowers, Mike McKean, Stacey Woelfel, and Dean Dave Kurpius. If not for the initial financial and intellectual support from Dean Emeritus R. Mills, this anthology would not exist.

Professors in the English Department—Nancy West, Julija Sukyo, Alexandra Socarides and Maureen Stanton—elevated journalism prose with literary voice and style. Professors in the College of Human and Environmental Sciences provided important research on how we live now, including new ways to think about exercise, diet, clothing, shelter and finances: Chris Hardin, Pam Norum, Ruth Tofle, and Catherine Peterson. KBIA assistant producer Sara Shahriari and MU photographer Shane Epping, besides editing their own passionate essays included herein, offered ideas and help with the marketing plan.

MU administrators kept us working against all odds: Professor Michael O'Brien, Dean of Arts and Science; Stephen Jorgensen, Dean Emeritus of the College of Human Environmental Sciences; and Interim Dean Sandy Rikoon. Special thanks to Professor Amy Lannin, Director of the Campus Writing Program, and her associates Professor Bonita Selting and Jonathan Cisco for their enduring interest and many productive brainstorms.

A team of remarkable graduate and undergraduate assistants worked far beyond expectations, burning nightlights while they tracked down lost addresses, researched tough questions, ran innumerable errands, fact-checked titles and names, and copied reams of manuscripts. Jeff Ingliss, Robin Jones Canalis, Callie Fromme, Kristen Hare, Emily Cashman, Danny Ramey, and Dalton Quick passed the baton to one another. The magazine office's dependable administrator and guru, Kim Townlain, kept both the right *and* left sides of our brains functioning while ushering us through six years of expense reports and institutional peculiarities—without ever, ever, losing her temper.

It would take a very long time and a whole lot of space to fully acknowledge how much I've enjoyed—how much I've loved, actually—the last two years of working with my superb editorial team: Amanda Dahling, Ginger Hervey, Marek Makowski, and Robyn Seale. We met weekly in the final months, editing and rewriting and quelling panic attacks. Long after their contracts expired and classes were over, they were still on the job. By then, they'd become part of the book itself. While I was consumed by other deadlines, they did all the heavy lifting to keep it on track. I'll never write enough letters to satisfy my debt to them.

Despite many fractious deadlines, negotiations, marketing problems, and final text preparation, the staff at University of Missouri Press worked with us 24/7 and were uniformly helpful. Director David Rosenbaum saved this book from oblivion by finding a "common theme." Although these writers work for different publications and address different audiences, they have one thing in common: Each cares about producing great writing. Many thanks to Mary Conley and Sara Davis, not only for overseeing the legal and editorial Must Do's, but also for their sublime patience while we did the Do's. Marketing director Stephanie Williams was the reward for having Done them. Her enthusiasm for this work was contagious.

If my gratitude to colleagues seems hyperbolic, please know: I could go on and on. This is the "too numerous to mention" section of every book acknowledgment, and I know I'll be sorry tomorrow when I remember more acts of kindness. It's been my privilege to have friends who sustain and inspire me: Dawn Fallik, Pat Smith, Amy McCombs, Marty Townsend, Suzanne Burgoyne, Heather Carver, Mary McNamara, KC Cole, Carrie Tuhy, Patricia O'Toole, Allison Cohen, Phyllis Wender … and so many more.

Wow. I must be taking a whole lot of people for granted, or I'd be writing every day to say how grateful I am for having them in my life. And in my work. Not only have they made six stressful years fly by, they also provided enough levity and gravity to keep me laughing and grounded.

Amanda Dahling

What a whirlwind this project has been! Without Mary Kay Blakely, *Words Matter* never would have happened. Without Mary Kay, there are lots of things that might never have happened. She's an inspiration for so many of us writers, editors and thinkers. For this project, she took a crazy, daunting idea and didn't let it die. I am grateful and indebted to her always for bringing me along for the ride.

Throughout the long process of making this book a reality, there have been many people behind-the-scenes helping make it happen. In my personal journey with this book, I'd like to send many thanks to those who offered me massive amounts of guidance and assistance as this book morphed from part of a master's project to a bound anthology: Jennifer Rowe, Dr. Amanda Hinnant, Walt Harrington, Mike Sager, Sid Holt, Wendy Call, George Kennedy, Martha Pickens and Kim Townlain.

The logistics of a book with so many moving pieces would have been insurmountable without the efforts of Ginger Hervey and Marek Markowski. There were times I could have and probably should have panicked about the task ahead of us, but Ginger and Marek were always there to offer a helping hand or another look at something. They've been the unsung heroes of this work.

But there would be no anthology without the brilliant writers showcased within its pages. Sincere gratitude goes to all of them for their patience and persistence as we continually went back to them again and again requesting revisions, signatures, contracts, answers to questions, bios and more in a seemingly endless list of needs. Their excitement and willingness to contribute were infectious throughout.

This book crossed paths with many people throughout its inception and completion. Huge thanks to those who've contributed from the beginning: Danny Ramey, Allison Cohen, Robyn Seale, Steve Weinberg, Sandy Davidson, David Rosenbaum, Mary Conley, Sara Davis, Kelsey Hurwitz and to all those I might be forgetting or that I might not even realize had an influence on this work.

And finally, I have to take a moment to thank both of my parents, Keith and Geri Dahling. They both passed away during the lifespan of this project, but my gratitude to them will forever carry me forward. Among all of the life lessons and experience they shared, my parents are largely responsible for my involvement in this wonderful book: My father helped me realize that journalism school might be where I belonged, and my mother instilled in me a love for language and books; she was the first person who taught me to respect words because they matter.

WORDS MATTER

INTRODUCTION

Mary Kay Blakely

After a bruising wrestling match during his senior year in high school, my son Ryan was mightily pleased that his team had defeated their top-ranked Connecticut rivals: "I *knew* we could beat those fucking fags from Darien." Almost immediately he heard the locker room phrase as it sounded in my ears and quickly apologized. Not for using the first F-word—"fuck" had become such a common expletive by 1991 that it resounded more than a hundred times in the movie *The Last Boy Scout*. By then it had penetrated corporate boardrooms, academic discourse, Oval Office briefings, perhaps even conversations in the royal family. It was the second F-word he was sorry about, knowing how deeply offensive it was to me. He said it didn't mean anything. "It was army"—just a meaningless word the guys used with each other. That afternoon in the car, I launched into another lecture about why words matter so much to me.

"Words are only language—only the stuff we think with," I said. "Words reveal what we value, what we respect, what we care about and what we don't. Words are never meaningless." Both of my sons were familiar with my thoughts on language, since I was a writer who began covering social issues in the local newspaper soon after they were born. In fact, I often included stories from their childhood in my op-ed columns because whenever I asked myself "how do you know this?" I'd come back to early explorations with my sons. Motherhood taught me most of what I needed to understand about life. As Annie Dillard and Virginia Woolf both explained this vocation, I write to find out what I think.

Writers have only words to influence people, personally and cultural-ly. Fortunately, words are usually more effective than weapons or phys-ical assaults, which can temporarily change behavior but rarely change minds. (Of course, propagandists and advertisers can influence behavior with words too, but if they withhold critical information about tobacco or internment camps or medicine, more wordsmiths will emerge and reveal it.) When my sons were still toddlers, I discovered that if I wanted them to adopt certain habits—hang up wet towels after baths, put milk back in the refrigerator, look both ways before crossing a street—they had to know *why* they needed to do those things.

Spankings could produce behavior changes more quickly, but only if I was within sight. To ensure that they would be healthy and safe when I wasn't, I had to rely on thoughts inside their own heads. Altering con-sciousness with words instead of punishment took more time and effort but ultimately worked even in my absence. More than two decades have passed since then, and the longer I've thought about our ever-expanding global culture, the more I believe words matter.

Not that writing becomes any easier with time. Author Michelle Hun-even confessed in a keynote address at a national writing conference in Los Angeles in that it took her twenty-two years to finish her first novel. She told her psychologist that she had to quit writing because she lacked confidence and self-esteem, assuming she'd internalized this criticism and disapproval from her parents. The shrink replied, "You can blame a lot on your parents, but not that—that kind of self-doubt and low self-esteem you're describing is just part of the creative process." This was a revelation to Huneven: "Those terrible feelings actually signaled that I was *in* the cre-ative process and not that I was failing at it."

Low self-esteem and self-doubt aren't critical to becoming a successful writer, but inevitably intrude on every ambitious writer's aspirations. The psychological trip from despair to grandiosity can be remarkably swift, however. As a beginning writer, I often doubted *any* editor could improve my work. I was truly lucky that the best ones understood this inflated self-perception and remained patient through my resistance to their help. A mature writer has to become adept at delayed gratification, which is much more difficult now that technology can provide instant gratification. As Huneven notes, "for posting mere snippets, we get liked, retweeted, favorited, shared, tagged, and notified; we get emails and instant messages and invitations to chat online."

My sister Regina is also a writer and shares the same "pickiness with words" that hounds me. She took a writing class a few years ago with author Lee Gutkind, founder of the literary magazine *Creative Nonfiction*, who had a "disarming habit of letting people apologize ad nauseum after reading their work," providing the other writers in class enough time to organize their responses. "He'd just smile in the direction of the babbling author and ask, with a bit of brilliant theater: 'Why are you so insecure?'" The class always laughed, my sister says, since everyone recognized insecurity as an occupational hazard. "Like a head cold, it was a virus with which we were all familiar, and his question was borderline rude but a relief somehow, like the one in a group who just tells the afflicted sniffler to blow his nose." We've all been there, she said, needing a few tissues.

Since most writers get drawn into the profession as readers first, we're strongly influenced by authors we've admired. It's not uncommon to think those published books and essays arrived intact, without a lot of revision and rewriting. It's an enduring myth that only bad writers have to struggle. A former student, Shane Epping—one of the writers included in this volume—sent me a short video featuring Ira Glass, founder of the public radio program *This American Life*. Shane thought I'd enjoy it, and I did. (For anyone inclined to be instantly gratified, here's the link: "Ira Glass on Storytelling," Vimeo, http://vimeo.com/24715531.) I now routinely share it with writing classes and have forwarded it to dozens of experienced writers as well. Glass regrets that nobody tells beginners that for the first few years they're doing creative work, "what you're making isn't so good. . . . It's *trying* to be good, it has *ambition* to be good," but it isn't. Most people experience bitter disappointment when they recognize that what they're creating isn't as good as they want it to be. "But your *taste*—the thing that got you into the game—your taste is still *killer*," Glass says. The most important thing a writer can do "to close that gap, he advises, is to create "*a huge volume of work.*" If you want to make your work as good as your ambition aspires, you can't quit. Glass admits that he struggled for *years* and assures beginners that it's entirely normal to experience disappointment. "You just have to fight your way though that, okay?"

I didn't have much faith that my talk in the car with my son would make a deep impression on him. For one thing, it occurred smack in the middle of the mother-loathing stage of adolescence, and, as author Kurt Vonnegut noted, "adolescence is children's menopause." But in a hospital emergency room a mere two months later, after another wrestling match that hadn't gone as well, the doctor asked if he could cut Ry's jersey before examining his dislocated shoulder. It would be less painful than pulling it over his head.

"Absolutely," I said.

"No way!" Ry said. He pointed to the embroidery underneath the team's name that he'd worked so hard to earn: "Captain." He then looked me in the eye and said he'd rather risk the pain than ruin the jersey.

"Words matter," he said.

So please know: if you start thinking that the words that matter so much to you can't possibly matter to anyone else, they probably do. Go back to your desk, sit down, let yourself swing from despair to grandiosity, blow your nose, and then continue working until you've produced a great volume of work. If you're tempted to quit because the first drafts disappoint you, it probably means your taste is still *killer.* Messy as it is, you may very well be inside the creative process. Don't quit. Just *fight your way through it.* 🪡

PART I

Profiles of People, Places, and Issues

PART I CONTENTS

When Daddy Comes Home
Walt Harrington
In light of an estimated 14.3 million dependent elderly by 2020, Harrington examines the beauty and struggle of one family's role reversal as an ailing father moves back in with his daughter.

The Town That Blew Away
Justin Heckert
In 2011, a rash of powerful tornadoes destroyed the tiny town of Vaughn, Georgia, and incited chaos after razing houses and a symbolic church. As they have always done, families work to survive and have no choice but to rebuild.

THE MIRANDA OBSESSION

Bryan Burrough

Paul Schrader took the first phone call at his hotel in New Orleans. It was 1981, and Schrader, who wrote the screenplay for *Taxi Driver* and went on to direct *American Gigolo* and other films, was in Louisiana to shoot *Cat People*, with Nastassja Kinski. The woman on the line introduced herself as Miranda Grosvenor, and before Schrader could get rid of her, she had somehow managed to keep him talking for 20 minutes, gossiping about Hollywood and a number of famous men she seemed to know all about.

Intrigued, Schrader invited Miranda to call back, and she did, again and again. "She would just call you up," says Schrader, "and she was very, very charming. Funny. Sexy. It was incredible. The information she had on people was very accurate. She knew who was where and who was going to do what project. Once that happened, you got into the game, too, because she knew half the dirt on someone, and you added 10 percent. Then she took that 60 percent and went to the next person. . . . And there was always sort of a tease, how good-looking she was, wait till you meet my friends. It was all about talking, flirting, power networking."

Repeatedly, Schrader arranged hotel-lobby rendezvous with the shadowy Miranda, but she never appeared. Perplexed, he phoned one of the names she had dropped, Michael Apted, director of *Coal Miner's Daughter* and *Nell*. Yes, Apted confirmed, he had talked on the phone with Miranda, too; no, he didn't know who she was, either. Apted mentioned that Richard Gere had a host of his own Miranda stories to tell. Schrader also reached Buck Henry, the screenwriter and occasional *Saturday Night Live* host, who confessed he too was captivated by Miranda's calls, though he also knew her only as a voice over the telephone. Amazed, Schrader nevertheless had neither the time nor the energy to unravel the mystery of his newfound friend. "This went on for five, six months," he says, "till finally it got so frustrating, all these aborted meetings, I just kind of let it go. I never found out exactly who she was."

Nor, apparently, did Robert De Niro, who, friends say, also took Miranda Grosvenor's phone calls. Nor Billy Joel, who tried out songs in progress on her answering machine and considered turning their strange relationship into a musical. Nor Peter Wolf, lead singer of the J. Geils Band, who attempted to meet her at a Louisiana hotel. Nor, in fact, did most of the dozens of well-known and well-to-do men on both coasts who answered calls from Miranda during the 1980s and suddenly found themselves drawn into the most fascinating, invigorating telephone conversations several of them say they ever enjoyed. It wasn't sex talk, everyone agrees, but it was flirty, gossipy, and more than a little mysterious. "You actually started living for these phone calls," remembers Brian McNally, the noted Manhattan restaurateur and hotelier. "I was absolutely—I mean, I couldn't wait for her call. She made you feel fantastic."

"A lot of nights she was my only friend," says Joel, who understood that Miranda was also phone pals with Eric Clapton, Steve Winwood, and Sting. "As they say, she did give good phone."

The story of Miranda Grosvenor, the riddle of who she really was and why she finally disappeared from the phone lines, has grown into a kind of urban legend in certain circles in Los Angeles and New York. The men who talked to her, a number of whom now decline to confirm they did so, came from all walks of the high life; they were actors and directors, rock stars and record producers, athletes and politicians, even a journalist or two. "[I believe] we're talking about hundreds of people," says Buck Henry. "This went on for 15 years. There's lots of people who think they have seen her, and it was not her. We're talking about someone who can con people into saying they saw her. It's very complex."

With her mellifluous, accentless voice—Henry thought she was British, others heard a hint of Manhattan's Upper East Side—Miranda Grosvenor was a silky phantom who told men she was beautiful and blonde, lived in the South, did some modeling, and looked after her fabulously wealthy father in New York City. Many men believed her; at least a few actually fell in love with her.

"Patrick believed she was the most ravishing woman on earth, with a red Ferrari, a powerful family, airplanes landing on the lawn," recalls Cynthia O'Neal, whose late husband, the actor Patrick O'Neal, became one of Miranda's most fervent phone pals a decade before his 1994 death. "She called him endlessly. I remember arriving at an airport someplace and Patrick was being paged. It turned out to be her. . . . In the early stages, Patrick was really, really—well, she was intriguing. It made me nervous. Personally— and I didn't say this to him, not till after, when Patrick would talk about her—I kept seeing this image of this lonely, very fat girl sitting in a room. I don't remember how it ended, but he never talked about it afterwards."

The name Miranda Grosvenor, in fact, is one that any number of famous and respected figures would just as soon forget. "No, never heard of her," Gil Friesen tells me from his car phone one morning in Beverly Hills. Friesen, a former president of A&M Records, is now president of the board at L.A.'s Museum of Contemporary Art.

"From the phone," I clarify, having been told that Friesen was on close terms with Miranda.

"Oooooh. . . Ohhhhh, my God. Yeah," Friesen says. "Oh, my God."

Friesen takes a moment to collect his thoughts as I list the names of some of Miranda's confidants. "Jesus," he finally says. "Well, Bob De Niro and Quincy Jones I can confirm. I know that through Quincy."

Friesen dates his relationship with Miranda to the early 1980s, her heyday. "She called me in the office," he remembers. "She just had an incredibly sexy voice and she had a great game, delivery, come-on. She said she was from—where?—Louisiana? I've never been there, but I was ready to go. . . . We were going to hook up in Florida and of course that never took place, because that was never her intention. Her game was just to have fun with this. You know, Quincy thought she was this really large woman."

Friesen laughs. "This went on for weeks," he continues. "She keeps you on the line because she has a very, very engaging way of making you feel that she is dying to talk to you. She knew the male psyche quite well. [Eventually] I think I just dropped it, once I put two and two together and realized this was one of the silliest things I had ever done. It wasn't going to go anyplace. It wasn't real. It was just someone with a switchboard and a vivid imagination."

Brian McNally, who has operated some of Manhattan's most glamorous restaurants, such as Odeon and Indochine, received the first call at his Tribeca loft in 1982. It was supposedly a wrong number, but then the woman on the line, who introduced herself as Miranda Grosvenor, seemed to have a spark of recognition. "Oh, you're the guy who has Odeon!" she exclaimed.

"So we started talking," McNally remembers. "She sounded very funny, charming, and incredibly sexy. The whole situation was sexy, though she never, ever spoke about sex. You couldn't get her on the subject. We talked for 20 minutes. So I said, 'Call back.'"

And she did. Before he knew it, McNally was hooked. Miranda seemed to know everything about everyone, especially in Hollywood—which director was considering which scripts, which actor was secretly dating whom. She alluded to friendships with Warren Beatty and Ted Kennedy. "It was amazing—she knew all these disparate sorts of people, all of them famous," McNally says. "Ask Buck [Henry], ask everyone—everyone was completely obsessed with this girl. It was just extraordinary."

Whatever doubts McNally had about Miranda's contacts evaporated when she phoned him one day at Odeon. A busy dinnertime crowd was buzzing around him when an aide handed him the phone, saying it was "Miranda from New Orleans."

"So who all's there today?" she asked.

McNally craned his neck and rattled off several names, including that of Alexander Cockburn, the Anglo-Irish journalist.

"Alex!" Miranda cried. "I know him!"

"No, you don't," McNally replied.

At Miranda's insistence, McNally walked over and handed the receiver to Cockburn.

"Oh, hi, Miranda!" Cockburn said.

"How did she do it? I don't know," says Cockburn, who spoke off and on to Miranda when he lived in New York in the early 1980s. "She would just ring up and say something flattering. She probably told Brian what great spring rolls he made. She would gab away, and she was very funny. She obviously had a romantic effect. We weren't talking about Socrates."

McNally says he began to have second thoughts about Miranda only after an episode in which he heard firsthand the effect she had on men. "She had a tape of Alex, on [her] answering machine, I think, and she played it for me," says McNally. "It was very funny. Alex was begging. 'Why haven't you called? You were going to call. I have your Solidarity T-shirt for you.'" McNally was disconcerted to discover that Miranda might be taping her calls. Still, he kept talking to her for months after. He couldn't help himself. It was Miranda who stopped calling. "*She* dumped *me!*" he yelps today.

"I got the call in the middle of the night—this was in '80 or '81," remembers Buck Henry. "It was a confusing long-distance call, apparently from somebody I knew. I called back, got an operator, but of course [I now know] it was all phony. It was an act. Ultimately I'm talking to this girl who says she has no idea who I am, and I have no idea who she was. During the conversation she suggests I am remiss not to know her, because she is this great-looking English girl going to school at Tulane."

Henry, like so many of his peers, was entranced by Miranda. "She was hip, funny, smart," he says. "If I brought up someone, she would know something about that person a civilian wouldn't know. What she did brilliantly was cross-reference everybody. She networked everything. I knew right away it was some kind of con, but I liked talking to her."

In the weeks to come Henry spoke often with Miranda, who always seemed to know his whereabouts, whether he was in New York or Los Angeles. Occasionally an operator would break into the call and say something like "Senator Kennedy calling from Aspen," an experience remembered by McNally and others as well. Yet Henry couldn't dismiss it as a put-on. Once, as he was fishing for information about her, Miranda volunteered that he would meet someone she knew the following Tuesday night. She suggested cryptically that he ask that person about the restaurant '21.' That Tuesday, Henry was on *The Tonight Show,* and during a commercial break it hit him. He leaned over and asked Johnny Carson, "Did you ever have anyone come up to you at '21' and say they're a friend of mine?" A look of recognition crossed Carson's face. "Yeah," he said. "A blonde girl, good-looking too."

"My mind reeled," Henry says. Ever since, he has made a hobby of collecting all the information he can about the woman who called herself Miranda Grosvenor. "I have a book's worth of material on her," says Henry. "I couldn't begin to tell you the whole story. It would take 10 hours to tell it all. . . . The stories are too long, and I want to save some of them. . . . And I've only scratched the surface. Some of it is really dark and strange."

The real story is indeed dark and strange. But it is also a love story. Or two. Or more.

On a cul-de-sac high in the hills above Sunset Boulevard, behind the gates of a sprawling Art Deco—style home Ronald Reagan built for Jane Wyman in 1941, Richard Perry gazes out at the evening lights of Los Angeles. Perry, 57, is a fixture in the L.A. music scene: one wall of his den is lined with the gold records he has produced over the years for the likes of Barbra Streisand, Carly Simon, and the Pointer Sisters; on another are dozens of candid photos of Perry with friends and collaborators, an arm around Frank Sinatra, cuddling with Diana Ross, sharing a laugh with Paul McCartney and Ringo Starr. Perry's once longish brown hair is now tastefully short and gray. He is an earnest, thoughtful man with a smooth baritone, a romantic who after two failed marriages lives alone in this one-acre compound, surrounded by Tiffany lamps, 1940s-era furniture, and two hissing cats.

"My story," he says, sinking into a desk chair and pouring himself a glass of 1989 Château Lafite-Rothschild, "begins with a phone call."

It has taken considerable prodding to get Perry to talk about the events that, friends say, preoccupy him to this day. He isn't proud of what happened, nor is he ashamed. But he knows what people may say about a man who fell for a woman he had never met. He doesn't want to sound pitiful. He doesn't want to sound cruel.

She reached him at home for the first time on a night in May 1982. Somehow, giving only the name "Ariana," she managed to keep him on the phone. In retrospect Perry realizes she had done considerable research on him. She knew his résumé by heart and within minutes had coaxed him into a conversation about his passion for 1950s doo-wop records. She knew all about Big Joe Turner and the Platters and even mentioned a classic recording he had never heard but later rushed out and bought, a duet by Ray Charles and Betty Carter. "I'm open and adventurous," Perry concedes. "I was having fun with it. I was getting off on this mystery woman."

They talked for 20 minutes, and he invited her to call back anytime. That led to another long talk and then another and another, until Perry realized he was looking forward to her calls. In a throaty, sexy voice, Ariana was funny and empathetic and made him feel wonderful about himself without being obsequious. She gave him a nickname, "Sicko."

In their second or third conversation she said she lived in Baton Rouge, Louisiana, but attended Tulane University in New Orleans. She said she had done some modeling.

Perry had just broken off a long-term relationship with an actress, and as spring turned to summer he found himself increasingly drawn to the witty, wise woman on the phone. They began talking two, three, sometimes four times a day. Before long Perry was scheduling his studio time around her calls; he made sure to finish work every night by seven, then he would race home, lay out his dinner, pour a glass of wine, and put Ariana on the speakerphone as he ate. They would talk late into the night.

"As it grew," Perry says after a sip of wine, "she would weave her spell and make you feel closer and closer and closer to her, until you're saying to yourself that this is the most extraordinary woman I've ever met in my life. I thought, I'm falling in love with her."

The photographs and letters didn't hurt. Perry had pushed to meet her, but she always had an excuse: She had to study. There was a problem with her father. She had to work. But she did send him a photo, cut out of a magazine, of a lithe, voluptuous model. A separate snapshot showed a white Ferrari parked on what appeared to be a college campus, with a blonde behind the wheel. Perry admits he swooned.

Then, at a recording-industry cocktail party, Perry ran into Gil Friesen. When Friesen asked how his love life was faring, Perry told him everything. An odd look crossed Friesen's face. "The same exact thing happened to me," he said. And then Friesen told Perry of the frisky calls he had taken from Miranda Grosvenor, who said she lived in Baton Rouge but attended Tulane. Both men realized it had to be the same woman.

"It was a knife through my heart," Perry says simply. Yet so deep were his feelings for the woman on the phone that he willed himself not to believe Friesen. "I was just livid, incensed," he says. "[I thought] Gil was doing this just to fuck with me. I felt no other human being could experience what I'm experiencing now. This is a once-in-a-lifetime event."

Shortly after his talk with Friesen, Perry discovered that his friend Buck Henry was also obsessed with Miranda Grosvenor. Henry's perspective, however, contrasted sharply with his own. Henry's initial infatuation had given way to a bemused disillusionment, and while he continued taking Miranda's calls, he had begun to investigate who she really was.

Henry's suspicions were triggered by a picture she had sent him, a photocopy of a leggy blonde model standing on a rock in a magazine fashion layout. "I thought it was a really bonehead move on her part," Henry says.

"The model was fairly well known at the time, and it took me about 10 minutes to find out who the model was. I thought, *Wait a minute. Something's going on.*" Henry confided his doubts to a friend, who mentioned that Jack Haley Jr., the *That's Entertainment* producer who was once married to Liza Minnelli, had taken Miranda's calls too. Haley told Henry, in Henry's words, to "watch your step, I think this is some kind of con job." (Haley confirms the story but remembers no details.)

Miranda, in turn, took pains to persuade Henry she really was a rich, gorgeous blonde, an effort that led to the Johnny Carson incident and an even stranger episode in New York. Henry was staying at the Essex House on Central Park South, to which he returned late one Friday night after a long rehearsal as host of *Saturday Night Live*. At the desk was a message from Miranda Grosvenor. The next morning the hotel staffer who had taken the message told Henry it had been left by a beautiful blonde woman who had stepped out of a fire-red sports car and was leading a tiny corgi dog.

Henry determined to find out who Miranda Grosvenor really was. He and his then girlfriend, *Time* magazine designer Irene Ramp, gave Miranda's phone number to a *Time* stringer in Louisiana. Somehow, presumably using a reverse telephone directory, the stringer was able to come back to Henry and Ramp with an address in Baton Rouge and a name Henry had never heard: Whitney Walton. The stringer also found a clipping from the September 20, 1978, edition of Baton Rouge's *The State-Times*, which quotes a Whitney Walton discussing how local elderly people can avoid being scammed by con artists.

The next time Miranda phoned, "I confronted her [about] Whitney Walton," Henry says. "She turned that into part of the made-up story. 'Yes, I'm also Whitney Walton. But so what? I'm adorable and so are you.' And then the relationship kind of petered out."

Henry wasted no time briefing Perry on his mystery love's real identity. "I told him she was a phony," says Henry. "He got angry at me and stopped talking to me. She got him thinking I was trying to wreck her relationship with him because I was so in love with her." Perry did take Henry's advice, however, to begin taping his calls with Ariana/Miranda/Whitney.

"Ironically," Perry says, "the first call I taped was the first time she told me she loved me."

> *The most important things lie too close to wherever your secret heart is buried, like landmarks to a treasure your enemies would*

love to steal away. . . . That's the worst, I think. When the secret
stays locked within, not for want of a teller but for want of an un-
derstanding ear.
—Portion of a letter from "Ariana" to Richard Perry, September
11, 1982

Autumn winds moan and thrash the pines outside Perry's window as he
answers a phone call, then flips on a CD of soft jazz. He says he remained
angry at Friesen and Henry, but their allegations nagged at him. Not long
after, he finally confronted Ariana. For the first time he asked pointed
questions: "What are you doing? How many other men have there been?
What's the point of all this?" Over the course of several calls, she seemed
to come clean. She said Whitney Walton really was her real name. Yes, she
had called dozens of famous men. She wasn't sure why she did it. It was like
a game. She called it "jacking" men. She referred to men who talked with
her as "jackable."

"She said her goal—her 'get-off'—was she felt she could make any man
on the planet fall in love with her," Perry says. "Whether it was a farmer in
Iowa or a senator in Washington."

Amazingly, Whitney's admission only deepened Perry's feelings for her.
Now, he told himself, he knew the "real" Whitney. "It didn't matter to me,"
he sighs. "I was so deeply involved."

By the fall Perry found himself drawn even further into Whitney's
calling game. She told him of talks with Robert De Niro, Bob Dylan, and
Paul Schrader and other Hollywood directors. He was surprised to learn
that one of her closest phone pals was his friend Peter Wolf of the J. Geils
Band; when he called Wolf, the singer freely told him of his own infatuation with "Miranda." Wolf related a story similar to Henry's Essex House
experience. In Baton Rouge for a concert, Wolf had arranged a rendezvous with Miranda at his hotel. When he arrived, he found only a message at the front desk, dropped off, the hotel clerk told him, by a striking
blonde in a red Porsche. Instead of being put off, Perry was in awe of
Whitney's talents. It seemed she really could get anyone to fall in love
with her.

MTV had debuted the previous year, and one night Whitney pro-
claimed to Perry her fascination with the lead singer of a Canadian rock
band whose video was in heavy rotation on the new channel. "This guy's
really cute," she said. "I'd love to jack him." A few days later she brought

up the singer's name again. He was visiting Los Angeles, she said. Would Perry agree to meet him? Maybe he could help the singer's career. Perry reluctantly consented, and the singer appeared at his house late one night, "completely love-struck," as Perry puts it, "to pour his heart out about her. He wanted to marry her." Perry consoled the young man, wished him well, and never saw him again.

That fall Perry, an enthusiastic University of Michigan alumnus, flew to Ann Arbor to watch one of his favorite football players, the celebrated Michigan wide receiver Anthony Carter. He had mentioned his interest in Carter to Whitney, only to have her insist she would arrange a chat. When Perry arrived in his hotel room, the phone rang. "Richard Perry, this is Anthony Carter," the voice on the other end said. "Whitney Walton asked me to give you a call."

"That blew my mind," Perry says. "She had gotten Carter out of a football meeting to call me, just to give you an example of her powers."

Not long after the Michigan incident, and only after months of pleading and cajoling, Perry persuaded Whitney to meet him in New York. He mailed her an airline ticket and reserved a room for her at the Park Lane on Central Park South; at her insistence, he promised to stay at a different hotel, the Sherry-Netherland, not far away, on Fifth Avenue. Friends urged him not to go, but Perry wouldn't listen. He was fully aware his heart might be broken, he told Henry. But he had to go. He had to know.

At J.F.K. airport in New York, Perry was met by one of Whitney's friends, who she had introduced him to over the phone. Walking to the baggage-claim area, he spoke frankly. "Look, if you really care about Whitney," he said, "if she's not the person that she has made herself out to be, tell me now, so I can prepare myself, so she won't have to see in my face the shock and letdown of knowing I've been conned."

The woman thought for a moment. "She's not," she said.

Perry brooded all that night, steeling himself for the worst, but allowing himself to hope for the best. The next afternoon Whitney checked into the Park Lane and telephoned him at his hotel room. They agreed he would go to her room at seven to meet her. She asked him to wear a blindfold. He refused. They compromised. She would leave the room darkened but with the curtains open. The only light, Perry recalls, "was to be the city lights coming in the window."

Just before seven Perry walked to the Park Lane. Within minutes he was standing before her door. His mind raced. He didn't know what to expect—a model, a college student, a maniac with a carving knife, or the woman he would spend the rest of his life with. He knocked. The door was unlocked and he pushed it open. She was sitting on the edge of the bed. He sat beside her and took her hand. As his eyes adapted to the darkness, he began to see her face.

You're right if you're thinking "Miranda Grosvenor" is hardly unique. Tales similar to hers—the latest versions include anonymous romances blooming in Internet chat rooms—float through dinner parties in Manhattan and Los Angeles on a regular basis. Right now Connecticut is home base for a woman who represents herself as a Saudi princess and who has lured several prominent Wall Streeters into business deals; she was recently unmasked by *The Denver Post* after making an unsuccessful $450 million bid to buy the Denver Nuggets basketball team.

During the late 1970s, a woman using nothing but a telephone and a sexy voice enticed a number of wealthy Los Angeles men to give her gifts of cash and jewelry. One young man, the scion of a prominent Southern California family, fell hard for her. A local prosecutor, urged by the young man's family to investigate, found the woman was a fraud. It didn't matter to the young heir. He met the woman and married her. The two lived happily ever after until, family friends say, the woman died in the mid-1990s. The story was ultimately turned into a screenplay that was never filmed. The photographer Peter Beard, who has dabbled in film projects over the years, read a screenplay with a similar story about 20 years ago. "I remember it well," he says. "The story had supposedly happened to Warren Beatty, who called the police, the F.B.I., and Missing Persons to find this woman who was calling him. We were going to try to get Beatty to [star in] it, make it like a nonfiction, drama thing. But it went nowhere. I'll never forget the last scene. Beatty finds the woman, rings the doorbell, and the woman comes out. She's a real hog. The movie ends with them embracing."

Screenplays, sadly, are not real life.

She was no model. As Perry's eyes adjusted to the darkened room, he saw a short, frumpy woman in her 30s, maybe 30 pounds overweight, with a large mole on her right cheek. She wasn't ugly. But she wasn't, he realized in a moment of self-loathing and almost unbearable sadness, a woman he could spend his life with. "I felt I had been conned," he says today. "Thank God I had been prepared."

They walked to the Plaza Hotel for an awkward dinner at Trader Vic's. Perry strained to keep his composure. "I didn't want to let her know I was freaked out, that I was devastated," he says. But after talking in circles for a time, Perry gave vent to his feelings. He told her he was deeply disappointed. She tried to explain. "[She said] we were in too deep for her to admit the whole thing was a fraud. She had gone too far, she didn't know how to deal with it. I had given her a dose of her own medicine. She said she was hoping I could see beyond the deception. But I couldn't."

They parted with a hug and a quick kiss, and Perry agreed reluctantly to meet her the next evening at the Carlyle Hotel bar. That afternoon Perry went to the apartment of singer Art Garfunkel to pour out his woes. Garfunkel, he was aware, had also taken Miranda's calls. In fact, Garfunkel said, he had been so enraptured by Miranda he had almost taken a Swiss vacation with her. The two men were so deep in conversation Perry almost forgot his second meeting. "Wait! You've got to finish the story!" Garfunkel yelled after Perry as he ran out.

Their meeting at the Carlyle, Perry says, "was not a pretty sight." Perry told her again that he felt duped. She begged him to look beyond her lies. "I never expected to fall in love," she told him. She began to cry. He told her he felt used and rose to leave.

She grabbed his arm and begged him to stay. He removed her hands. "I'm terribly sorry, Whitney," Perry said. "But I don't think I was treated fairly. I'm not in the habit of giving my heart easily. And you should have respected that. I can't ever really trust you again." And then he walked out, leaving her in tears.

Perry returned to Los Angeles. Several weeks later he received a handwritten note at his home. It said simply, "You have broken my windows and crashed through all my doors. W."

The episode lingered with Perry for months, in scenes he would replay in his mind again and again. In time he got over it.

Then, two or three years later, Perry was dining at the Ivy, a restaurant in Beverly Hills, when he heard someone call his name. He turned, and, to his surprise, there was Whitney. She was sitting on a banquette with a man. He walked over and saw it was Quincy Jones.

"Quincy and I are buying a house in Bel Air!" Whitney exclaimed.

In the end, Whitney Walton isn't that hard to locate. A public-records search turns up a current address in Baton Rouge, near the Louisiana State University campus, just down the street from the Mississippi River levee; the phone number, ironically, is unlisted. An Internet search of local newspaper archives uncovers a half-dozen mentions of a Whitney Walton during the 1990s, including a letter she wrote to thank people for donations to Head Start and other programs benefiting disadvantaged youth. On the flight down to find her in Baton Rouge, I imagine her as a sedate housewife, dressed in blue blazer and white Keds, active in local charities, her secret past as Miranda Grosvenor shed and half forgotten, perhaps a crazy prank she dreamed up with sorority sisters.

A call to the local Head Start office leads to a run-down elementary school in a poor area of north Baton Rouge within sight of the levee. Directed to a door marked SOCIAL SERVICES, I stick my head in, peek over a room divider, and ask for Whitney Walton. "I'm Whitney Walton," a woman sitting behind a corner desk says. She rises to join me in the corridor outside, and I see she is a weary-looking woman around 50, maybe five foot six and 250 pounds. She wears shocking-pink stretch pants and a matching top, a Slinkylike assemblage of gold bangles and chains around her right wrist, what appear to be diamonds twinkling at her earlobes and knuckles, and the fading remnants of a blond dye job. There is a large mole on her right cheek.

I begin to explain my quest. Before I can finish, she hisses, "Keep your voice down!" and then leads me into an indoor play area. There, as we sit on folding chairs, I tell her the whole story, of an enchanting woman who called herself Miranda Grosvenor and who once made powerful men swoon with the sound of her voice.

Her reaction is immediate and irritated. "It rings no bells with me," she snaps. "I don't know anything about it." I begin to list the names of Miranda's many confidants. "I don't know these people," she interrupts.

There is no surprise in her reaction, no dismay, no sense of hearing an outlandish story for the first time. Only anger and a dash of sarcasm. I press, saying I am certain she is Miranda Grosvenor. "It's not me," she says flatly. "There's a lot of people named Whitney Walton. This is intrusive. This is invasive. I'm a social worker."

A crowd of kindergartners file into the room and begin to play. Eyeing the children's teacher, she again admonishes me to keep my voice down. She quickly grows impatient, refusing to answer questions about her background and issuing an unyielding wall of stern denials. After a bit, I rise to leave and apologize for bothering her. She stalks back into her office.

In a half-hour with Whitney Walton I sense not the slightest whiff of joie de vivre, of curiosity, of playfulness or whimsy, any of the qualities men have attributed to Miranda Grosvenor; in fact, it is impossible to reconcile this woman with the stories told of her. As I drive off, a question nags at me: Is there some chance this Whitney Walton isn't Miranda Grosvenor?

Then, later that night, unable to sleep, wondering how to handle the contradiction, I return to the tidy off-campus duplex where Whitney Walton lives.

In the rear carport sits a fire-red Porsche.

'Oh, I remember Miranda," giggles Barbara Davidson.

"Oh, and she used Ariana," says Genny Abel. "And Brianna."

"She was proud that she knew famous people," says Davidson. "It was her social life."

"It was her life," says Abel.

Abel, a smiling woman in granny glasses and a navy "Take Back the Night" T-shirt, is director of Baton Rouge's battered-women's center, in a brick building on a shaded street north of downtown. She and Davidson, her co-worker, joined the center in 1982 and were assigned to a three-woman office with Whitney Walton. Walton, after earlier jobs as a librarian and a consumer-fraud investigator for the city, had joined the center a year earlier as a counselor.

"The first thing I remember is she had a big poster of Vitas Gerulaitis, the tennis player, on her door," says Abel. "I remarked on it. She said they were great friends. They talked on the phone a lot."

For the next three years, until she left in 1985 to become a social worker, the two women say, Walton spoke endlessly of her many famous friends. To convince them she was telling the truth, she played her answering-machine tapes for them at the office. The two women remembered that Walton's friends included Peter Wolf, Buck Henry, Art Garfunkel, and others, including two other tennis pros, Yannick Noah and Guillermo Vilas.

"But her big romance," Abel says with a grin, "was Billy Joel. She let us listen to their calls. He was always calling to see how she was. It wasn't sexual; it was intimate, like he was courting her. He wanted to send her stuff. He did send her a Rolex with diamonds. [He asked] did she get it. He talked about buying her a grand piano. And an emerald ring. She didn't want an emerald with diamonds in it. She wanted a plain emerald. He couldn't find one." At various times, they say, Walton returned from vacations claiming she had been with Joel in New York. Once they listened as she called Manhattan real-estate brokers to help him find an apartment in the city.

Abel and Davidson had no doubt it was the real Billy Joel because, among other things, he sang to Walton's answering machine, experimenting with music and lyrics as he went. When the album Joel was working on at the time was finished, the two women believed that its title, *Uptown Girl*, referred to Walton, not Joel's new love at the time, Christie Brinkley. Walton, they say, returned from one vacation, in St. Barts, claiming she had spent time with Joel and had been present when he met Brinkley. But then she also claimed that Peter Wolf had spent a week staying in her small Baton Rouge apartment, where she lived alone with two tiny dogs.

"She complained about that," says Abel. "She said she didn't like him touching her things."

"We never knew whether to believe her or not," says Davidson with a roll of her eyes.

"It was just so bizarre," says Abel.

"I knew her as Whitney Walton," says Billy Joel. "At first [when she called] it was a pain in the ass. [I said,] 'I don't know you, what's the catch?' [But] she seemed to know a lot of people in my business. Stevie Winwood. Sting. Eric Clapton. [So] I thought she was on the level. . . . This was just before I started dating Christie Brinkley. I was dating Elle Macpherson at the time."

There ensued the familiar pattern. They talked a little, and then more. He appreciated her quick mind and began rehearsing lyrics and rhythms over the phone with her. "Musicians," he says, "get calls from all kinds of wacko people. . . . But this girl was different. . . . She was awfully good company." Joel pushed to see her.

She demurred. If he wanted to know what she looked like, she suggested he go to the drugstore and buy a bottle of Clairol ash-blond coloring; she was the model on the box, she said. Rendezvous were arranged, but she never appeared. Joel insists he never actually sent her any gifts of note—only a stuffed animal perhaps.

But then one day, he says, "someone showed up at my house with a gift, I don't know what it was, a toy or something. It was a friend of hers. Her car was out front. There was a person sitting in the back of the car. I couldn't see who it was. I assumed it was her." He says she grew oddly possessive. When he dated other women, says Joel, "she would get jealous. . . . I think I sent her a tape of a song. It was called 'And So It Goes.' It was actually written about someone else. . . . I sent it to her to kind of say I was seeing other people."

After she failed to appear at their third appointment, "I just said that's it, this is some kind of phony," Joel remembers. "When it was ending, she said she was going to start seeing Sting." He pauses. "I was even thinking about making a musical about this, because every time I tell people this story, they never believe it."

Probably no one other than Walton knows exactly why Miranda Grosvenor and her alter egos retired, if that's what happened. Buck Henry heard an unconfirmed story that Miranda may have "disappeared" in the wake of threats from the late Vitas Gerulaitis's lawyers; the Gerulaitis estate's current attorney says he knows nothing about it.

Few of the men Walton courted are willing to shed any light on what transpired. Her relationship with Quincy Jones apparently ended abruptly after Richard Perry saw them together; though a Jones spokesman refuses to comment on the matter, a Los Angeles friend says Jones sent Walton packing within days of seeing Perry at the Ivy. Warren Beatty, Peter Wolf, Richard Gere, Michael Apted, Art Garfunkel, Bob Dylan, Ted Kennedy, Eric Clapton, Sting, and Robert De Niro all declined to be interviewed. But if Miranda Grosvenor is dead and gone, her memory lives on. What men such as Richard Perry remember most was her eloquence. In the absence of any tape recordings—Perry says he lost his—her words can be found only in letters, including one Walton wrote to Perry after their awful encounter in New York.

"On a good day," she wrote, "I feel like a shipwrecked person spotting the sight of some nearing shore: a taste in the wind, a softness in the light, a sudden passage of words. Love is so easy in the movies. No conflicts are too hopeless to resolve, no obstacles too painful to overcome, no resolutions too final for last minute reconsideration. Love means forever in the movies. Not to worry—what was ignited when I loved you continues to burn."

Somewhere. 🪷

Bryan Burrough on fresh writing
and the importance of transitions

I've been writing the same story for twenty-five years. They pay me to write the same story. Well, I don't do the same *story*; I do the same *structure*. It typically starts with a real-time lead, an anecdotal lead. It breaks out into a part that at the *Wall Street Journal* we used to call the "nut graf"; at *Time* magazine I think they always called it the "billboard," which is essentially a quick one or two paragraphs saying "this is what the story is," a section where you say this is why the story matters. And then you get out of the way and tell the story as fast as possible.

I find that the best writing is if you write when the material is fresh. I try to write my stuff as fast after gathering it as possible. I get off the phone; I've just interviewed someone for thirty minutes. I'm writing that up when I get off—no later than the next morning, because I want the sense and nuance and inflection. If I wait six months—I don't know about y'all's notes; mine tend to suck. I remember really well for two hours, maybe even two days.

So at the beginning of the first day, when I get the assignment, I start two files on my desktop—a dot-reporting file and a dot-writing file. Everything I gather, obviously, goes in the reporting file, but unlike a lot of people I don't wait to the end to start filling up the writing one. I start immediately. Let's say I get a nice interview and I've got eight grafs. I write it up. Everybody knows that the worst part of any narrative project is when you don't really have the confidence that you're going to get enough to do it. And it feels good when I can say, "Look. I have eight paragraphs."

Every morning, I go up into my dot-writing file, whatever it is, and I just play with words, play with words with the goal of chopping as much as I can, just cut, cut, cut, cut, cut, until I get down to the best stuff. I'm absolutely ruthless. You can't fall in love with anything you write, because shorter is always better. I know this is Journalism 101, but some of us forget it. Your words are not nearly as great as you think they are.

The biggest challenge is that people are busy, and they are dying to put down your article. They don't really want a new character; they want to find out what happened to the other character. They don't want to turn the page; they're dying to go do something else. So I put enormous energy into devising ways to trick them into staying with me.

The end of a paragraph is where you're going to lose people. So I'm nuts for transitions that are good active words at the beginning of a paragraph.

What's the greatest single transition word? *And* is weak, because nobody cares. *But* is the best one. *But* says, "You don't know everything yet. I'm going to correct something you think. You can't walk away."

The problem with *but* is, obviously, that it's overused. So you don't want to be one of those every-other-paragraph *but* people. If you're really not into *but*, and you need something at the beginning, *however* is acceptable. I like *however*.

The absolute best transition word ever, and you can only use it about once every two or three stories, because people will catch on: *suddenly*. It's a word you cannot walk away from; who's ever going to walk away from a graf that starts "Suddenly"? Suddenly something happened—I've got to know that.

I put stories together like DNA, like papier-mâché. It just grows and grows and grows, and at some point, it fills the file, it gets up to about where I think it ought to be. Then I read it aloud, and then I let my wife read it, and if she thinks it's as good as the last thing I did, then I know I'm done.

(Content adapted from Burrough's presentation at the Mayborn Literary Nonfiction Conference in 2010; original/unedited transcript via Neiman Storyboard.)

HARVEY'S TWO FAMILIES

Ken Fuson

For the past sixty-seven years, the only proof that anyone in his family cared about Harvey Quillin was a faded birthday card in his file at a Taylor County care center.

> *Dear Son:*
> *I'm wishing you a very, very happy day and sending you my love. Will try to come see you, but don't know when we can. I hope you are well.*
> *Love from Dad.*

The card arrived in 1951.

Harvey never heard from his father or his mother, or from any other immediate relative again.

If this bothered Harvey, if he felt lonely, confused or bitter, he kept those emotions private. Harvey is mentally retarded. It's possible that he simply failed to comprehend the concept of family. The missed birthdays, holidays, Thanksgiving dinners—perhaps he didn't know any better.

Harvey is 77 years old. He can't read and has never held a job. He has been the responsibility of the state, or Taylor County, since he was 10 years old.

All those years, Harvey has just existed, a forgotten branch on the family tree.

Finding him would require a wrinkled sheet of notebook paper, a yellowed newspaper obituary and the dogged persistence of a distant cousin who hoped to make her family whole.

31

What little is known about Harvey Quillin's life is contained, along with the birthday card, in his file at Taylor Ridge Estates, the residential care center in Lenox, Iowa, where he now lives.

He was born in September 1923 in Montgomery County to Vascoe and Claudie Quillin. His parents divorced in 1934, when Harvey was 10. That year they admitted their only child to the Glenwood State Hospital-School, when he was diagnosed as mildly to moderately mentally retarded.

Had Harvey been born today, he likely would have gone to school, and certainly could have learned enough skills to hold a job. Society and the law are different now. More opportunities exist for the mentally disabled.

In those days, "People thought they were possessed by devils," says Sandy Helm, the assistant administrator of Taylor Ridge Estates. "They didn't want them around. They were scared to death of them."

Parents often were ashamed of their handicapped children. They were advised to place the children in state institutions. Several of Taylor Ridge's older residents, like Harvey, were abandoned and never heard from their families again.

Nobody knows why Harvey's parents divorced, or where his mother went next. Harvey's father eventually moved to Kansas and remarried a woman named Alice. It's her handwriting that appears on the birthday card that Harvey received in 1951, his last contact with a family member.

That same year, Harvey was transferred from Glenwood to the Taylor County Home, located in an enormous two-story house between Bedford and Lenox. Most Iowa counties had such a home—called "the poor farm" by locals—that served as the last refuge for the indigent, disabled and unwanted.

In 1976, a staff worker described Harvey as a "rather slender man with dark hair and dark brown eyes that are lit with mischief. His face and smile express much energy that is truly delightful. From time to time, he would raise his right hand and that would then twitch."

The writer noticed something else.

"According to the staff at the County Home, Harvey talks in many voices to himself. When interrupted he will stop and acknowledge your presence. I overheard one of his conversations and it was fascinating. His voices had personalities of their own. He sounded as though he really enjoyed the companions that he had created in his mind."

Helm, too, has heard Harvey's imaginary conversations.

"You'd swear to God he was talking to a woman," she says.

She doesn't believe Harvey has a multiple personality disorder. He simply has an uncanny ability to mimic voices.

She now thinks Harvey's conversations might have served a greater purpose than entertaining himself. "I just wonder if it was a replacement for a family that he didn't have."

Genealogy unites a family

In 1951, the same year Harvey moved into the Taylor County Home, a second cousin named Doris Russell left her Missouri home to follow her husband, an airman in the U.S. Air Force, around the country.

Back then, she says, "I didn't give all that much thought to my relatives. I was too busy changing diapers and wiping runny noses on my four children."

Russell's interest in genealogy began in 1990, then blossomed into a full-fledged hobby four years ago when her husband retired and they returned to Missouri. They live in Raymore, a suburb south of Kansas City.

"It's like putting a puzzle together on the table," she says. "You put one piece in, and it looks like a picture, and that makes you want to find the next piece. Then you're up until midnight, trying to put all the pieces in."

Russell, 67, was working on her mother's family tree last year when she discovered a wrinkled piece of notebook paper. On it, her maternal grandmother had listed the names of seven siblings, including when they were born, when they died and how many children they had.

The grandmother's siblings included twins—Virgil and Vascoe Quillin. The list indicated Vascoe had a child, but there was no other information.

A blank branch on the family tree.

"It just plagued me," Russell says. "I don't know why. That's what happens when you get into genealogy. You become obsessed with it almost. The puzzle isn't done until you've got it."

Who was this mystery child? She questioned relatives. Several said they thought Vascoe had a son who was mentally disturbed, or got into trouble, or something. They couldn't remember. An older relative thought the son's name was Harvey, but he wasn't certain. A few relatives, including her own mother, advised Russell to quit, as they put it, "looking for the dead."

Russell pressed on. She assumed the mystery child was dead. All she wanted was to fill in the blanks—the date of birth and death—on the family tree.

She knew that Vascoe Quillin, the child's father, had died in 1955 in Chetopa, Kan., a small town on the Kansas-Oklahoma border. During a vacation last spring, Russell convinced her husband to stop there. It was a long shot, but perhaps she could find a record of Vascoe's death at the local funeral home.

Yes, the funeral home owner said, checking his records, here it is.

He referred her to the local historical society. There, Russell found a 45-year-old newspaper obituary for Vascoe that included this line: "He had a son named Harvey in Conway, Ia."

Russell says, "I went crazy, I was so excited."

Conway is so small, population 55, that Russell had to call the post office in nearby Bedford to find someone who might remember Harvey Quillin.

She was given the phone number, but not the name, of a Conway resident. She recalls their conversation:

"Did you ever know a Harvey Quillin?"

"Never heard of him."

"Did you live there in 1955?"

"Yes, I did."

Russell groaned. How could you live in a town that small and not know someone? She asked one final question.

"Was there anyone in town that took care of troubled children or homeless children?"

"We had a county home out here, but it closed in 1981. They moved everybody to a place in Lenox."

On May 18, Russell dialed the phone number of Taylor Ridge Estates. Her fondest wish was that somebody could tell her the date when Harvey Quillin died.

T.J. Henriksen, the business manager of Taylor Ridge Estates, took the call.

"Well, we've got Harvey right here," she said.

Russell says: "I nearly fainted. I cried. I thought he'd be dead."

Sandy Helm, the assistant administrator, talked to Russell next. "She was just screaming with excitement," Helm says. "I had goosebumps."

Word swept through the care center. "You're not going to believe this," Helm told the nurses. "Harvey's got a family!" Everybody had tears in their eyes.

Now it was time to inform Harvey.

He is a tall, chunky man with short, coal-black hair and a face dominated by big black glasses. He will talk to people he trusts, like Helm, but when he gets nervous, Harvey's arms begin to shake and his conversation is reduced to one-word replies, usually, "Yeah."

"He just lets you know that he appreciates the things you do for him," Helm says. "I don't know if he can really express himself, but you can tell what he's thinking by the look on his face.

"When Harvey smiles, everybody in the room smiles."

Harvey likes watching baseball, playing bingo and listening to the schoolchildren when they come to sing for the 50 residents.

Only two other residents have spent more time under Taylor County's care. For birthdays, or Christmas, or the annual Family Day picnic, the 35 staff members often bought Harvey a gift. Otherwise he went without. He didn't complain. Perhaps he didn't know any better.

"Everybody enjoys Harvey," Helm says. "He's just a likeable guy."

She wondered how he would react to Russell's phone call. It had been so long since he had a family. Would he understand? Would he care?

"Harvey, I just talked to a woman who says she's a member of your family," Helm told him. "She wants to come see you."

Harvey stared blankly at her. Helm understood. "I don't think he believed it, either."

A week after the phone call, on May 25, Russell and three relatives from Missouri arrived at the care center to visit Harvey for the first time. They brought chocolate chip cookies and a stack of black-and-white photographs.

Helm led the family into a conference room and watched. Harvey was polite but cautious. His arms trembled. He said nothing. Russell began showing photographs.

Harvey still said nothing.

Russell placed another old photograph on the table. It showed three young men, all wearing coats and hats. "Harvey, do you know any of these people?"

Harvey's arms began to shake. Tears filled his eyes. With a trembling index finger, he slowly pointed to the young man sitting on the far right in the photograph. Then Harvey, who rarely talks to people he doesn't trust, said this: "That's my Dad." He had pointed to Vascoe Quillin.

Harvey cried. Helm cried. Russell and the other relatives cried. After all those years, Harvey remembered. "Now what does that say to you?" Russell says. "Forget genealogy. A child never forgets his parents. Sixty-seven years later, Harvey knew who his dad was. Oh, I think there's a sermon in this one."

Is it also possible that Harvey knows that he was abandoned by his parents? That he has been holding in that hurt all this time? That he remembers more about his past than he can adequately express or that anyone has previously imagined?

Harvey's family went to work. They replaced the stiff institutional chair in his room with a green easy chair. They filled his bare walls with family photos, postcards and greeting cards. They sent candy and gifts. They have visited four times since May, and a pre-Christmas trip is planned.

On Harvey's family tree, these relatives are distant cousins. While previous generations in the family forgot about Harvey, they embrace him. Times change. Attitudes do, too.

"Whenever they walk in, his face lights up," Helm says. "We have seen a change in him since his family found him that's for the good. He's more open. He'll talk more. He smiles more."

In September, for the care center's annual Family Day picnic, Russell and a dozen other relatives headed to Iowa to surprise Harvey with a birthday gift: His first television. He couldn't talk. He just smiled.

"This is more than a fill-in-the-blank on the family tree," Russell says. "I believe we all deserve to be loved. I just believe Harvey deserves to have a family before he dies.

"He's not forgotten. I really think he knows that, too. I may be wrong, but I think he does."

Harvey's fellow residents were thrilled for him. During the picnic, a woman born with Down syndrome cornered Russell. She was excited and out of breath. "We didn't know Harvey had a family!" she said. Russell replied, "Well, we didn't know there was a Harvey."

Before she left the care center, Russell approached Helm for a private meeting. She knew Harvey has prostate troubles and congestive heart failure. He gets along fine now, but he's almost 80.

When Harvey dies, Russell said, there is an empty plot in Missouri where he could be buried among other relatives. Helm presented another option. The care center and Taylor County already had made provisions for Harvey. If the family consents, he will be buried among the other long-time residents of the county home. Like Harvey, many had been abandoned and forgotten, symbols of a long-ago time in Iowa history.

These were Harvey's friends, the people with whom he played bingo, watched baseball games and listened to school kids sing Christmas carols for the past 67 years. "They and the staff people were his family for years and years," she says. "They loved him and he loved them."

All those years, everyone thought Harvey Quillin didn't have a family. Now, it turns out, he has two.

Ken Fuson on finding the universal truth

An opinion is not a story. Everyone has an opinion, and they share them 24/7 on Facebook, Twitter, et cetera. Readers want stories and they always have. Study the elements of storytelling, and see what works and doesn't work for you. You will know if you are connecting with readers. Think, *Will readers be invested in this? Is what I am writing about getting at some intangible and universal truth?*

I was at a workshop with Chip Scanlan, who was then working for the Poynter Institute, when I first heard the suggestion that reporters should look for the universal truth in their stories. In other words, does the story have the potential to touch on an aspect of the human experience that touches us all? There are certain themes—growing up is hard, you're never too old to learn, your life can change in the blink of an eye—that seem to surface repeatedly in stories. I don't think the theme changes with the audience and publication; the story is the story, but writers can look for stories that reflect different themes depending on different audiences.

With the Harvey story, the universal truth is fairly obvious: everyone needs a family. The twist here is that Harvey is mentally challenged. Did he understand the concept of "family?" It wasn't something he talked about, and nobody knew for sure. Some of his helpers thought it might have been a blessing in a way because he would never know that his parents had left him all those long years ago.

For me, the dramatic high point of the story is when Harvey points to the photograph of his father and recognizes him. It wasn't that Harvey had found his family. They had found him. When I give talks on storytelling, I often refer to a children's book, *Are You My Mother?*, written by P. D. Eastman for Random House, because it's such a great example of the complication-resolution form. I thought Harvey's story contained some of the same themes found in the book—that sense of being lost, then found. What made Harvey's story different, though, was that he was never truly lost. He had found another family that loved him in the other residents and the employees at the care center. However, it was very clear that he knew the difference between that family and his biological family and was thrilled to be reconnected.

In this case, the universal truth that everyone needs a family applied both to Harvey's relationship with his blood relatives and to his relationship with the care center, and I tried to organize the story in a way that would help readers see that.

Language, imagery, and creative writing still matter because they still matter to readers. There is always going to be a market for a well-told tale. This has been true since our ancestors sat around a fire and told stories to each other.

THE PRICE OF FOOTBALL FAME

Wright Thompson

There's something perfect about an old football player standing in a lobby telling a dinosaur joke. It's Canton, midsummer, where the greatest men ever to put on a helmet—at least the ones (a) alive and (b) (sort of) mobile—gather in a hotel, and a town, that oddly reflects their bodies: once powerful, now crumbling, still commanding respect. They are all, at this moment, waiting on a bus to take them to a kickoff luncheon. Joe Greene has a fancy camera slung around his neck, looking like the tourists pressed against barriers outside. John Hannah stops to talk, and he describes a cartoon he recently saw: two dinosaurs stand on top of a shrinking island, water rising, rain pouring down, looking at the back of Noah's ark. One dinosaur turns to the other and, in the lobby of the hotel, the same thing happens: Hannah delivers the cartoon's punch line to Mean Joe Greene.

"Oh, s---," he says, "was that today?"

Most days, the old stars are mostly forgotten to history—left behind—but for a few days in July, the ghosts of seasons past reappear in the McKinley Grand, a downtown Canton hotel. The first thing I noticed was a no-frills table for check-in, with dilapidated cardboard boxes holding gift bags. The boxes are divided alphabetically, i.e.:

Hendricks-Kelley

Rooney-Bruce Smith

Jackie Smith-Taylor

Football fans would lose their minds in the small, generic bar: Dave Casper debating religion with Roger Wehrli, John Randle holding court in a corner, five or so Hall of Famers on stools, telling stories. John Madden

41

is on a bench outside with the cigar smokers. Is that LT walking through the parking garage? Is that Earl Campbell in the wheelchair? Is that new inductee Jack Butler sitting in the chair next to the front desk? Yes, it is. Greene, a fellow Steeler, walks over. Butler apologizes.

"I can't get up," Butler explains.

There are detailed studies being done as we speak about the danger of football, but if you want to understand the lives behind the data, sit in the McKinley Grand during induction weekend. Watch the guys walk across the lobby. Bobby Mitchell inches with a cane. Campbell needs to be pushed. They wobble, waddle and lean. Some sort of swing themselves across the room, like a gate opening and closing. A small group seems untouched by their careers—Wehrli looks like he could still play—but mostly, I watch them struggle between the front door and the elevator. "They're all like that," a security guard says. "It's sad."

In addition to the cancer and cardiac screening done, there's a display providing information about new joints, which are heavily in use and demand. "You don't want them going through a metal detector," new inductee Chris Doleman says of the old-timers.

The water is always rising on the men who gave their youth to football, and on their small island, much of the talk eventually circles back to the price they've paid and continue to pay; when Madden sees Curtis Martin by the front desk, they exchange numbers and Madden says, "I want to talk to you about some safety things, if you have a minute."

Health worries have long been about scar tissue, about smashed joints and ripped tendons, about arthritis and gout. And they remain about those things despite the public debate about concussions. I get the sense that, right now at least, there is more conversation about the brain among reporters than players. Among people who knew Junior Seau, there'd always been worry about how he'd adjust to life after football, and what would happen to a man whose identity revolved around being the first to the facility, and hitting full speed even in shorts and shells. For reporters like me, Seau is a cautionary tale about concussions. For ex-players, it seems like he's a cautionary tale of something else entirely.

Still, this new fear is there, fueled by the recent suicides, by Seau, by the evolving understanding of concussions. So in addition to the heart tests and brochures about titanium hips, there is something new in Canton: a presentation about brain health and a neurological questionnaire. Madden finds someone with the Hall of Fame and requests they announce where to turn the survey in. Lynn Swann had asked him, and he didn't know.

"He said it's a little personal," Madden explains. "You can't just drop it anywhere."

And the water rises a little more.

Me: Was it worth it?

Willie Roaf: Oh, yeah. It was definitely worth it. I wouldn't change anything. It's worth it to end up in a group like this. There's not but 150 of us even living. It was more than worth it.

Me: Do you worry about hidden brain injuries?

Roaf: Nah. . . . you can't . . . I mean, you can't worry about that day in, day out. I didn't have a whole bunch of concussions. I had some knee scopes, ACLs. I didn't have too many concussions, where I think I have to worry about that. I'm not that bad. Well, I don't know. Ten . . . 20 years, we don't know. But now I'm fine.

Upstairs in the hotel, on the second floor, Roaf's family sits around the room. They know what it cost to be here, heard about shots of painkillers, received the groaning phone calls. "That's the side of football you don't see," sister Phoebe Roaf says. "That's not the glamorous side. That's the real side."

She's the one Willie texted when he got to the Hall of Fame and saw an enormous banner depicting him, one that would permanently hang in a new wing. He'd looked up at it, at himself, and this is what he wrote to his sister: "in hall forever."

Football was how Willie Roaf stood out in a family of overachievers. His mother was the first African-American state Supreme Court justice in Arkansas history. One sister went to Georgetown. Phoebe holds degrees from Harvard and Princeton. For him, starting at an early age, football wasn't just a thing to do; it allowed him to find himself. "What I recognize now which I did not then," his dad, Cliff Roaf, says, "is he decided he would use sports to gain his status in this family order. He knew I had played sports. He loved me and I loved him. This was his way of honoring me. He knew that he had to reach a bar of excellence in something. He chose this, and he has reached the pinnacle of this game."

Cliff is emotional in the hotel room, because he sees in his son the realization of generations of dreams. What is an achy joint compared to completing a journey begun hundreds of years ago? "This wonderful creator did not forget what he promised to generation after generation after generation," Cliff says. "God promised people in our families that if we loved him, and served him, and honored him, he would bring blessings to our children and their children and their children. That is what is the essence of Will Roaf."

That's the question left unasked in all the studies about football. Would Willie Roaf's life have been better if he'd never been allowed to play such a violent game? Who would he be? Who would Curtis Martin be if society had "protected" him from the crushing hits? He grew up in a violent neighborhood. His father tortured his mother, literally, making her stand in scalding water, and if she flinched, he burned her with cigarettes. Five-year-old Curtis saw this. He saw him punch her in the face, saw her with black eyes and a bloody face. His grandmother was violently murdered. His aunt was murdered, too. When he was 15, someone put a gun to his head and pulled the trigger seven times. It misfired each time. Finally, his mother begged him to go out for football, just to have a few more hours out of the dangerous streets. That's why he played. His anger came out through the violence. Baseball didn't have what Curtis Martin needed. The violence kept him alive.

They've reached Canton. They've made millions of dollars and earned the right to walk—or limp—across the lobby with the rest of the legends. They gained much, and gave much, too.

"He's so-so," Phoebe Roaf says. "Pretty much every joint, lower back, both hips, both knees, both ankles, constant pain. That's the side you don't see. It wasn't for free."

Me: Was it worth it?

Dermontti Dawson: It was worth it. I wouldn't change anything. I have a lot of people ask me, my son played football, knowing what you know now, with all the concussion stuff that's going on, I said I still would play; you play for love of the game. That's just a risk. It's gonna happen. I may feel good now, but give me 10 more years and see where I am then.

Me: I saw your helmet on display in the museum.

Dawson (laughing): Oh, man. You see the gouges?

The black Steelers helmet, in a display case just outside the circular room filled with busts, is cut, smashed and lined with rough creases. The top of the four-barred face mask, around the temples, is now bare metal, the plastic coating ripped off by helmet-to-helmet hits. The damage is mostly to the part that covered Dawson's forehead. The yellow stripe down the middle is torn, the 6 and the 3 partially ripped away. Even one of the plastic brackets holding the face mask in place has been hit so often, and with such force, that it's crooked. But if you walk around the display and look at the back, it's smooth. From the back, it'd be hard to tell that this helmet had been used.

The Pro Football Hall of Fame is a celebration of this violence in the same way baseball's Hall of Fame, a timeless brick building in a timeless, quaint town, is a celebration of baseball's pastoral past, even if that past is gone at best, a myth at worst. It's fitting, then, that the Pro Football Hall of Fame is just off an interstate that runs through the collapsed industrial center of the country. Everything about Cooperstown says permanence. Everything about Canton says transience. The town is surrounded by decay: north to Cleveland, west to Detroit, east to Youngstown, south to West Virginia. An important line connects Dawson's helmet to this boxy museum to the manufacturing towns where pro football was born.

This building isn't a shrine to flash and athleticism; it is a shrine to grit and determination—to dinosaurs. One of the most powerful bits of history, preserved like a relic, is the piece of paper sent to the NFL by the Minnesota Vikings that deactivated Brett Favre after his record streak of playing through pain. Football is more about that piece of paper than one with daring plays scribbled on it. Sure, the game can be safer, and the league can police the hits, protect the quarterbacks. And yes, there can be tests and studies. But one hour in the Pro Football Hall of Fame and the NFL's conundrum becomes clear: The game was born out of violence, and its mythology not only tolerates that violence, it celebrates those who survive it. The damaged men in the hotel lobby aren't legends in spite of their limping.

In many ways, they are legends because of it.

Curtis Martin: Literally, football saved my life. Not just a quote or just saying it. Football really saved my life.

Me: Do you want your kids to play?

Martin: Initially, my thought would be: I don't want my kid to play because I know what I had to go through. But I'd say I would want my kid to play in the sense that I don't think there's any better game to learn about life. Football taught me how to be a businessman. Football taught me how to be a caring individual, a giving individual. Football has done so much for my life that I would trade everything. I would trade the Hall of Fame for what football taught me as a man.

After the speeches ended, a crew of workers began tearing down the stage, pulling up the floor from the high school football field, rolling up cables, unplugging lights. It was time to leave. For a few days, I'd been hanging around former football greats, struggling to articulate even to myself exactly what I was looking for, or what questions I wanted to answer. In the empty stadium, the thought crystallizes: What if brains are the new knees?

In 2012, the legends struggle to walk to the elevator. In 2062, will they even know what an elevator is? It's an overdramatic question, but it's the simplified version of everyone's fear, the worry at the heart of the neurological questionnaire. Is there a generation of football stars—household names and faces, modern celebrities—who have already been ruined and don't know it yet? What if Favre can't cut his food at the reception? Might Peyton Manning come to Canton and not recognize Eli? Will Ray Lewis remember dancing during player introductions? That's what everyone is really asking, right? And nobody knows the answers, so people look for clues.

I stared at the gouges in Dawson's helmet, and thought about the player he'd replaced on the Steelers' offensive line: Mike Webster, a Hall of Famer who died at age 50, five years after his induction, depressed and suffering from dementia, living out of his pickup truck. Football killed Webster, and Dawson watched it. He's 47 now. Every player knows what could happen, and they hope they've been spared. Right now, Dawson is fine. He thinks he'll stay that way.

For a night, at least, those questions could wait. The players, and their families and friends, went down the hill to big, white tents. Food filled long tables, and drinks moved across the well-stocked bars. Music thumped out into the darkness, and a journey that began when these men were just children came to an end. Tomorrow would be the first day of the rest of their lives. 🪦

Wright Thompson on writing what most
are thinking but not saying

Great stories can't be predictable, reporting what people already know. So it's important to notice what nobody's talking about but everyone has to be thinking about—or *should* be thinking about. To avoid "the stench of journalism"—reporting the facts and only the facts—I look for the narrative line for every feature, the compelling story beyond the who/what/when/where/why of the inverted pyramid.

When I was covering the 2012 induction at the Football Hall of Fame in Canton, Ohio, I—like every serious sportswriter in the country—was already familiar with research on the long-term effects of concussions. I had to assume most ESPN readers were aware of it too. Yes, the glories of professional football live on, and yes, the injuries also live on. After watching older players make their way through the lobby—using canes and crutches and wheelchairs—I interviewed many Hall of Famers as well as their siblings and parents, and kept asking, "Was it worth it?" Most of the sports legends thought it was. They loved the game, the success, the camaraderie. They loved becoming who they were through this game not *despite* the violence but *because of* the violence. There were so many titanium joints, hips, ankles, and knees in the room, accompanied by pains they could live with. But losing their minds? No one could say, because while nearly all of them had had at least a few concussions, none had yet experienced brain damage themselves. They were aware of others who had.

After several days of trying to articulate exactly what I was looking for, I knew I was close to the narrative line when I asked myself: "What if brains are the new knees? In 2012, the legends struggle to walk to the elevator. In 2062, will they even know what an elevator is?" I recognized this was an overdramatic question, but it identified everyone's unspoken fear. Here was the story behind the story—the story that everyone was thinking about but not talking about: did this generation of football legends already have brain damage but not know it yet?

THE VIEW FROM WITHIN

Seth Wickersham

January 2008, Seventeen Months to Go

Michael Vick arrives at Leavenworth in time for lunch. He's led by guards to a small cafeteria and left alone, inmate No. 33765-183. A few days earlier, word passed quickly through this Kansas federal prison that Vick would be serving the remainder of his 23-month sentence for dogfighting conspiracy here, making him the most famous athlete ever to pass through its doors. Vick doesn't pause to scout his new surroundings; he turns around, drops his eyes, grabs a tray and slides down the lunch line. But he feels the stares burning his back, and he hears every whisper. *Oh, he's a small dude. I thought he was bigger.*

Vick is handed a plate of pork and a roll. Just as he's about to face the other inmates, he pauses and thinks, here we go. He pivots and finally scans the room. Black prisoners sit on one side, whites on the other. A few inmates brazenly eye him; the rest act preoccupied. The black side is full, so Vick, not wanting to make a scene, joins the whites. He says nothing, tries his best to look at nothing and no one. He bites into the pork, but it tastes weird. Not at all like pork.

Vick expected Leavenworth to be like what he'd seen on TV: barren halls, dank cells, the entirety of the outside world closed to him and the partitioned remains guarded by expressionless men of the law. But Leavenworth doesn't quite feel like prison. For one thing, it has a visitors' lounge—a square room with glass doors that open to a courtyard dotted with round tables. Nothing divides visitors from prisoners.

It was different at Northern Neck Regional Jail in Warsaw, Va. That's where Vick began his sentence in November 2007, where he could talk to guests only through glass. His 3-year-old daughter, Jada, would ask him why she couldn't see his feet. After a visit, he'd go back to his cell, small as a dorm room, with a toilet, shower and sink. When the door closed the first time, the reality of it all set in. *What the hell did I get myself into?*

He was supposed to stay in Virginia for all of his 23 months, but he heard that a federally sponsored drug-rehab program could shave maybe a full year off his time. (He'd gotten caught smoking pot before his sentencing, a violation of his pretrial agreement.) So he applied for the program and received a transfer to Leavenworth. Vick said he had assurances from officials there that he would not spend time in its infamous Big House. He would be housed in a smaller neighboring facility on the prison grounds.

And so on Jan. 7 Vick flew from Virginia to Kansas in a small plane and climbed into a car. An officer drove him over the rising and falling wheat-color countryside, frozen for the winter, past the cows and into the town of Leavenworth. But then the car pulled up to the Big House—concrete and capitol-like, with 40-foot walls and a long row of stairs that flopped like a tongue from its domed entrance. Vick panicked and thought, *Man, I've been told a lie.* A guard took him inside, handed him a khaki button-down shirt and pants and said, "Do your time and get out of here." Vick was placed in solitary confinement, peach-color cinder blocks surrounding a sink and a toilet. He stayed in solitary for a few hours while his papers were processed, and then he was led, without explanation, to the neighboring camp he'd been promised.

After lunch, after the terrible-tasting pork, he sees his cell for the first time and realizes this is worse; this is actually much worse than solitary confinement. There are no cells at the smaller camp. There are only bunk-bed units, like a barracks block, eight inmates per group.

Night after night, cockroaches roam the floors. Guys shuffle around a lot. Vick witnesses certain things—"things that should stay in prison," he will later say, refusing to comment further—that disturb him too much to sleep. At first, he tries earplugs. Then he applies for a midnight-shift job, mopping floors for 12 cents an hour.

On a typical day, he mops in the predawn morning, then watches TV until sunrise and sleeps. He wakes around noon. Uncertain about what else to do, he joins games of chess; a lot of the guys here play. Before Leavenworth, Vick had never tried the game, but in no time he's able to beat every inmate—except a guy named Huey. Vick never learns anything more about Huey than his name.

At one point, a guard advises Vick to "stay away from everyone and don't make friends." Vick is a target, and there are fights many days. He notices guys studying him, 27 years old, hair unbraided, goatee fuzzy. So Vick remains wary of the others, which is easy enough. Even on the outside he was a closed man, leading a closed life.

In the silence of night he mops floors with a man named Dink-Dink from Kansas City—to whom Vick speaks just enough to not share anything.

February 2008, 16 Months to Go

Why me? That's the thought that keeps racing through his mind. He can't figure out why he landed such a stiff sentence. Twenty-three months in prison for dogfighting? None of the other three defendants in his case got as much time. Why me? He begins to keep a journal, to chronicle it all, to see whether putting it on the page will help him make sense of what his life has become—a life in prison that everyone but him believes he deserves. "I felt like the law didn't apply to me," Vick would later say.

At times, the journal helps. Familiar faces do too. A few weeks after Vick's incarceration at Leavenworth, C.J. Reamon, round-faced and lanky with a trim goatee, known to Vick as Charlie, enters the visitors lounge and sees his friend.

"Man, they got you out here?" Charlie says.

"Yeah, Charlie, they got me way out here."

Charlie, whose uncle Tommy was Vick's high school coach, worked at the Delta counter at Norfolk International Airport. One day in 2002, Charlie asked the TSA agent if Vick could skip the security line. The agent said no, so Charlie slipped Vick through a back door and was caught. Before Charlie could be fired, though, Vick said, "Look, come work for me. I'll take care of you." Charlie quit and was so excited to be Vick's personal assistant that he commuted between Vick in Atlanta and his wife, Vanessa, in

Virginia. Vick paid Charlie in cash and in gifts, like new rims. Anything that needed to be done, Charlie did.

Well, almost anything. Charlie was Vick's only posse member who wasn't involved with Bad Newz Kennels. While Vick attended fights, Charlie stayed home with Vanessa. In spring 2007, Vick confessed to Charlie how bad it would be if "this stuff went down." But Vick didn't quit. He knew dogfighting was illegal; he just didn't believe it was so wrong. After police raided Bad Newz Kennels but before the arrest, Vick transferred $1.1 million into Charlie's bank account so he could pay the bills and support Vick's mother, Brenda, brother Marcus, girlfriend Kijafa Frink and their two daughters, Jada and London, a newborn. Charlie then drove Vick to jail, slowly as he could. When Vick exited the car, Jada crawled out the window, screaming, "I want my daddy! Daddy, please come back!" Kijafa pulled Jada back inside, which left Charlie to be the last one to hug Vick before he was booked. Charlie didn't let go until Vick was pulled away.

Now, sitting opposite Charlie at Leavenworth, Vick rubs his face. He's irritated. It's 11 a.m., and he's barely slept. Vick points Charlie to a vending machine in the lounge, past a red line that inmates aren't permitted to cross. "You got any change?" Vick asks. Charlie fishes out a few quarters and returns with a microwave cheeseburger and a Sprite.

Charlie says he and Kijafa are looking for a rental near Leavenworth with a big basement because Charlie's scared of tornadoes. Their plan is to trade shifts every two weeks. There are instances in the months to come when Kijafa and Charlie's visits will overlap. To pass time, they'll watch movies or eat tater tots at Sonic or tell funny stories about Mike— like the time when, as a kid, he Krazy-Glued one of his eyelids shut. Telling stories doesn't always help, though. Kijafa cries thinking that her kids are growing up without a present father. She's scared that intruders hide inside her home, so she often asks Charlie to search it before she enters, something he doesn't tell Vick about when he visits. Charlie doesn't complain to him either about leaving his family to tend to Mike's.

During visits from Charlie and Kijafa, Vick never apologizes for the mess he's heaped on them, doesn't really say thanks. But that's the Mike they know; he can be self-absorbed. Vick just tells them to "hang in there," never realizing that he's not the only one who must survive Leavenworth.

About a month after that first visit from Charlie, Kijafa's phone rings. It's Mike. His voice is muddled, but his words are fast, the way he gets when he's angry. He starts talking about Leavenworth's drug-rehab program. "I didn't get in," he says. He's furious. The entire reason for transferring from Virginia was to get into the program, leave prison early and sign with a team for off-season workouts. Now he's stuck in Kansas, a thousand miles from his extended family and friends, living in those damn barracks. "Call my lawyer," he tells Kijafa.

She dials Vick's attorney, Billy Martin in Washington, D.C., who says he'll look into it. Martin calls the Feds repeatedly over the next few days and finally gets an answer: Vick won't be admitted for reasons the Feds don't divulge. A week later, Kijafa visits Vick, and they sit in a nook in the lounge, away from sight. He's slouched and angry. But he says, "I've got to let it go."

April 2008, 14 Months to Go

Vick enters the TV room to watch the NFL draft. He's still under contract with the Falcons until 2009 and occasionally trades letters with the owner, Arthur Blank. He hopes to return to the team; the Falcons, however, are working to trade his rights. When he sits down, the draft is already an hour old. The Falcons held the third overall pick, so he asks another inmate, "Who did the Falcons take?"

"Matt Ryan."

Silence. The guys look at him. Vick's been fired, in front of everybody. His face stiffens, trying to hide his humiliation. He stares blankly at the screen for as long as he can, an attempt to prove that he's unaffected. He finally gives up around 2 p.m., leaving the others so he can call his mother on her birthday. He fakes a cheery voice. "Happy birthday, Mom," he says. Brenda changes the subject too quickly. "I got something to tell you," she says.

"What happened, Mom?"

"Grandma had a stroke."

Vick had been afraid that Caletha Vick would die while he was in prison. She'd suffered from dementia for years and was in poor health. Hours before Vick surrendered to authorities, he sat next to Caletha, not sure what to say. If he told her where he was going, he worried she'd have a heart attack. So he said he was off to training camp and kissed her goodbye. Vick later learned that after he left, Caletha turned to Brenda and said, "He said he's going to camp. But he's going to jail."

Five days later, Caletha dies. Vick requests permission to attend her funeral, but officials tell him that funeral visits are permitted only for the deaths of immediate family members. And that's when it hits him, harder than all the other times before this: Man, I really f--ed up. He is an embarrassment to himself and his family, a tainted man who can't even pay respects to those who loved him. He opens his journal, considers an entry. Screw it. He tosses it in the trash.

June 2008, 12 Months to Go

Vick plays in a basketball game, part of a prison-organized tournament. When his team wins, another inmate accuses Vick of paying off the refs. He tries to shake him off, but the inmate, in front of all the others, yells "F*** you!" over and over. Vick's prepared himself to walk away from a confrontation like this, but now, in the moment, it's not so easy. He figures if he ignores this guy, he'll be branded as weak.

"I'm a grown man," Vick snaps. "You're not talking to me that way."

"What do you want to do?" the guy says. "You got more to lose than me."

"I'm in the same position you're in," Vick says.

They stare at each other for a moment, then Vick lunges. But before he can swing, another inmate grabs him and pulls him back, reminding him, "Vick, you can't do this!"

Vick backs off and looks at the man who saved him from the fight, from perhaps a transfer to another prison, coupled with a longer sentence that would have kept him out of football another year. It's Dink, his floor-mopping companion.

In every prison, there's a loyalty among inmates that Vick had resisted, a pact forged by their common circumstances. Vick realizes at this moment that with these guys, he'll forever be a part of their lives. Over time, silent games of chess become small talk. Small talk leads to deeper conversations. Vick finds many other inmates candid. Genuine. Honest. Loyal. Smart. They read all day, inspiring Vick to read more too. Dink is easiest to talk to; he and Vick can chat all night. Another inmate, Dino from Chicago, is so upbeat he can always make Vick laugh. But they all talk about how Vick shouldn't be here, how he's a victim of his own celebrity. Vick agrees.

He watches football with the guys every Sunday of the 2008 season. He tries to teach them the game. He describes why a receiver runs a particular route and why a linebacker shoots the C gap. But inmates argue each point—everyone's an expert, even in prison—and Vick gives up on the tutorials. After mopping floors at night, he watches highlights on TV, completely disgusted by what he's lost.

He had to declare bankruptcy in July. By the end of the year, Charlie is forced to relinquish Vick's boats and cars and what's left of the $1.1 million. A bankruptcy committee permits payments only to Vick's girlfriend and mother. Short on money, Charlie starts driving buses. Vick's brother Marcus paints boats. Vick's not only wrecked his life; he's wrecked his family's too. His daughters used to cry after visiting him. Now they don't, and Vick can't decide which hurts worse. This isn't the man he promised Kijafa he'd be.

He comes to know that he must do more than survive Leavenworth. He must learn from it. So now, when the guys tell Vick that he shouldn't be here, he doesn't indulge them. He looks them in the eye and says, "You're wrong."

February 2009, Four Months to Go

The weeks pass until it's Super Bowl Sunday. The Cardinals and Steelers are set to kick off in a few hours when Vick receives word of an unexpected visitor: Kynan Forney, his former right guard in Atlanta. Both were drafted in 2001: Vick first overall, Forney 219th. Forney was eager to buddy up to Vick, like vintage guard-quarterback relationships go. But Vick always put him off, just like he put off every other lineman, just like he put off most teammates.

Forney hadn't talked to Vick since his arrest. Worried that nobody else would make the trip, Forney decided to see his former quarterback.

Vick enters the visitors lounge. Wow, he's cut, Forney thinks. Shoulders bigger, stomach leaner. "Man, you look good!" he says. Vick tells him he's been doing a lot of push-ups and sit-ups recently. Forney rises for the vending machines, and Vick follows until he hits the red line. With a hopeful look he says, "I can't cross."

"Yo, why you saying things sideways?" Forney asks. "If you want something, just tell me!"

Vick tiptoes the line as if trying to stay inbounds. He selects chili cheese Fritos and an iced tea, and as he waits, someone asks him for an autograph. He signs it agreeably, then sits down at one of the tables with Forney, munching on his chips. After a few minutes of small talk, Vick blurts out, "I should have been watching tape."

"What do you mean?"

"I was doing just enough, going off instincts. We could have been much more dangerous. I'm one of the best quarterbacks in the game with this skill set, and I'm in prison."

Forney is shocked but doesn't show it. Vick's just figuring this out? Maybe he should have told Vick to study more, but no, it was understood in the Falcons' locker room that Vick's 90 percent was better than most quarterbacks' 100 percent. Next time, Vick says with an intensity that Forney never saw in Atlanta, he'll be a better teammate.

May 20, 2009, 17 Hours to Go>

At 11 a.m., guards approach Vick's bunk. "You, Mr. Vick, come stand in the corner." What the hell? I didn't do nothing, Vick thinks. One of the guards says, "You're leaving tomorrow at 4:30 a.m."

Vick is leaving prison early for good behavior. He'll be released in the middle of the night to avoid cameras, the guards inform him. Ecstatic, he calls Kijafa and tells her to be at the gates. "You sure?" she says. Yeah, he's sure. Vick returns to his bunk and unzips a green bag to pack. Inmates had advised him to leave everything from prison, so Vick ditches his khaki shirt and pants, shoes and socks. But he doesn't want to forget this place either. He packs some prison underwear and T-shirts.

That night, he lies awake, too excited to sleep, until the guards arrive predawn, right on time. The doors open and he exits, wearing an untucked white T-shirt, jeans and white sneakers with untied laces. He embraces Kijafa. She clutches his hand, already walking ahead of him and telling him to hurry, as if it's an escape.

A black Chrysler sits in the parking lot. Kijafa drives away while Vick leans against the window, looking at places both familiar and foreign—the yellow of a McDonald's sign, the orange of a Hardee's, the halogen glow of a gas station. They check into a hotel. Vick runs his hands along the walls of the room, just to feel something other than concrete.

A few hours later, in the midmorning sun, they're back on the road. The states along I-70 slip into each other: Kansas, Missouri, Illinois, then Indiana. Vick sees a grassy stretch of land in some forgotten rural county that's covered with swaying knee-high grass. He asks Kijafa to pull the car over, and they walk out into the field. The horizon goes on forever, which is both inspiring and comforting to him. Kijafa senses what he's thinking.

"Want land like this?" she asks.

"I'd get 150 acres," he says, then adds with a scoff, "Just need to make sure we can afford it."

Vick stands there a minute longer, listening to the whoosh of passing cars. The dull panic that he felt outside the prison, as if not another moment of his life could be wasted, falls away. Back in the car, he's calm, finally—every mile taking him farther away from one place and closer to another. ▨

Seth Wickersham on good stories versus great stories

Writing is a process. Writing a complicated, layered magazine story is difficult and requires all kinds of elements. But when it comes down to the pure style of the writing, a few factors have to exist. You have to internalize your material. You need to know it cold so that when you're writing, your natural voice takes over, and you instinctively know which details to include and which to shed, and the pacing and physics and subtleties of the piece fall into place. I always use the analogy of giving a toast at your best friend's wedding. You know the person so well that you don't need to glance at notes; you speak from the heart. You want to try to know your material for a magazine story as well as you know a friend.

The next step is taking creative risks, knowing that some will work and some won't. When I began writing at the *Maneater* and especially the Columbia *Missourian*, I wanted to be distinctive. I tried too hard, reaching for metaphors and jokes and different ways to tell very mundane stories. I once wrote about a football player who had an alcoholic father in second person from the point of view of the alcohol. I had a sort of blind confidence and audacity. Then I interned at the *Washington Post*, and reality set in. I didn't take as many chances, but I still tried to distinguish myself, and it was a rocky process. I had to learn how to be more direct and concise. It took dozens of stories, but I made progress. I returned to the *Missourian* and started taking smarter risks. I was hired at *ESPN* magazine, and the process began all over again.

It's a process that really doesn't end, that evolves as you accrue scars and experience life and gain perspective. Writing is a craft, which means that it's inherently difficult and can always be refined. The best writers grind; they write and rewrite. They keep pushing when they feel brilliant and when they feel like a hack.

You want each story to check all the boxes. One of the lessons I've had to learn the hard way is that not all stories can check every box. The reasons vary, but usually it has to do with constraints: time, access, space. Sometimes the first step in writing a good story versus a great story is knowing when the story is merely a good one. There are only so many holes you can fill unless you have all the material you want, and the simple fact is that some topics or subjects are richer than others.

Truly great stories are rare. That's why they're great. Knowing the difference between a good story and a great story also helps you maximize the material of a great story. Develop your own standards, and you'll know the great stuff when you see it. Years ago I wrote a story about the most influential book in football history, written by the legendary coach Bill Walsh. Almost every coach had it on his shelf—550 dense pages, available only online for hundreds of dollars, almost more of a textbook than a literary tome. Now, anybody who knew Walsh knew that he was a tortured football genius whose need to be perfect all but ruined him. The book was really a biography masquerading as a textbook, and it was a guide to ruin your life as much as it was a guide to win football games. I knew all of this before I made my first trip or phone call. One of the most important aspects of any story is to know what you're looking for, so that when you see it, your reportorial antennae are up.

I thought of ways to flesh out the themes I wanted to explore. I wanted to report the tragic history of how the book came to be and find a tragic young coach who sought to be great, but instead came to realize that it corrupts from within. I found an ambitious young coach outside of Philadelphia who was using the book to coach a high school team. I spent four or five days with him, watching the process erode him. Those themes would mirror the themes that emerged from my reporting of how the book came to be. When I wrote the story, I alternated sections between the present and the past, each one subtly foreshadowing the other. I don't know if it was a great story, but it's one that I'm proudest of because I was able to check all of the boxes. It was memorable because it was rare.

CONFRONTING
A DIFFERENT KIND OF LOSS

Jane Gordon Julien

Stanley Rosenzweig stands in his shiny kitchen in Manhattan, reflective surfaces all around, by the stainless-steel island that friends refer to as looking like "an autopsy table." Mr. Rosenzweig, an easygoing, upbeat man who once went online to rent a Moses costume to jazz up a Passover Seder, is telling a joke, which he does frequently.

It goes something like this: A man doesn't feel well, but he looks well. He goes to doctor after doctor, all of whom say he's fine. Finally, one of the doctors agrees to do tests, and after reading the results he says to the man: "You're fine. Go home." Once home, the man drops dead. On his tombstone was the epitaph he had already instructed his wife to write: "I told you I was sick!"

Mr. Rosenzweig weighs his words for a moment, then says, "This story does not apply to me."

Not so much. A little bit, maybe.

In the late 1960s, Mr. Rosenzweig and a girl he loved, Zelda R. Stern, parted ways—twice—after meeting at Temple University in Philadelphia, two young lovers too young for love. They met again through a mutual friend more than 30 years later, in 2000, after Ms. Stern had forged careers in Manhattan as a social worker, psychotherapist, published feminist writer and philanthropist, and Mr. Rosenzweig had prospered as a seller of specialty foods. He had remained in the Philadelphia area, married, had two sons and lost his wife to cancer in October 1999. Ms. Stern had remained single.

The couple married on Sept. 9, 2001, and for nine months reveled in their rediscovered love. Then, during a routine physical, Mr. Rosenzweig's physician told him he needed to see a urologist. On a Sunday evening in June 2002, the urologist called Mr. Rosenzweig in Los Angeles, where the couple was visiting Mr. Rosenzweig's son. His words are burned into their respective memories: "You have cancer."

After years of gazing at Mr. Rosenzweig's photo and wondering where he was, then finding him, Ms. Stern was prepared to fight. "I said to him: 'You made me a bride. You're not going to make me a widow.'" Tears welled in her eyes as she spoke about it. "I refuse to lose him."

Almost 10 years later, Ms. Stern, 62, and Mr. Rosenzweig, 63, are like the college kids they were when they met. They hug, they kiss. They sit on the sofa, her legs wrapped around him, his arms wrapped around her, in a combined living and dining area filled with framed photos of the couple on their wedding day.

He is alive and fairly well, considering that his illness—metastatic prostate cancer—has subjected him to numerous surgeries, chemotherapy, the removal of his prostate in August 2002 and the spread of the cancer to his lungs and pelvis. "I call it the 'Where's Waldo' of cancer, since we never know where it is going to pop up next," Ms. Stern said.

And all things considered, he has Ms. Stern, along with good Manhattan physicians, to thank. He is unlike the man in his joke for a couple of reasons, primary among them that Ms. Stern galloped to his aid when his resolve faltered, which was almost immediately. Besides losing his wife to lung cancer, Mr. Rosenzweig lost his mother to breast cancer when he was 14. "I see cancer as a death sentence," he said.

But for Ms. Stern, cancer was a fight she had been training for for years. Feisty and fearless, she is a feminist who embraces Orthodox Judaism, which has been known to look askance at unmarried, liberal-thinking women. Now married but always a liberal thinker, she made a name for herself as a philanthropist who supports the Jewish Orthodox Feminist Alliance, of which she is a founding board member; the Yeshivat Maharat, which trains Orthodox women to be clergy; and other organizations that empower Orthodox Jewish women. She was not immune from the effects of cancer, either: it had taken the lives of her mother, maternal aunt and maternal grandmother, when they were all about 60.

After the couple learned of the diagnosis of Mr. Rosenzweig's disease, Ms. Stern used her considerable connections as a former social worker, then psychiatric social worker, to find him good care. She lined up six oncologists for the couple to interview, called on the support of her network of Jewish friends (the couple belongs to three synagogues, including one on Long Island, in Lido Beach, near their summer home in Long Beach), and countered Mr. Rosenzweig's resignation with her own dogged determination. He told her, "All right, all right, I won't make you a widow." Ms. Stern, smiling, said, "He is so accommodating."

They also began planning overseas trips in earnest. "When you have an illness like this, you don't wait," she said. "We didn't know how much time we had. Everyone should do that—maximize their time. But they say, 'What's the rush?' and then they never get around to it. So for us, this was very motivating." They have traveled the world in the last 10 years, and just recently returned from trips to Portugal and Israel.

Mr. Rosenzweig's health problems are like a rip in an otherwise seamless piece of silk. Ceaselessly polite and kind, the pair defer easily to each other. She laughs at his jokes, he strokes her hair and kisses her cheek frequently, as though he fears she may vanish again.

When they moved into Ms. Stern's apartment together in December 2002 (she was having it renovated before she re-met him), his adjustment to life in Manhattan was just a ripple in a river. He misses his garage, which was attached to his house. Now he has to walk four blocks to retrieve his car, which he pays ("Pays!" he crowed indignantly) to park.

What he did not have to relinquish: his tinkering ways. He changed all the light switches in the apartment, changes the water filters, and handles all repairs at the Long Beach house. "Zelda won't let me do big plumbing," he said, grinning.

Geography had little meaning for him. "I am very much in love with Zelda," he said. "I'm very thankful to have found her. We have a lot of fun together, and that is such an important part of living."

She had avoided marriage for years, fearing it might pose challenges she couldn't navigate. "Our marriage has brought me great relief and a feeling of being free," she said. "Stanley does much more of the food shopping than I. He loves shopping. I can entertain, especially for Shabbat meals, so, so much more than before, because I have someone with whom to share hosting responsibilities."

"I tell him how much I love him," she said, "and that he is in the best hands as far as medical care. And I tell him, which he knows, that I will always, always fight to make sure everything goes right."

Standing in his kitchen, he tells another joke, employing her as his straight man: "My wife, my wife, it's like we were married yesterday." She smiles wanly and says, "Oh, is that right?" To which he responds, "Oy, yes, and what a lousy day yesterday was."

Mr. Rosenzweig grins, because he knows for certain that this story, above all, does not apply to him.

Jane Gordon Julien on digging to find the story and the right words to tell it

There will never be a substitute for the great storytelling channeled by the classics. Voice and meaningful themes will never be outdated.

If I read too much contemporary fiction, I have trouble finding the right words to write my stories. If I read Dickens, Tolstoy, Victor Hugo, Louisa May Alcott: the words come. The masters settle into the brain and start working whatever magic they can. Yes, shorter attention spans and click-bait are seizing this generation. Read the classics anyway. Having words at your fingertips helps every writer. Getting the juices flowing requires reading great writers.

As you write, your voice will evolve and seep through. I started my career with pure journalism, followed by more appreciation of color, followed by a more devoted approach to storytelling.

And what makes a great storyteller of fiction is the same for what makes a great storyteller of journalism. Don't be afraid to dig, ask more questions, dig some more. People are forgetful, they file memories away in the attics of their minds, and until someone pushes them to blow off the dust and pull out the files, the story is only half done. I do multiple interviews, asking them questions they can't possibly answer right off the bat, and asking them to think about it and I'll check back in later. I've drawn out some of my best information with this approach. Gather more than you need, and boil it down after.

Seeking out a story requires curiosity. Random conversations, interviews I am doing on a completely different subject, chance events: these are all fodder for stories. The themes will present themselves. After working with journalists for so many years, I have found that one of the greatest dangers to a potential story is their going into it thinking they already know what it's about. This deprives them of an open-mindedness that may take them in much more interesting directions. I think many stories offer a multitude of themes that an enterprising writer can tailor to numerous publications.

Writing and storytelling are a commitment. What's that saying, "Just sit at the typewriter, open a vein and bleed"? Attributed to a gazillion people but it's painful to do—and painful not to do. Like falling in love, good writing makes you feel more than anything else. That's what the classics do well.

VINYL HERO

Doug Meigs

Vinyl records have consumed his life. More than 300,000 albums engulf his apartment and five warehouses. Paul Au Tak-shing is the steward of Hong Kong's biggest record collection.

He slept with his records on the streets of Sham Shui Po, the city's poorest district, off and on for 20 years. He moved permanently indoors in 2004. Now, the 52-year-old hawker sleeps shoulder-to-shoulder with his merchandise. Mountains of vinyl crowd his dreams. His bed occupies the apartment's single patch of empty floor, a 7-by-3-foot gap, which doubles as the only place where customers can stand during business hours.

Au usually wakes in the early afternoon. He folds his aluminum and nylon cot, and squeezes it into a utilitarian bathroom. He unofficially opens shop from 2–10 p.m., but entertains customers at all hours, seven days a week.

Call his phone number and ask about buying records. He'll reply, "What sort of music do you like?" He has a bit of everything—and it's not organized. If your interest is obscure, he might have to go to his New Territories warehouses, where the bulk of his collection rests under dusty sheets alongside a stockpile of turntable equipment and discarded vintage clothing.

He lives near exit C1 of Sham Shui Po MTR station. Hong Kong's budget-shopping Mecca sprawls in every direction. Pedestrians swarm the labyrinthine neighborhood. Stockades of garment, stereo and cell phone peddlers line the streets. Piles of random junk (shoes, appliances, fishing poles) spill from rusted green stalls at the Apliu Street flea market. Across Cheung Sha

Wan Road at the Golden Computer Shopping Center, the latest computer gadgets race into obsolescence.

Take the elevator up to see Au on the dingy fifth floor of the Wai Hong Building. Nine crates packed with vinyl huddle in the stairwell. More record boxes crowd the hallway. An arrow sign—drawn onto a blue-colored disco LP—hangs from the wall. It directs visitors past a neighbor's home.

Unless he's taking a walk, or scouting for more records, Au is listening to music inside his shop. A friendly voice welcomes visitors in Cantonese, Mandarin or English. He wears jeans and a black Guns N' Roses T-shirt, a cap over his short hair, scruffy stubble covering his chin. He is thin and wiry, and stands 5 ft. 3 in.—an ideal size for such cramped quarters. He has kept fit carrying countless record boxes for the past 26 years.

He entertains customers and friends with an encyclopedic knowledge of classic rock. He cracks jokes and laughs easily. He laments the tragedy of vinyl records, an example of society's eagerness to discard quality goods for the sake of new consumption trends. He lives modestly, with minimal electricity and no air-con (unless a customer insists).

About 45,000 records remain on hand. The genres span experimental jazz to folk. Top sellers include 1980s pop hits and albums from Taiwanese songstress Teresa Teng. He also sells strange items (for example, a Chinese children's choir singing about Superman).

When Au lists his favorite musicians, he names two local Hong Kong metal bands from the 1970s: Ram Band and Chyna. He has lots of their albums, but they seldom sell. "I love the records so much, but they are not going fast enough. Nobody wants them. I have got a problem with no solution," he says, surveying the overcrowded flat. Two bedrooms store more piles of records, but they are virtually inaccessible. The only way into the rooms: up and over.

Make a random request in Au's shop. Name any band or album (as long as it is not too contemporary) and he springs to action. Barefoot, he climbs cardboard Tsingtao boxes full of vinyl. He steps gingerly over Michael Jackson, Leslie Cheung and Peking opera stars.

Customers buy records from Au every day, even on public holidays. But the patronage is not enough to stem the tide of incoming vinyl. He accumulates more than 10,000 records every year. His 525-sq.-ft. flat is overflowing. Soon he hopes to secure a new warehouse, but money is tight, and real estate prices continue to rise.

"I told myself six years ago that I was not going to receive any more re-cords, but I just could not resist," he says. "These people come and tell me, 'If you will not receive them, then they will go to the dumpsite.' What can I do? I'm an orphanage; this is an orphanage. I receive them. I cannot re-sist. So they are here. I have given up my comfort. These are my children," he says. Like real children, the albums have value beyond any dollar sum.

Now that an (almost) infinite amount of music can fit on a small mobile phone, vinyl records seem like clunky dinosaurs—especially in congested Hong Kong where space is so limited a commodity. Sacrificing space for vinyl doesn't appeal to many casual music listeners. However, audiophiles tout vinyl's analog superiority over digital.

Records are manufactured using a sound-sensitive stylus/needle, which cuts a spiral groove in a wax disc. The wax disc becomes a mold for vinyl versions. When the vinyl copies spin beneath a needle on a turntable, the needle vibrates in the exact same way to create an "analogous" sound wave. Speakers amplify the vibrations processed through a diaphragm. Digital recordings use a sequence of numbers to imitate analog sound. They do not capture the exact sound wave.

Au's bias for vinyl goes beyond the analog vs. digital debate. "From CDs, the sound is quite sharp, and its quite clean, but mostly it's not my lifestyle; I live with the records," he says, laughing. "It's like the five senses: I see them, I hear them, smell them, touch them. Records are my passion. I'm quite nostalgic. I'm still living in the 1970s."

He was born in 1957 in Cholon, the Chinatown on the outskirts of Sai-gon, Vietnam. His parents were Chinese. His grandfather was a wealthy soap factory owner and leader of the Cantonese community. Au's father grew up among the local colonial French elite. The factory and fortune disappeared before Au's birth. He grew up lower middle class, studying English with other *fan su tsai*—a derogatory Cantonese phrase translating directly to "foreign book boys."

The Vietnam War raged in the countryside. Boys from Au's neighbor-hood went to the battlefields, and they did not return. Fighting spilled into Chinatown during the Tet Offensive in 1968. Grenades exploded and gun-fire rattled in the street outside his family's home. One day a suicide bomb-er detonated a truck full of yellow dynamite across the street.

Au and his three younger brothers spent hours in front of the televi-sion. They developed a fondness for American culture from watching the

American military television channel. They watched *Batman* and *Gunsmoke* and absorbed American music.

Years passed, and the war continued. American rock culture progressed with hippies' messages of "free love" and "peace." Lyrics carried heavy anti-war sentiment.

His first record was a scratched and worn copy of Creedence Clearwater Revival's *Cosmos' Factory*. The band is famous for Vietnam protest songs *Who'll Stop the Rain* and *Fortunate Son*. Au's father told him, "We're waiting for the war to end; life will be better."

Every Lunar New Year, Au and his brothers saved red packet money to buy bootleg vinyl records. Their collection was small, but some friends had original pressings of Deep Purple, Led Zeppelin and *Woodstock: Music from the Original Soundtrack*.

Au remembers zonked American GIs at open-air festivals and bars in Saigon. The soldiers drank liquor, smoked pot and listened to Vietnamese hippies covering the same anti-war songs contemporary back in the States.

Like the US draft-dodgers, Au also avoided enlistment. Americans fled into Canada or Mexico to escape service in Vietnam. Au came to Hong Kong. Months before turning 18, his family paid smugglers to transport him to the British colony where an uncle lived.

He hid with a group of boys in a seaside farmhouse for one week. The smugglers arrived in a sampan and took the boys to a cargo ship. Another week passed on the South China Sea. At night they arrived near Hong Kong Island. Fishing junks ferried them to the shore of Shek O Country Club. The smugglers contacted his uncle, who reluctantly paid the smugglers' ransom. Au soon realized that he was alone in a strange city.

Two months after arriving in Hong Kong, the war ended. South Vietnam fell to the communists. He had no contact with his family. "Every day I was waiting until I lost hope," he says.

He moved into a rooftop squatter in North Point. He worked odd jobs until 1980, when he became a clerk in a Wan Chai record shop. Vinyl records and rock culture gave respite from the loneliness. In retrospect, he says they were the best years of his life.

"I'm now only half hippie. I cannot be 100 percent because half of me has stepped into the market already. I have to pay the rent, installments on warehouses. It's money, money, money every day. I wanted to have a free shop out on the street, with no rent, but in Hong Kong, that's not possible. I'd be arrested." Not that he hasn't been arrested. He estimates 50 arrests since he began hawking records.

Au arrived in Sham Shui Po in August of 1983, when he rented a squatter shack on the roof of a nearby building. "That place was hell," he remembers. Wind and rain passed easily through the wood and sheet metal.

In the fall, he stumbled upon an illegal hawker selling vinyl records along Nam Cheong Road (now called Nam Cheong Street). While flipping through a box, he noticed albums that he wanted. Each was HK$2 or HK$3. He found some duplicates and thought he could sell them to cover the purchase expense. When he tried to buy, the hawker offered the entire crate for HK$50. So began a cycle of accumulation that surpassed 300,000 albums in 2002.

"Street hawking is easy," he says. "Anyone can do it. You just put your things on the side of the road." Broke and jobless, he began selling records with the hawkers in 1984. He was arrested for the first time a week later. It was early in the morning. A voice screamed, "Run Ghost!" in Cantonese. Au looked up, and he saw the uniforms of the Urban Services Department approaching. Hawkers scattered. Some pushed trolleys. Other deserted their wares. Au's box was too heavy to carry.

He started to run, then stopped. He returned to save a few records. The officers caught him. They confiscated his box and issued tickets for obstructing the street and selling illegally. "I should have been smarter; I should have left," he says. "Whether I go or stay, I still lose the records."

He returned the next day with another crate. Another arrest followed two weeks later, when Urban Services teamed with police to ambush the hawkers. Everyone got ticketed.

Sometimes raids repeated morning and afternoon of the same day. "It was like playing cat and mouse," he says. "Just when you thought it was safe, they'd come again." He doesn't fault the government employees for doing their job. Some even became customers, buying records during off-duty hours.

Hawking gave a meager profit, an adrenaline rush, and sometimes a broken heart. In the spring of 1985, Au had to pretend that he was a passerby as officers tossed 1,200 of his records into a lumbering garbage compactor.

Like common rubbish, the crushed vinyl mixed with kitsch, clothing and furniture fragments sold by other illegal vendors.

Legal expenses increased with every ticket. A judge called Au's name for the last time in 2003. The fine was about HK$2,000.

Licensed hawkers now sell vinyl records in the street market during the day. Sometimes Au visits their stalls. They offer mostly ragged albums, haphazardly shoved into mountains of secondhand scraps. On a recent visit, Au discovered some familiar items for sale.

The albums included rare 45s that he remembered stashing 20 years back. He returned to the warehouse where he kept his. He found the place ransacked. Burglars had raided his treasure. He spent most of July seeking legal recourse. To no avail. "They told me to just leave it alone, there's no evidence," he said. "But I won't give up. These are my records; they are my life blood."

A few of the current vinyl sellers have been hawking on Apliu Street since the 1980s, when Au was still sleeping on the street.

He slept beside records hidden in an alley from 1984 until 1989, when he began renting his first apartment in the neighborhood. He slept inside until too many record crates accumulated. Then he returned to the street. At night, when his wares were less obstructive to the public, he would pull boxes onto the street. He sold late, listening to music with friends and drinking beer.

Local broadcaster TVB profiled his lifestyle in 1991. "Because of that program, everyone knew about a silly guy like me," he says. Coincidentally, the program was broadcast at a time when vinyl was being disposed of en masse—people were replacing their music collections with CDs.

"Hong Kong people, they are very narrow-minded," says Au. "They thought, 'Oh, records are no longer for sale,' and suddenly, they threw away all their records and record players."

In the 1990s, men in suits frequently stopped their fancy cars near Au's spot on the street. They would pull hundreds of records from a BMW or Volvo and drop the pile at Au's feet. "They'd say, 'Okay, pay whatever you want.' At that time, I was not paying much," he says.

He also claimed large stockpiles from record distributors, closed discos and local shops. He bought piles of turntable needles, when music stores stopped selling them. A garbage collector on Broadcast Drive sold him discarded albums from RTHK and Commercial Radio. He also got a gold Kenny G album (the kind that record execs display on their office walls). He displays the plaque prominently in his shop.

"I didn't refuse. I took everything. That's why my numbers grew too quick," he says.

Amid the chaos, Au bought a Harley Davison motorcycle and met his girlfriend. They have a daughter who is now 12 years old. She lives with her mother, and they visit Au every Sunday. "I don't have time for them. I feel guilty. I don't live with them. I live with the records," he says.

He bought another warehouse in Kwun Tong in 1996; he tried sleeping there, but it was too remote. He again slept on the street sporadically until 2003. He began buying from international sellers after 2000. Distressed Japanese shops and a British record dealer sold him crates. Each crate might contain 40,000 albums.

In 2001, he had 30 trolleys packed with 25,000 records outside his apartment. The vinyl queue stretched down an alleyway, and rounded the corner, to cover two sides of the building. Street cleaners would warn him in advance, and he would spend the entire night moving the trolleys into scattered piles so that in case of a raid police would not confiscate everything. During typhoons, he didn't sleep at all. Every hour, he would monitor the waterproof tarps he had draped over his vulnerable treasure in the alley.

His previous apartment in Sham Shui Po was a loft above a doctor's office. The stairwell up to his apartment was perpetually stuffed with a wall of records. The doctor always complained, and they argued frequently.

Finally, the landlord refused to renew his lease for 2004. Au suspects "that fucking doctor" conspired against him. Moving took months. He planned to build rows of shelves, to make space for customers and his family. But the records came in too fast. Soon, there was barely room for himself, never mind his girlfriend or daughter.

The last time he bought a warehouse was 2008. He sliced his rocker locks for the occasion; too much hair would have made the moving process uncomfortably hot and sweaty. He hadn't cut it in 30 years. A photo on his wall shows the old Au: he is straddling his prized Harley Davidson motorcycle (which he sold in 2002 to buy his second warehouse). Thick black locks dangle past his shoulders. A thick beard and black glasses darken his face. He looks like Axyl Rose's twin.

Before moving to his upstairs apartment, Au's street-side presence was his advertising. The Internet replaced this function. One of Au's customers is the webmaster of Vinyl Paradise (www.vinylparadise.com). H.C. Lee created the Chinese-language site to catalog his personal collection of 30,000 albums, and to help other record aficionados.

Lee drops by Au's shop on an afternoon in June. A first-time visitor is already inside perusing jazz records. "Oh! I read about this store on your site," she says.

Vinyl Paradise notes 29 record shops in eight districts, including six hunting sites on Apliu Street, but it does not reference the mainstream retailers around Hong Kong.

At any of Hong Kong's HMV stores, visitors can find a token selection of new records from international mainstream and indie acts like Radiohead or Portishead. The Tsim Sha Tsui location only stocks around 50 albums, other HMVs carry even fewer.

The editor-in-chief of *Rare Record Collector Magazine,* Ian Shirley, said the future for vinyl is an exclusive, small-yet-stable, niche market. For the second consecutive year, vinyl sales in the US and Canada have set a new sales record. Nielsen Soundscan, a 19-year-old industry tracking system, reported 2.5 million vinyl albums sold in 2009.

Physical album sales continue to fall, while online sales struggle to offset the difference. Digital album sales constitute 40 percent of all American album purchases. Meanwhile, many local DJs are moving away from the vinyl discs once essential to their art.

Local DJ AKW says he still carries 50–100 vinyl records to every set, but relies increasingly on the thousands of digital files stored conveniently on his laptop. He explains the professional perks of digital: new software from Traktor and Serrato replicate the feel of records for scratching, and he can browse/purchase new dance music instantly with websites like Juno.

"In a club at four in the morning, people are drunk and high, and 90 percent aren't paying attention to the fine print of the track," AKW says. To be honest, it's only vinyl freaks who will notice the difference."

Vinyl is also moving online, with eBay and other auction sites. "Hong Kong is part of the world record dealership now, which includes Japan, Australia, Russia, France . . . everywhere really," Shirley says from his magazine's office in London.

In recent years, Au says competition has increased in Hong Kong. More local record dealers work from home computers, or in remote locations in New Territories.

He finds himself at a disadvantage. He doesn't use the Internet for buying or selling, and doesn't own a computer, although he has a phone from PCCW that can access YouTube and occasionally watches music videos.

A friend made a Facebook fan page for Au, and visitors sometimes show him the site on their smartphones. One customer printed it for him, and he has the pages in a plastic sleeve. He points at a critical wall post from a netizen named Alex Leung: "His collection of LPs is not that great." The comment irritates Au. If he had a computer, Au says he would write back: "My collection might not be great, but what I'm doing might be great." Leung's post has since been deleted.

Eliza Wong is the co-creator of the Facebook page. She says Au is a "1980s culture warrior." Wong knew of Au's shop for many years and wrote about him for *U Magazine* a local Chinese-language publication. "The difference between his store and others is the attitude: you love one thing, you do one thing and you persistently go for it," she says.

Au's reputation continues to grow. Record shops from Beijing, Shanghai and Guangzhou buy inventory from him. A collector from France—who has the largest collection of Pink Floyd albums—visits Au once or twice a year to find Asian pressings of international bands.

Other collectors visit him for old bootleg records. Chinese buyers have snapped up most of his Communist memorabilia, while local DJs visit for funk and soul. International DJs come for obscure Hong Kong pressings of the same. DJ Nu-Mark (of the hip-hop group Jurassic 5) visited Au at least twice during a weeklong visit for a 2008 performance.

On June 3 this year, Au flew to Beijing to speak at a "Project Shine" seminar about vinyl records, at the Today Art Museum in the Songzhuang Art Zone. Event organizers paid for his airfare, food and accommodations. He played psychedelic rock records and talked about the history of vinyl in a lecture hall.

Energized by the crowd's enthusiasm for vinyl, he returned to Hong Kong on June 8. The day was busy. Midnight approached and customers continued to arrive.

A rotund Mainlander wearing a pressed polo rummaged for Cantonese opera. The man bought a stack, then another customer arrived. Sham Shui

Po resident Tom Chu Chi-fung has been waiting/hanging out for an hour already. Au multitasked, chatting with Chu, assisting the new customer, switching albums on the turntable.

Au can accommodate limited groups inside his shop—he claims to have once packed 10 visitors inside. However, when too many customers arrive, he often recommends they walk about the neighborhood till the shop empties. Chu says he once waited four hours before Au was free.

Twenty years ago, they met on the street. Chu was a 16-year-old student. Au introduced him to Led Zeppelin, Harley Davidsons and hippie culture. "Before I just came to talk, I didn't have much purchasing power. Now I usually buy something," Chu says.

He owns roughly 100 records. He bought a turntable and 95 percent of his collection from Au. And he keeps coming back. The story is representative of many of Au's customers.

Chu finally leaves after 2 a.m. Rain poured all night. The following day is less hectic for Au. The rain continues. He awakes, tidies his shop. No customers visit in the evening. He has time to contemplate the future.

Au worries about the fate of his records, his lifetime investment. He would consider selling his collection, if he could find a buyer who would care for it properly. Otherwise, they are his daughter's inheritance. If he buys another warehouse, he would like to make room for his family in the Sham Shui Po flat. Maybe they could help with the business.

He saves about HK$8,000 per month. His net profit from the past years would disappear if he bought a new warehouse. The dilemma repeats itself each time his Sham Shui Po location overflows. He suspects the landlord won't sell his current flat, and if rents rise, Au might have to move.

Au walks around the neighborhood. Rain continues to fall gently on the brick street. He carries a cordless phone in his pocket. His 77-year old mother calls from Toronto, where she lives. He tells her about Beijing. Since emigrating from Vietnam to Canada with his brothers in the early 1980s, she calls several times a month.

She visited in 1987, and he recalls her reaction to his lifestyle: "She said 'Wow, what kind of man are you, you are like a beggar in the street. You should not live like this.'" She worked to sponsor his Canadian immigration in the late 1980s, but he gave up on the process. He wanted to stay with his records. They still argue about the subject.

Back inside his apartment, Au unfolds his cot. The cozy nest of vinyl resembles a caged-home. Walled inside his record collection, he falls asleep. Sometimes he dreams of the US, a country he has visited only through music.

On other nights, he suffers nightmares: he rushes to check on the 30 trolleys stretching around the building. Police are confiscating the boxes. People are stealing them. Typhoon winds batter them.

Nightmares are common for those fighting to preserve Hong Kong's tangible culture. Developers threaten the *tong laus*. Central Market is endangered. Useful buildings across Kowloon are disappearing, as skyscrapers begin towering above height limitations once required for air traffic at the now-demolished Kai Tak Airport.

Au struggles to preserve Hong Kong's tangible musical heritage. Vinyl records played an essential role in music history, but they are becoming cultural artifacts—expensive to store, technologically outmoded.

Still-useful vinyl records and turntables make way for mp4s and the next generation of iPhone. The changes are especially visible on the streets of Sham Shui Po. Roughly a dozen record shops once sold new vinyl in the blocks surrounding his home. Cell phone shops replaced the stores.

What is the cost of cultural preservation? Au knows. He has endured loss of comfort and family structure to build his "orphan home for records." Hong Kong residents and politicians often complain about insufficient heritage preservation, but they seldom live with the real costs. Au is an exception.

Visitors sometimes laugh and gawk like tourists, he says. "They say, 'You're very rich!' But that's just sarcasm. They want to say, 'You have a bunch of rubbish.'" They don't understand his mission.

A stack of business cards beside his record player read, "Vinyl Hero." The card depicts a retro American cartoon character, Archie, and his friends playing in a band. Au copied the album cover of a 1970s pirated compilation made by a local bootlegger called "Hero." Au pasted the word "Vinyl" above "Hero," and hoped that the creator of Archie wouldn't sue for copyright infringement.

Au is a vinyl hero. He sacrifices everything to save records. "My girlfriend is always complaining that I love these records more than I love my daughter," he says.

He invites anyone who is willing to come and adopt the "vinyl children" from his shop. "They can still sing, they still have life," he says. "This is their last stop. The next stop is the dumpsite. In fact, many should have been in the dumpsite long ago. I just prolong their life. I love them too much."

More people are buying records in Hong Kong, Au says. He's happy about vinyl's resurging popularity. But he suspects the trend will pass. His passion will not. The vinyl hero says, "I'll sell records until I die."

Doug Meigs on revision versus rewriting

Writing is a process, and revision is a critical aspect of any good writing. But I don't consider revision and rewriting to be the same. Completely rewriting an article is an impossible luxury on deadline. For me, rewriting is the fate of a truly terrible SFD (shitty first draft), or it could be an essential step toward submitting a repackaged, rewritten piece to another publication.

I practice revision at every stage of my writing process. If I've pitched a story to my editor, then I already possess a basic knowledge of where I want to take the narrative. I might draft an outline of the basic structure with sentences or fragments ordered in bulleted-list form. Part of my story pitch might be flushed out in the lead or in a nut paragraph below, or it might be dropped somewhere into the rough outline. This outline will continue changing as I continue reporting.

During interviews and research, my story's bare-bones outline is rearranged into a new skeletal form. I flesh out the meat of the story. I fill in holes of logic or missing information. New questions arise with added research.

Longer narrative pieces might evolve in segments. For assignments with word counts longer than one thousand, I sometimes flush out a complete super-rough draft for a macrostructure—with gaps remaining for missing quotes and context to be inserted later—and then continue refining the paragraphs, transitions, and micro-components at the sentence level.

Author Kurt Vonnegut wrote in his semi-autobiographical work *Timequake* that writers fall into two categories: "swoopers" and "bashers." Swoopers write a story quickly, higgledy-piggledy, crinkum-crankum, any which way. Then they go over it again painstakingly, fixing everything that is just plain awful or doesn't work. Bashers go one sentence at a time, getting it exactly right before they go on to the next one. When they're done they're done.

Vonnegut admits he is a basher. "Most men are bashers, and most women are swoopers," he writes. However, I would probably fit with the swoopers. Vonnegut's gendered perspective could present a false dichotomy. Or maybe his characterization depends on depth of reporting. I would approach an eight-hundred-word deadline piece altogether differently than I would a two-thousand-word narrative feature. For daily deadline news or smaller pieces, the only way I can write is by bashing it out on the keyboard.

Editors introduce another level of revision to the process of rewriting. I have encountered four types:

1. Fact-checkers—editors who might ask for specific revisions.

2. Loopers—editors who foster a feedback loop with the writer, making editorial changes and asking for feedback and confirmation before publication.

3. Baskets—minimalist editors who fiddle only with punctuation or a few clauses, transferring the copy from e-mail inbox to page.

4. Transformers—editors who can be demons or saints, most frustrating when they appropriate text into their own voice and writing style.

These are generalizations. Most editors' style seems to vary depending on tightness of deadline. Yet I have encountered all of the types across the world, on staff and freelance, from Omaha to Hong Kong.

Until a story is in print, the revisions never stop.

REWRITE

Robert Sanchez

Todd Stansfield is awake, just barely. A sedative enters his bloodstream through a needle that's stuck into one of his torn-up arms. His joints ache. His chest is a road map of stitches from the surgeries he underwent three weeks earlier. He's dropped 30 pounds from his already lean frame; his arms and legs have become emaciated sticks of skin and bone. The 16-year-old's head pounds from the screws bolted on a brace attached to his skull.

It's early July 2004. The room at Littleton Adventist Hospital is bright. The lab coats and steady march of friends and family—too numerous to count—flow in like an ocean tide. Most everyone is warm, positive, enthusiastic. *How ya doing, Todd?*

The tracheotomy hole at the base of his neck makes it impossible to answer; the air tickles his throat. So he points to a small board of letters that the doctors gave him to communicate. His girlfriend, a blond high school cheerleader, sits at Todd's side and asks him to spell out how he's feeling. *Point to the letters, Todd.* He strings together a few random letters. Katie looks confused. He's not making sense.

He's been awake only a few days, but he's already come to fear the night here. Not because of the darkness that envelops the hospital room, but because of the loneliness that surrounds his mind. At night, Todd is left only with questions.

Todd survived a car crash—he'd gotten that bit from his older sister—but that was it. So far, there have been no stories of how he'd nearly died during surgery, or how his car was so badly burned that it didn't even look like a

81

car anymore. No one told him about the *others*—his three high school buddies, and that old man in the other car. They didn't make it.

No one told Todd about the funerals and how hundreds of people showed up for them, packed the churches. No one told him about the investigation and the questions that sheriff's investigators had been asking around town: *On a scale of one to five, how responsible is Todd? Do you know what the boys were doing? Do you think Todd would drive that fast?*

Ninety-three miles per hour. It was all over the news by now: Sixteen-year-old driver, 10 days with a license, four dead. Todd will have to get better before they deliver that news. Until then, Todd is here in a hospital bed, listening to the sounds of the machines that are making sure he's still alive.

While everyone quietly worries about his future, Todd worries about his family. His parents and his sister are at his side every day. He can see the concern on their faces. Todd's sister wonders if her little brother knows how he got here. *Do you know what happened to you, Todd?*

There is a pad of paper nearby. Todd scratches out a letter. I. . . . Then another. W. . . . His sister watches. A. . . . S. . . .

During his brief existence, this is the first time Todd would see the power of the written word, the deeper meaning behind a phrase, the staggering punch of a simple, declarative sentence. These would be the first words of his new life.

I was in a car crash.

The city college of New York is on a hill that overlooks Harlem, a graph-paper grid of streets sketched among the buildings that constitute the Upper Manhattan skyline. Green lawns dot the neo-Gothic campus; redbrick walk-ups, tenements, cafes, and bodegas line the sidewalks that border the 164-year-old school. To the east sits the historic St. Nicholas Park, where Alexander Hamilton's post–Revolutionary War home is located. On this busy fall afternoon, students race across the streets on their way to class or to catch the subway home—or to the library, or a bar, or a museum. Amid all of the frenetic activity—the wailing police sirens, the low rumble of trash trucks that barrel through the intersections—Todd Stansfield stands alone.

Todd is 23 now. He's 5-foot-9, lean and muscular with dark, thinning hair, and a jaw of right angles. His piercing blue eyes look like crystal, so clear and so bright that you trust him immediately. He is polite, perhaps overly so, always wanting to please. He has an almost permanent acquiescence about him—the way he turns his eyes away. People feel his wariness. Todd Stansfield is barely an adult, but he is a convicted killer. A felon. And he worries that is all anyone will ever see.

In Parker, Colorado, where he'd grown up, Todd felt embarrassed and ashamed. He'd been storefront gossip for years. He was the boy who'd ruined all those families' lives. He was the boy who'd ruined his own future. He'd done jail time and finished high school, then graduated from college in three years—all while following his probation rules religiously, locking himself inside his parents' home by seven every night, just like the court told him. He'd wrapped himself in a cocoon of penance, and he'd been good at it. He was one of the best kids his probation officer had ever met. She thought of him as her own son: He was thoughtful, honest—an amazing young man, she said. Still, that wasn't enough. At home, nothing could change what he'd done.

So in October of 2009, Todd left for New York City. He moved into an apartment with his sister, Lindsay, a hospital pharmacist, who'd offered to be there for him. Todd started to rebuild his life.

Almost a year after his arrival, Todd enrolled in CCNY's graduate writing program with dreams of one day becoming a professional author. He'd been writing for years now, first at the request of a psychologist, then for his own sanity. He could put things on paper that he'd never say to his parents.

I hate the silence; memories are so easy to come by when there is nothing to listen to. . . . God, my words are aggravated. It's amazing, I never thought in my whole life I would end up here.

Back on the CCNY campus, Todd makes his way to North Academic Center, where he shows a security guard his student identification and takes a series of escalators to the sixth floor. The heat is stifling inside his narrow classroom, and the 18 students are fanning themselves with papers and manila folders. A classmate wearing a short skirt shows up late and takes a seat at the head of the long table in the middle of the room.

The students soon review their classmate's work. Her writing is raw, with lots of sexuality and violence, and the students enjoy it. Todd raises his hand with a comment: He isn't buying one scene in which the protagonist—a young girl—is physically abused in public. "I think that part is unbelievable," Todd tells the woman. She opens her eyes widely at the suggestion.

Todd eases into his words. The story is good, he tells her: "I just think that someone would help a girl if she were in trouble. I wouldn't stare and do nothing."

"Well, that's how it happens, and I think it's very real," the woman shoots back.

There's an uncomfortable pause. The professor at the other end of the table speaks up. All the students' stories will need some work if they want a chance at getting published. "Writing is like driving a car in the fog," she tells the class. "You're looking at the yellow lines and trying to feel your way home. You need to anticipate the curves in the road."

June 18, 2004. The rural landscape washes past the car windows as the two-lane road rolls like a wave—blacktop cresting, then falling away to hundreds of feet of open asphalt. Crest. Drop. Crest. Drop.

Open fields swell around the vehicle. The last trace of sun casts a dim light over the wild grasses, which are damp from summer rain showers around Parker. Inspiration Drive shines like polished glass under the car's headlights. Todd presses the gas pedal in his 1990 Lexus sedan. The engine roars.

Crest. . . .

Todd is behind the wheel of his new car, 10 days since he earned his license and made his dad so proud. *Take the car out for the night. Be back by 11. Have fun.*

Drop. . . .

Up front with Todd is 16-year-old Tony Majestic. Athletic and handsome, with short dark hair and a crooked grin, Tony can disarm nearly anyone at Ponderosa High School. He's the class cutup, bold and brash, and his friends love him for it. A few months earlier, Tony stepped into the batter's box during a high school baseball game and blew a kiss to the opposing pitcher. The next pitch drilled Tony in the ribs. Coach made Tony run sprints after the game, and Tony laughed the entire time.

Crest. . . .

Behind Tony, Michael Budge is the yin to the other boys' yang. Friends with Todd since the two met in middle school, the 17-year-old prefers hanging out at his church to almost any other place. He doesn't display the same self-consciousness that seems to preoccupy other boys his age. On weekdays after school, he'll round up friends and take them to study, then to read from the Bible and pray. He often speaks of making a difference. While other kids talk a good game, Michael measures his life with action. The previous summer, he saved $1,000 so he could travel to Mexico for two weeks and help pour a concrete foundation for an orphanage. A few months later, he started to grow his hair out. Every week, he'd sneak up behind his mother, pluck out one of her hairs, and compare the length to his.

Drop. . . .

Next to Michael is Sean Student, the new kid in the group. He turned 17 two days earlier. At six foot three and 210 pounds, he's a physical presence, the captain of an elite traveling hockey team that keeps him out of school and in the Midwest two weeks out of each month. College programs have already shown interest in him. This past season, he logged 41 goals, 43 assists, and 118 minutes in the penalty box while playing through minor injuries. Most important to his mother, Sean has a 3.8 grade point average. This summer, he'll leave Parker for a new high school and an even more high-profile team in Iowa. For now, though, Sean just wants to concentrate on being a teenager. He wants to spend time with his friends.

Crest. . . .

Who knows what they were doing on Inspiration Drive? Years later, Todd couldn't remember. There'd been dinner earlier in town with a bunch of other friends and talk of going to a movie. No drinking. No drugs. Just teenagers out having a good time.

Drop. . . .

The speed-limit sign reads 40 miles per hour. Todd's foot is down. Forty-five. Fifty. Fifty-five. Sixty. Sixty-five.

Up ahead, Marvin Gilchrist is driving home. The 77-year-old former volunteer fire chief had left a friend's house a few minutes earlier. He'd eaten dinner, had some wine, and watched the Colorado Rockies on television. He made a right onto Inspiration Drive and gained speed in the burgundy Chrysler convertible he'd bought his wife for their 50th anniversary the previous year, a few months before she died of complications from cancer.

Crest. . . .

At 8 p.m., a driver behind Gilchrist sees a pair of headlights cross into the oncoming lane. It's like slow motion: Todd's car skids sideways toward the convertible. The Lexus' passenger side slams into Gilchrist's hood, contorting the vehicles into instant heaps of tangled metal and glass. The Chrysler is blown backward onto the dirt shoulder. Gilchrist is dead.

The Lexus rolls and lands upright, next to Gilchrist's vehicle. Michael and Tony's side of the car is annihilated. The glass is gone. Their doors are smashed in. The roof is caved. The car catches fire.

The witness pulls off the road, gets out of his car, and rushes toward the crumpled vehicles. The twilight is broken only by the fire. He sees Michael and Tony. There aren't any sounds as the flames reach the boys. They're both dead. The man then runs to the other side of the Lexus and sees Todd and Sean. They're both alive. He pulls them out of the car.

A few hundred yards away, a neighbor hears the crash. He races to the scene and sees the two bloodied boys unconscious outside the burning Lexus. He blasts the car with a fire extinguisher, but it still burns. The boys are dragged away from the vehicle.

Someone calls 9-1-1, and within minutes firefighters and Douglas County sheriff's deputies flood the site. A paramedic intubates Sean and works on him for almost five minutes. The injuries are grim: His pelvis is fractured; his face mashed. He's loaded into an ambulance. A few feet away, Todd's unconscious. The paramedics strap him down and send him away too.

It took a team of doctors at Littleton Adventist Hospital nearly six hours to put Todd back together. Both of his lungs were collapsed. His neck was broken. His diaphragm was ripped. Most of his organs were pushed into his chest. He almost died on the table. Severe life-threatening injuries, not expected to survive, a doctor wrote on Todd's file. He's now in the hospital's intensive care unit.

In another room, Sean is unconscious. His family is led to his bedside. Karen Student has seen her boy almost every day of his life, but now she only recognizes him from the bottoms of his size 13 feet and from his short-cropped brown hair. Both of his eyes are blackened.

The family sits and waits. By 5:45 a.m., doctors tell Sean's family that there's nothing more they can do. They agonize over the decision they have to make. Eventually, Sean's parents sign some papers and Sean is taken off life support. Karen sits in a chair next to her son's bed, holding his hand. It's cold to the touch. It takes him 35 minutes to die. When she finally lets go, Sean's hand is warm again.

Todd Stansfield grew up at the corner of Seibert Circle and South Edinborough Way in Parker. Kids in the neighborhood played roller hockey in the street, tossed water balloons, and challenged one another to video games in their parents' basements. At night, they would raid friends' refrigerators and hang out in backyards—boys atop sleeping bags, staring into the vast darkness and talking about the girls they wanted to ask out.

Todd was the younger of Todd Sr. and Maryanne Stansfield's two children, born March 11, 1988. At first, he was simply known as "The Baby" because his parents hadn't settled on a name. Maryanne wanted to name the boy after her husband because she was certain the little bundle in her arms would embody her spouse's greatest attributes—loyalty, friendliness, and most important to her, dedication to family. Todd Sr. wasn't sure. How could you tell what kind of kid he was just by looking at him? So the boy's parents took him home. About three weeks after his birth, it was official: Todd would be his name.

Todd's father was an insurance salesman, and his mother stayed home until Todd turned seven, then took a part-time job with United Airlines so the family could travel the world together on a discount. During the summers, the Stansfields visited places like Australia, England, and France.

When he wasn't globe-trotting, Todd was busy playing sports. In elementary school, it was soccer. In middle school, football and track. By Todd's sophomore year at Ponderosa High School, he'd eased his way into the popular crowd. He was an A and B student who'd become captain of the school's varsity track team and was just three seconds short of qualifying for the state meet in the 800-meter event. As part of his training, he punished himself with five-mile runs, some in 95-degree heat, others in the cold of winter. Michael Budge once saw Todd sprinting along the path behind his home. He went inside and told his mother that he'd never known anyone like Todd before.

Todd was also the starting fullback on the junior varsity football team. Though he weighed only 150 pounds, No. 22 regularly ran over teenagers 50 pounds heavier. He scored more than ten touchdowns that season—including three in the JV championship versus Highlands Ranch High School, which Ponderosa won. It would be his last game.

Todd woke up three weeks after the accident in the intensive care unit at Littleton Adventist. He regained a bit of weight and was transferred to Craig Hospital in Englewood, a world-renowned center for spinal cord injuries. Six weeks after the crash, he was relearning how to walk and could speak well enough to carry on a conversation. His parents thought he was finally ready to know.

One morning at Craig, Todd Sr. led his son, still in a wheelchair, into a conference room and closed the door behind them. Maryanne was already there. A social worker and a psychiatrist, both from Craig, were also there.

Todd's father spoke. Three friends were with you: Tony. Michael. Sean. You hit another man in a car. They're all dead. Todd, they said you were going 93 miles per hour.

A man in a dark suit—Todd soon learned he was an attorney—came into the room. Todd would be charged, the man said. Don't worry about that now. Focus on getting better. Later, Todd wrote:

> *I didn't cry, not at first. All I could think about was the hours I had spent trying to remember my accident. The harder I tried, the more I found myself imagining it happen [sic] than anything. I crashed into a tree a hundred different times, in daylight and at dusk, in rain and sunshine. I never imagined crashing into another car, another person.*

In the 16 months before Todd's accident, at least nine teenagers died in Colorado vehicle crashes. Most involved reckless driving; some were alcohol-related. In this particular case, four people were dead, but Todd had survived. And now, it appeared, he would pay.

Returning home from Craig Hospital in late August of 2004, Todd felt like he was in a foreign body. His arms were pockmarked from the broken glass; the brace was still screwed into his skull; the tracheotomy scar was bright red and had just begun to heal. Todd drifted between depression and angst. He'd closed himself off to most people—including his parents—and fixated on his guilt and his fear of a potential prison sentence. Prosecutors by now had intimated that Todd could be tried as an adult, and the sentence could exceed 20 years. Vehicular homicide charges were filed in November. Maryanne worried that her son would get raped or killed—or both—in prison. Inside the Stansfields' once peaceful home, Todd's father yelled about the unfairness of it all, about how prosecutors seemed to want a fifth victim.

While facing the felony charges against him, Todd had signed a bond that prevented him from getting within two blocks of his old high school. After he left the hospital, he'd been homeschooled. That winter, Todd and his mother met with Ponderosa administrators to discuss Todd's options. The vice principal suggested Todd attend a private, Christian high school a few miles from home.

Shut out of his school and shut off from most of his friends, Todd enrolled in Lutheran High School Parker. His parents hired a psychologist who encouraged Todd to write about the grief he was facing. He put pen to paper, and a month later he'd written more than 10,000 words. He met regularly with his psychologist and continued to write. He even started a story about his friends. Months later, he couldn't find the courage to finish it.

His dead friends' parents, meanwhile, had already begun defending him. Tony's parents didn't want to see their son's friend hurt further. Ivan Majestic and his wife, Mary, had gotten to know Todd over the years, mostly over breakfasts of Cheerios when Todd stayed the night at their home. Ivan called Sherri Budge, Michael's mother, and asked if she thought two wrongs could make a right. Sherri did not. The day after the crash, she'd visited Todd at the hospital; he was in a medically induced coma. Sherri held Todd's hand. "I want you to know that Michael loved you," she said. "We both love you."

Even before they spoke on the phone, Ivan and Sherri had misgivings about the investigation. During a briefing a few days after the crash, investigators presented their theories about the wreck, including Todd's speed. Sherri brought her two brothers along; one was an engineer who helped design vehicle air bags, and he questioned the angles of impact, which would have affected the speed calculations. The measurements had been taken at night, when clues could have been missed. The road was opened for morning traffic and cars were rolling over the accident scene. This isn't conclusive, Sherri's brother said.

Tony's and Michael's parents were prepared to fight, but Sean Student's family had receded from the spotlight. Sean's mother, Karen, showed up at court hearings but stayed away from the other families. Sean's father and younger brother were rarely seen. While the other boys' parents fought to keep Todd out of prison, the Students wanted to remain neutral, to let things play out in court.

Sherri and Ivan obtained the investigation files and pored over the 400-plus pages. The pair noticed that investigators hired an independent crash-scene reconstruction team—and just as Sherri's brother had suggested, the initial speed calculations appeared to be incorrect. A new calculation dropped Todd's speed from around 93 miles per hour to a range: 68 at the low end, 71 at the high end. No one had told the families about the adjustments. Todd was still nearly 30 miles per hour above the speed limit, but it was dramatically lower than what they'd been led to believe.

Then one night, Ivan called Sherri and told her to flip to the coroner reports. "Do you see what I see?" he asked. Marvin Gilchrist's blood-alcohol level was 0.076, just below the limit of 0.08. If Gilchrist had been pulled over seconds before the crash, or if he'd lived, he could have been charged with driving while ability impaired.

By mid 2005, the case was still hung up in court and there was no resolution in sight. Were Todd's case to go to trial, Gilchrist's blood-alcohol content could be admitted in court. Ivan and Sherri had taken the Douglas County sheriff's investigative findings to the media and now were openly criticizing forensic work on the case. Juvenile justice groups jumped in, too, organizing protests outside the courthouse during Todd's hearings and circulating a petition against prosecuting him as an adult. A similar case in Jefferson County in 2003—in which a 16-year-old killed three friends and injured nine others—resulted in 12 years of probation.

In August 2005, 14 months after the wreck, prosecutors and Todd's attorney reached a deal. Todd would plead guilty to two felony counts of criminally negligent homicide—one for the deaths of the three boys, and one for the death of Marvin Gilchrist—but he would avoid prison. He would serve 90 days in a juvenile jail, 12 years of probation, and complete 1,200 hours of community service.

Gilchrist's family was outraged. For months, they'd advocated that Todd be tried as an adult. They'd gotten friends to write letters saying the boy should pay for his crime. Now their father was being treated as the reason for the wreck. They felt like pariahs, having to be led through a back door of the courthouse to avoid protesters who showed up for the sentencing on September 16.

Inside the courtroom that day, Todd wore Tony's orange short-sleeved shirt. Before the sentencing, Todd stood and tried to apologize to the families. He broke down. Instead, he faced the judge. "I'm so sorry for all the pain and suffering this accident caused," Todd sobbed. "I know this has been stressful on victims' families. I'm so sorry. . . . I think about them every day."

On his first night in jail, Todd was put into an 8-by-11 cell. When he was allowed to, he would write with the nub of a pencil:

I wake today with hopes for a better tomorrow / A day when the sky will be painted by God's blushing sunrise / A day when worry will be limited by the very happiness I seek / A day many dream of and few ever experience / A day when I will be healed from these self-inflicted wounds.

Todd kept up with his classwork and graduated in May 2006 (his plea agreement prevented him from walking during graduation ceremonies), then he enrolled at Metropolitan State College of Denver where he studied business. Every day, he rode public transportation home, where he studied, wrote, and checked in with his probation officer—four times each night—before he went to bed. His mother worried about him. Shortly after Todd's 21st birthday, when a court-mandated driving restriction was lifted, Maryanne told her son that he should drive the family car around the neighborhood with her. Todd was uneasy, but he made it a mile before returning to the driveway. He handed his mother the keys.

"That was good," Maryanne said. "What did you think?"

"I think I'm fine, Mom."

Todd drove infrequently after that, and rarely more than a few miles from home.

By the spring of 2009, Todd had finished college. His sister, Lindsay, had already invited Todd to live with her in New York. His mother pushed the idea, but it wasn't until October of that year that Todd got clearance to transfer his supervision. In New York, he'd have to have regular urine tests and occasional strip searches. He'd also have a 9 p.m. curfew. Todd couldn't wait to move.

Ivan Majestic sits at the kitchen table in his home just outside Parker, a ranch house with a deck, a barbecue grill, and a long dirt driveway, flanked on each side by brush and yucca. He's staring at the hutch in the corner of the room, at the bronze urn behind the glass.

The urn is beautiful, a miniature mountain with an eagle soaring at its peak; the bronze reflects the sunlight. The hutch is like a time capsule, a shrine to a boy who will never grow old. There's a photo of Tony in his baseball uniform—hands on hips, a wide, bright, mischievous smile splashed across his face—and another picture of him dressed up for Halloween as Dorothy from The Wizard of Oz. At the bottom, in a sealed white bag marked "MAJESTIC, ANTHONY," are the belongings Tony was carrying the night he died: keys, wallet, spare change. On another shelf is a ball Tony gave to his dad on Father's Day nearly 11 years ago. The date is written in black ink across the cowhide: June 18, 2000. Four years, to the day, before the crash that would take his life.

There's the old cliché that time heals all wounds. But sit here with Ivan Majestic—at the table where he watched his boy so many years ago—and see him stare at the urn that holds what's left of his son. When you lose a child, he says, you mourn the death of the present and of the future. All the what-ifs in life. What would Tony have done after high school? What would he be doing right now? "There's a range of emotions," Ivan says. He has a tattoo of his son's face on his left arm. "There's denial and anger. Some people get depressed. It changes you. Am I a better or worse person today? No. Am I a different person? Of course I am."

A few miles across town on a snowy winter night several weeks later, Marvin Gilchrist's son sips a beer while his wife sits by his side in a Mexican restaurant. It's been more than a year since Scott Gilchrist learned that Todd left town to start a new life—news that makes him question whether justice was served in his father's case. "I don't know that Todd is truly sorry," the 55-year-old auto-body shop owner says. Scott is stocky, and a gray goatee hangs below his chin. "You always hear people say there's a reason for everything. Well, what was the reason for this?"

He says that, yes, his father was an old man; that, at the age of 77, who knows how many years Marvin Gilchrist had left? His father was drinking, yes, but he wasn't drunk. The sheriff's investigators said it wouldn't have mattered. How many people could have gotten around a car going that fast, slipping sideways into an oncoming lane? "It's ridiculous," Scott says, shaking his head. His wife reaches for his hand. "It's like every time we went to that courthouse, with all those protesters supporting Todd, that we were being victimized again," Janet Gilchrist says. "It's like everyone forgot what had happened. Four people died, and Todd was behind the wheel. Todd had sole responsibility over that crash."

The two think about what could make their lives easier, or at least could help them move beyond the anger they still feel. Janet says she'd like to hear from Todd, "but only if he's really sorry." Scott says he will never be able to forgive Todd, especially since the move. "It's too late," he says. "Why did Todd have to go to New York? So he could get away from this? When do I get to run away?"

Todd showers and pours himself a glass of milk inside the kitchen of his Manhattan apartment. He stands next to the refrigerator, stripped to the waist, his exposed flesh a scarred patchwork of lines and squares and circles. There's a buttonhook from the middle of his chest down to his belly button, where a surgeon cut him open and sewed his diaphragm together. There's a raised patch the size of a quarter over his stomach, where a feeding tube was inserted. Two other circular scars dot his ribs on the right—another on the left—where more tubes inflated his collapsed lungs.

Todd moves to his bedroom, turns on an overhead light, and half-closes the door. It's a weekday morning and Todd hunches over his desk, a glass-top no larger than a briefcase. He sits at the keyboard in the yellow light of his bedroom and waits. Todd wishes he could remember that night. It's haunted him all these years—in his bed at home in Colorado, in his jail cell, and now here, where he'd gone to escape the ghosts but now finds himself chasing them with his fingertips.

Think of how great it would be to see the future. Where would I be? Where would my friends be? Who would they be? None of this . . . would exist.

A few blocks away, Lindsay walks her chihuahua-terrier mix, Bella, through the streets and heads to a dog park near the Queensboro Bridge.

Her hair is shoulder-length and brown and is pulled into a ponytail. She works the 2 to 10 p.m. shift at a nearby hospital, which means she has only a sliver of time each weekday to see her brother. When she returns home from work at night, she takes the dog for a walk. Like clockwork, Todd heats water for tea and serves it to Lindsay in a cup and saucer when she gets back. Later, they turn on the television and watch reruns of *The Office* before heading for bed.

The two rarely talk about the crash. The times Lindsay has tried to bring up the accident, Todd's gone quiet, then started to cry. "I want to talk to Todd, but he shuts down," Lindsay says. "How's he really feeling? I'm not sure, because we haven't been able to go there. I think Todd struggles with opening up about the accident. It hurts to think what kind of pain he must be in."

Every few months, Todd's parents offer to pay for therapy, and Lindsay's encouraged it. Not long ago, Maryanne asked Todd if he wanted to fix the marble-size tracheotomy scar at the base of his neck. Todd wore T-shirts under collared shirts after the crash in an attempt to hide the hole, but now he tells his mother that he's accepted the scar as part of who he is. "It makes you wonder if this is how he's punishing himself," his mother says. "The only thing I want is to see my son smile again. I want my old Todd back."

Inside his room, Todd throws on his scrubs—a white smock and powder-blue pants—a gray fleece jacket, a backpack, and heads out the door. There are 18 subway stops between Todd's place in Midtown Manhattan and New York Methodist Hospital in the Park Slope neighborhood of Brooklyn, where he volunteers 200 hours a year as part of his probation requirements.

When Todd exits the train, the morning wind along Seventh Avenue is blowing hard. He raises his shoulders to escape the chill and heads through the hospital's glass doors and up an elevator. He goes to the volunteer office to check in and soon is back down a phalanx of stairs, out another door, and into a second building where the physical therapy department is located.

"Hey, Todd!" someone calls out.

There are 10 padded tables lined up in the long, narrow room, with weights and a treadmill up front, and a sitting area in the back where rehabilitating patients get heat and ice treatments after workouts. Todd makes his way to the chairs to begin his work, and one of the therapists steps in his way.

"Whatcha reading now, Todd?" the woman asks.

"Orwell," Todd says. "Some Gertrude Stein."

"Stein," the woman says. "Haven't read her since high school. Let me know what you think."

Within a few minutes, Todd is all helpfulness and courtesy. He organizes the exercise balls, strips linens from tables, and tosses the laundry into a bin. Soon, he's icing a man's knee and a woman's shoulder. He cleans the underwater treadmill in the back room, ices another knee, and heats a back and a shoulder and an ankle and a calf. All the while he's getting directions from the half-dozen-or-so physical therapists around the room. *Todd, can you take this patient? Todd, can you reserve that table? Todd. . . .*

None of the therapists knows what Todd's done to be here, and Todd's not telling them. He just wants to work. So when people ask why he was here 250 hours last year—50 more than his sentence called for—why he pulled entire shifts for no pay, he answers simply, "I like it."

Around noon, Todd spies a group of therapists huddled near the front door. Someone turns off the lights. One of them, a man, calls out.

"Todd," he says. "Come on. Let's go eat."

"I'm alright, but thank—thank you."

"Seriously, Todd, you need lunch." The rest of the group waves him over. Todd's face goes flush. He's frozen.

"I'm good," he says.

"Really, Todd, come on."

"I—I can't."

He lies that the volunteer office doesn't want its workers mingling with paid hospital staff.

"Well, if you change your mind, you know where to go," one therapist says. "We'd love for you to join us."

Todd gives a half-smile and watches the group head out the door. He exhales and walks to one of the chairs in the back of the room. He puts his head in his hands.

When Todd finishes graduate school, he'd like to find a job at a university where he can teach other writers, where he is happy and carefree and can focus on nothing but a perfectly turned sentence. He'll work in a place that is friendly and inviting. He's sure of that. He'd like to move back to Colorado. It won't be to Parker—at least that's what he says now. Give him until 2017, though—after his 29th birthday, when his probation ends—and maybe he'll change his mind.

By then, perhaps he'll have a place of his own, with an office and a wooden desk and a big leather chair. Maybe he'll have a car, too; one he will drive carefully down some street on his way to having morning coffee with a girlfriend or a wife who loves and understands Todd for who he is.

And then, maybe . . . well, who knows?

Until then, Todd works at the hospital. He goes to class. He has an internship at *Fiction*, a well-regarded literary journal. He is home before curfew. He writes, trying to work out the great riddle of his life one letter at a time.

And he dreams. Todd has seen his friends again. He's written about it. They're sitting inside his car.

And all at once, it becomes clear to me what I have to do; this is my second chance, and I am not going to waste it. But first, I wait to see those three perfect smiles just one last time. Slowly, I smile at each of them and they smile back at me. I nod my head and clear the tears from my eyes. With my right hand, I take the key out of the ignition and with my left I open the door. My face is still facing theirs and with my last words, I say to them, "I love you guys."

In his dream, Todd throws his car keys into a nearby field. And then he runs away.

Robert Sanchez on the value of being
a relaxed and confident reporter

I try to make my reporting and writing as familiar as I possibly can. Obviously, with experience, you make tweaks along the way. That's one of the most enjoyable parts of being a journalist: there's always the opportunity to get better.

Even now, looking back on this story, I think I'm a much better reporter and writer. As I've gotten older, I've come to relax a little more about my reporting style—and who I am as a journalist. Once you have one successful story, then another, then another, you begin to believe in yourself a little more. This business always comes with self-doubt, but I've always embraced that as a way to improve.

If you're a little more relaxed, a little more confident in your abilities, that will come across in interviews. The worst reporters and writers are the ones who always have their heads buried in their notebooks. It's almost like they don't trust themselves. Look up. Make eye contact. Check out your surroundings. How does your character comb his hair? What color is the district attorney's tie? What kinds of flowers are growing in the garden next to the school? The best, most poignant, moments are often small ones. But they stick in your head. You can't forget them. And that's what will make your stories memorable.

Also, make sure you shut up once in awhile. I like to think of my interviews as conversations—that my discussions are more about hearing ideas and opinions, rather than an interrogation. I talk far less than I once did. My audio recorder helped me with that. I'm now a much better listener.

Because of my reporting changes, I've found writing to be less of a slog and more of a fun challenge. Don't get me wrong. Writing is tough. But you can make your life a little easier through solid reporting. I always tell young journalists that, at least in the magazine world, you get one chance to tell a story. You want to make sure you have the right topic, the right characters, the right voice. The first step is always reporting. The writing flows from that.

The best advice I can give is to follow your instincts. Sit and really listen; look around. Your instincts will get better as you get more experience, but learn to trust yourself today. You'll thank yourself for it tomorrow.

SKID ROW KARAOKE

Randall Roberts

Gentleman Robert, wearing a pinstripe suit and maroon fedora, crooned the words to Tommy Edwards' hit "It's All in the Game." He wandered the room, singing to a few dozen people at a church on skid row.

Jonathan James Brown donned a cowboy hat and sang the Muppets' "Rainbow Connection," enunciating each word just like Kermit.

Linda Harris spun circles through the room, dancing with friends. Later, when her name was called, she grabbed the microphone and gestured with the confidence of a diva as she sang "I Hope You Dance."

For 15 years, these moments have arrived every Wednesday, courtesy of Pastor Anthony Stallworth, his wife, Lucy, and a karaoke machine bought by Rage Against the Machine guitarist Tom Morello. The stars of the evening come from the neighborhood's hotels, shelters and sidewalks.

Performances are ragged, raw and often inspired. On some nights you won't find a more electric room in Los Angeles, and the crowd bears witness to a brand of musical epiphany seldom seen at a cutting-edge Echo Park club or the stage of the Hollywood Bowl.

Pastor Tony, as he's known throughout the neighborhood, came up with the idea: "We're a place where the homeless can come, they can sing a song, they can feel like somebody after being rejected everywhere else, get a free cup of coffee—and people applaud for them."

The show begins at 7:30 inside the Central City Community Church of the Nazarene, a storefront at 6th and San Pedro streets. The karaoke is held in a nondescript sanctuary, packed with chairs and two tables where singers select songs from thick binders. At its peak, about 100 people pack the room; it's standing-room-only.

Every karaoke night, Pastor Tony holds an optional prayer session in an adjoining room. One sweltering summer night, a dozen people gave voice to their troubles. A young woman prayed for nothing but strength; she was homeless and was kicked out of a library where she was studying. A disc jockey, blinded in one eye and vision-impaired in the other, prayed for audio gear so he can earn a living.

After hearing the prayers and conveying them to Jesus, Pastor Tony led this offshoot flock to the karaoke room to do the Electric Slide.

Much of my time as a music critic is dedicated to discovering artists and trends, and appraising concerts and recordings, but I've made a point every so often to go to places where songs can resonate with an unusual depth.

When I recently heard the soft metal classic "Carry On Wayward Son" over a gas-station speaker, I didn't think about Kansas. Instead I saw the aging metal head from skid row, playing air guitar and bringing a surprising urgency to the line, "Lay your weary head to rest."

The repertoire in each three-hour show is wide-ranging. "It's a little bit of everything, some do country, some do rock 'n' roll," said Lucy Stallworth, the evening's disc jockey and emcee. A few rap songs get tossed in—at least those that pass a prohibition on lyrics containing profanity or sexual content. Lucy stacked the scribbled karaoke requests as a woman yowled her way through Christopher Cross' "Ride Like the Wind."

A few minutes later, a missionary group from Colorado stood up to perform Queen's "Bohemian Rhapsody" and sang in harmony the opening lines—"Mama, I just killed a man"—which made Lucy laugh. "We don't really have a rule against murder in song," she said. "Maybe we should."

Jennifer Campbell is a skid row poet, and when she performs here she prefers what she called "dusties—old music from the '60s and the '70s like Mary Wells, the Temptations."

She considers karaoke essential to the neighborhood's well-being: "It's a healing agent. Every Wednesday, we can look forward to gathering here peacefully."

John Malpede, who for the last 26 years has run the Los Angeles Poverty Department, a nonprofit activist theater group on skid row, sees the emotions tapped during karaoke carried beyond the church doors. "It's not just that it happens there. It's that people take that with them when they leave. It really changes the vibe of the neighborhood," he said. "You see people perform there, you see them later, they see you."

Two decades ago Pastor Tony himself was in a rough spot. He was living on the streets of San Diego, addicted to crack, sporting a crusty beard and pushing a cart. He was saved by the kindness of a stranger who directed him to a treatment center and introduced him to Jesus. Now Pastor Tony leads a congregation that numbers about 250.

As he walks through the karaoke room each week with a donation basket collecting money to pay for water and coffee for the crowd, his blue eyes sparkle in gratitude with each offering. He wears his hair tight, pulled back into a neat ponytail.

And when he busts out "Jungle Love," by Minneapolis funk group the Time, he can make the room forget everything except for the "oh-ee-oh" refrain.

One night soon after I started attending in 2008, I was captivated by an unlikely performance of Olivia Newton-John's "Magic," a light-as-a-feather aspirational song about hope in the face of desperation.

Sung by a wiry-haired woman, slightly addled—maybe crack, maybe mental issues—"Magic" became something different. Holding the microphone like a long-neck Bud, the woman found comfort in the words, her face turning peaceful, soft. "You have to believe we are magic," she sang, her voice barely scratching out the melody, "nothing can stand in our way."

Over the years I kept returning. Thrills came randomly. Sometimes an alcoholic James Brown impersonator arrived in a purple cape to do "I Feel Good." After he was finished, he vanished into the night like a funk superhero.

The church has accumulated hundreds of karaoke discs stuffed into thick cases and acquired a sound system big enough for the sanctuary.

Morello donated the karaoke machine after he heard of the need through a friend with the outreach group Food Not Bombs. He said people on skid row are marginalized, and not just physically.

"They're completely erased from history in a way," he said. "You fall below this certain poverty line, you no longer have any voice—certainly no voice in electoral politics, and no economic voice to buy a lobbyist to serve your cause.

"One small way that these people maintain a voice is through song."

When Robin Martell stepped up in front of the crowd, his voice was a golden falsetto. He first came to karaoke about a decade ago when he was starting out as a singer and ran with a few well-known names.

"I was like a hardhead, hanging out with Bobby Brown and El DeBarge," he said. "I went from jumping out of limos and major tours to jumping in and out of tents and alleys for crack."

Martell pulled himself out of his addiction and now tours as a backup singer for the funk band Lakeside. He returns occasionally on Wednesdays to remind himself where he's been. You can hear the confidence of a clean voice in his take on Gladys Knight's "Neither One of Us (Wants to Be the First to Say Goodbye)," which he sang in pitch-perfect tone, making eye contact with audience members when an older, fragile-looking woman, seemingly smitten, stood up, grabbed a microphone and began an impromptu duet.

Some in the crowd sang along, others mingled in the back sipping coffee and chatting. Teens from a visiting church group whispered and laughed among themselves. When Martell finished, the audience clapped vigorously.

Every Wednesday at 9 p.m., when the room is most crowded, Lucy cues up Will Smith's "Wild Wild West." After the chairs are pushed to the sides, the crowd steps joyfully to an imperfect line dance.

Among those leading the dance the night Gentleman Robert performed was Harris. She said that she used to be shy onstage, but about a decade ago, she started pushing herself to act in skits and plays with the Poverty Department. Now she's a regular on karaoke night and often sings the country song "I Hope You Dance."

"When I perform this song, it opens up my heart," she said, "and allows me to know that doors may close in my face, but another one opens. And no matter what, I'm not ashamed. I cry when I cry, but to know that I can get up there and do what I do knowing that you're not looking down on me, or through me, or around me, but you're looking at *me*."

This evening, she sang like a star: "Give the heavens above more than just a passing glance/And when you get the choice to sit it out or dance/I hope you dance."

As the singing wound down and the final melody played, the micro-phones were turned off, the door locked, and Harris walked into the night. 🪶

Randall Roberts on themes

One of my favorite editors had an excellent tip both for organizing a first draft and for determining themes: he said to imagine sitting at a bar with a friend, and tell the story as you would were you casually chatting. A narrative arc will usually reveal itself, which will help organize the information. And that conversational but authoritative tone is one I always strive for in my longer stories.

I use a couple other old-school methods for contemplating themes. I focus hard while I'm transcribing notes and interviews, paying attention for ideas that are repeated by different sources, connecting dots that might not otherwise reveal themselves were I winging it or if I haven't done ample reporting. If that doesn't work, I often find that taking a long, hot shower will usually produce a few bankable ideas.

I'm in the process of trying to master the essay, or what we usually tag a "critic's notebook." As the *LA Times* pop music critic, I'm charged with writing both quick-react bloggy stuff about whatever's trending and interesting, and long-form essays, reviews, profiles, and trend pieces on music, musicians, and the state of the biz in various subgenres—hip-hop, rock, mainstream pop, EDM, country, and international music.

The essay part is new territory for me. I had come to understand the structure and possibilities of reported profiles and features through the hundreds I've written since I went pro. That stage involved working daily to master the art of nonfiction storytelling, followed by a period in which I edited a roster of writers and their stories and posts but did little actually writing myself.

I didn't like that. I've come to understand that I'm more a writer than editor by nature. The joy for me, and the sense of purpose, comes in imagining and then conveying a story, one that these days often celebrates the creators who decorate our lives with beauty.

Long-form critiques and essays still make me bite my nails, though, which is what makes it exciting for me at the present.

My next stage is a book: nonfiction, about the secret and not-so-secret history of weed and music.

SEXUALITY
A View from the Chair

Kevin Dubouis

When Max Lewis came out of Ragtag Cinema, a woman jokingly offered to rub his ears. He tried to turn his wheelchair to meet the generous fellow moviegoer, but it was too late. The woman had his earlobes in-hand and was caressing them. "Oh," Lewis said, giving her a shy smile, "thank you."

That night in August 2012, the theater on Hitt Street showed *The Intouchables*, a French movie featuring Philippe, a millionaire who relearns the joys of life after a paragliding accident paralyzes him from the neck down. With the advice of a caretaker, he figures out how to enjoy sex again. Philippe hires a sex worker who massages his ears, one of the rare zones that remains sensitive to stimulation.

Lewis, a 46-year-old Columbia resident, also has come a long way in rediscovering a healthy sexual life. A diving accident in 1986 left the then-19-year-old Lewis paralyzed from the neck down. When the doctors told Lewis he would never walk again, the reality of the disability sank in. In his early days at the University Hospital, he thought he might never have anyone else in his life. He couldn't imagine ever participating in and enjoying a sexual relationship again. "But the problem is that my hormones, my emotions, my feelings, my attractions toward women did not stop," Lewis says. He thought his life was over.

Once he understood that his paralysis was not what defined him as a person, he accepted his disability. He was quadriplegic, but giving up on life was not a possibility.

A stereotype about people in wheelchairs is that social life and romantic relationships are difficult at best and nonexistent at worst. People with disabilities desire to build connections with others just like anyone else. In addition to the physical barriers preventing certain sensations, an emotional barrier can create the loss of confidence and comfort that prevents them from exploring their social and sexual possibilities.

Rehab usually helps patients and their loved ones not only set but also reach physical, mental and emotional goals. The ultimate purpose is an easier reintegration into their communities. With efforts and communication, people in wheelchairs can overcome these barriers and embrace love, sex and their disabilities.

Four months after the accident, as part of his therapy at Columbia's Rusk Rehabilitation Center, Lewis watched an erotic movie featuring a person with a disability. The therapists wanted him to know how he could be transferred from the wheelchair to the bed and what positions were safe and comfortable for him during intimate moments.

It was the first time Lewis had encountered any material about disability and sex. Although it would require some adjustments, having sex seemed doable to Lewis.

During his stay at the hospital, he received a lot of attention and care. He became friends with nurses and doctors, and soon he fell in love with one of them.

When Lewis first saw his nurse in the summer of 1986, he was still at the Rusk Rehabilitation Center and didn't have much contact with her. Three years older than Lewis, she was beautiful and smart, he remembers. But Lewis felt clumsy and inappropriate on his four wheels. He felt no one would really want to date him.

"My biggest obstacle was probably the fear of being turned down," he says. "I am aware that there's the disability aspect, but I've always thought that you'll never know if you don't try."

In September, when he was able to get out of bed and go to rehab, he started seeing her three to four days a week. He'd talk to her about the hospital, the drugs, the pain, the therapy and about his life. He felt he could be himself with her.

Because nurses are required to take special care of patients in rehab, the two spent several hours every day chatting, laughing and getting to know each other.

But nothing serious came of it. For one, she was a nurse—and nurses often develop a level of health care intimacy with their patients. Second, she was married.

"Hey, I'll walk with you," Lewis said to her one Friday as she started for the back door of the hospital to go home.

"I want to tell you something, I've been wanting to tell you something for a while," he said before pausing.

He finally added with more confidence: "I find myself being attracted to you. I really, really like you."

"I appreciate it, Max," she answered immediately. "It's really nice of you. But I'm married, and that would be unprofessional for me."

"I know that, but I just want you to know that I find you very attractive," he said.

He had done it. He was proud and happy, yet he felt a little sad. "She was married, and she'd told me before," he says. But he couldn't help himself and continued pursuing her.

He told her again and flirted more and more with her. About a month later, the attraction was reciprocated. Although it took the nurse some time to accept the affection and feelings she had for Lewis, the two started dating and soon began a sexual relationship. He would wait for her to have a break, and she would stay after work for him. They hid, but Lewis was in love. The relationship lasted six months and ended a short while after he left the hospital. She moved away from Columbia with her husband, and Lewis had to move on. Fifteen years later, Lewis met Wanda Jesse, to whom he is now engaged.

Cassy Kubala, an occupational therapist at the Rehabilitation Institute of St. Louis, has heard stories about nurses who had relationships with patients. The 30-year-old has, herself, been dating Jesse Cuellar, a quadriplegic, for more than three years since just after his accident. But he wasn't her patient, she says. A therapist friend thought their personalities would match and introduced them after Cuellar was discharged from the hospital.

Cuellar was 27 when he lost his balance, fell off a roof and broke his neck. Now paralyzed from the neck down, he is still learning how to live in a different body. "He kind of got annoyed sometimes because I have the tendency to ask him if he's doing OK," says Kubala, who had never been with a quadriplegic partner before. But Cuellar's answer is always, "Live in the moment; I'm fine."

Kubala has always enjoyed working with people who have spinal cord injuries. They bring back memories of her quadriplegic grandfather who lived several years with her when she was younger. She only knew him in a wheelchair because he suffered a ruptured brain aneurism before she was born. Her familiarity with the disability and the fact that she's now in a relationship with a quadriplegic man have made her a better clinician, she says.

When it came to having sex, she's learned everything with Cuellar. "It's definitely been a learning process," Kubala says. Because her boyfriend is quadriplegic, she has to do the positioning and most of the hip movement during sex. With time and practice, they've found what works and satisfies both of them in bed.

"I can still pleasure him even though he doesn't necessarily feel it," she says. "And for him, he can still pleasure me even though he can't necessarily control what's going on or be as physical as he'd like to be."

Teaching the partner of a person with quadriplegia how the disability affects sexuality is as important as teaching the person in the wheelchair, says Kubala. She monitors Cuellar's blood pressure, a problem for many quadriplegics and paraplegics. An overfull bladder, urine drainage bag, leg straps that are too tight, pressure sores or any minor stimulus can cause blood pressure to rise. Also known as autonomic dysreflexia, this complication can be life-threatening, Kubala says.

According to the website of the University of Miami's Miller School of Medicine, "the stimulus sends nerve impulses to the spinal cord, where they travel upward until they are blocked by the lesion at the level of injury. Since the impulses cannot reach the brain, a reflex is activated that increases activity of the autonomic nervous system."

Having sex sets off a rapid heartbeat that, if uncontrolled, can trigger a sudden change from very low to very high blood pressure and lead to convulsions, stroke, hemorrhage or even death.

At The Rehabilitation Institute of St. Louis, an education and prevention program puts individuals with spinal cord injuries into real-world situations prior to returning home. For example, many people who use wheelchairs need to learn about bowel and bladder management because they often cannot transfer independently and struggle with how to use the bathroom. Sex education is a small part of this program but is emphasized individually rather than as a group. Teaching the patients and their partners how to recognize symptoms of automatic dysreflexia is part of the center's spinal cord rehabilitation program.

Kubala says in the past, patients have asked the institute if they could have privacy with their partners to try the techniques they were taught in rehab. Although the center does not allow privacy for sex, it does allow partners to practice the other techniques learned. Kubala thinks talking about sex to inpatients is essential because it could be more challenging for outpatients to figure it out on their own.

Dani Vanderboegh, a 29-year-old MU graduate student originally from the St. Louis area, figured out the sex part on her own. She broke her back in a snow-sledding accident when she was 19, and she has since been paralyzed from the waist down.

After 12 hours of surgery and on morphine, Vanderboegh spent time talking to a quadriplegic woman who shared her room at the hospital. They talked about what life would be like for her outside the hospital. She knew her life had changed, and she was getting ready to confront the world in a wheelchair.

Although she was assured she would be able to enjoy intimate relationships despite the disability, Vanderboegh wondered if anyone would ever see her personality behind the wheelchair and be attracted to her. She thought she'd live in celibacy, but she discovered quite the opposite. Just a year after her accident, a young man asked her on a date. She knew she wasn't interested in him, but she needed to reconnect with her sensuality. She also wondered if sex would be the same.

Once they began having sex, she realized they were not sexually compatible, and the relationship became awkward. At the time, she thought it was her fault because she was the one with the disability. After a month, she broke up with him.

She now realizes that her disability was not the problem, but rather the relationship. And she had learned something from the experience; she could still feel something between her legs. Experts explain that women with spinal cord injuries can achieve normal orgasms if there is some residual pelvic innervation, though orgasm remains relatively rare.

Because she accepted her disability and was determined to enjoy life, Vanderboegh started dating someone else. But a month into the relationship, a bacterial infection she had contracted in emergency care took her back to the hospital. Her boyfriend supported her the entire time, and together they dealt with her health issues.

They dated for more than three years, enjoyed sex and even lived together. In bed, it wasn't awkward. "I think he was just waiting for a red light," she says, recalling the time when she was in bed with her boyfriend. "I don't ever remember him asking questions. Maybe at some point: 'Can you feel this? Can you feel that?' But it wasn't a big conversation."

Lewis also didn't have a big conversation with his fiancée, Wanda Jesse, a 47-year-old who works in the canteen department at Truman Memorial Veterans' Hospital. At the beginning of their relationship, he asked her, "Hey babe, do you want me to see the doctor about getting some Viagra?" She said yes, and shortly after, they had sex.

Jesse entered Lewis' life more than four years ago when he took care of a legal issue she was involved in. She remembers the immediate connection she felt with him. They didn't date right away but kept in touch through friends and met occasionally.

Jesse kissed Lewis first. For a long time, they kept their relationship low-key because they wanted to see where it was going. After keeping it a secret for two years, the couple finally told their friends and family. They got engaged last January and would like to live as a family, have their own house and maybe adopt a child. "The biggest problem we have right now is that the bed is way too small," Lewis says with a smile. They both live in Paquin Tower, but Jesse has a bigger bed, and Lewis says that the lift he uses to get in bed would not raise him high enough to reach her bed.

Despite the limitations, they know communication is the reason why it works between them. With his fiancée, Lewis has been able to experience what experts call "paraorgasm" or "phantom orgasm." Research shows there's more than the physical response to orgasm—a person's mind plays a role in getting excited and stimulated.

The Christopher & Dana Reeve Foundation, renowned for its 2006 campaign that featured the Superman "S" shield on logos to raise public awareness about spinal cord injury, explains on its Paralysis Resource Center website that the orgasm occurs "through reassignment of sexual response to areas of the body unaffected by the injury. This is described as a pleasurable, fantasized orgasm that mentally intensifies an existing sensation."

Earlobes and neck are Lewis's sensitive zones that when stimulated can give him a lot of pleasure. Jesse didn't know whether Lewis could have sex when she first met him. For that reason, she doesn't blame friends who ask whether she has ever been intimate with Lewis.

But sometimes reactions from people are more difficult to accept. Jesse's brother and a friend have asked Jesse why she would ever date a man in a wheelchair. They think she could do better; they say she deserves better than sacrificing her life for Lewis. But Lewis and Jesse are happy together. "I think we have more of a happier and dynamic lifestyle than the majority of people out there," Lewis says. "Personally, making love is about the gift of giving. When you strive and you aim to give pleasure to the other, that exponentially elevates your love life as long as that gift of giving . . . doesn't abate."

Kevin Dubouis on asking intimate questions
and writing about taboo topics

In December 2012, a friend of mine and I decided to work on a documentary film together. Because I had no broadcasting skills to offer, I was in charge of conducting interviews and writing the script.

A year prior to this decision, we had met Max Lewis—the main character of my piece "Sex and (Dis)ability"—during a class presentation. As part of an open discussion about what it means to belong to a minority group, Lewis talked and answered questions about his disability. Later on that year, my friend and I talked about the experience we had respectively had with Lewis and decided that others should know about him. He's always been very involved in social activism and is a board member of several committees, but we felt there was something grander about him. We talked with Lewis about spending time with him to document his life. Without hesitation he agreed to show us what it means to live with quadriplegia.

I would never have written the piece if I hadn't worked on that documentary film. It took hours of interviews and even more time spent with Lewis and his family for me to feel comfortable enough to ask questions related to Lewis's sexual and emotional intimacy.

Several weeks into the project, it became obvious that this part of Lewis's life was missing from the conversation. We knew that he had a fiancée but no kids. We knew that she would sleep over at his place after pizza nights, and he would stay late playing cards at her place once in a while. In short, they were a normal couple. But because of Lewis's disability, I had more questions. Would people have wondered how sex worked for them if Lewis wasn't disabled? Probably not. And my friend and I pondered initially on whether we should let our curiosity invade Lewis's private life.

I felt I had gotten such great access to Lewis that I couldn't miss the opportunity to explore this—let's face it— taboo subject. I was not sure it was going to work, but I took it as a challenge and went forward.

A few days later I asked Lewis to meet me at a café downtown to continue our ongoing interview. I still remember how nervous I was. We had certainly established a level of trust in a few months, and my friend and I both knew what we were trying to achieve with the documentary film. However, I was about to add another component to the conversation and was scared I might put Lewis off and change the dynamic of my relationship with him. How would you feel if I were asking you questions about your sexual life?

When I first asked whether he was sexually active, there was no recorder on—just he and I chatting and drinking tea. He smiled but took my question seriously. When I realized that he was comfortable talking about the challenges he has faced, I quickly turned the recorder on and let him lead the conversation. I discovered a whole new world during this conversation: the realities of his life but also those of other people with disabilities.

His openness allowed me to move forward, and I started contacting more disabled people. They all wanted people to know that they or their partners enjoy very fulfilling sexual and emotional lives beyond the disability. Like with any challenge, they have found ways to overcome the disability and create a zone of comfort for themselves. To be honest, I was surprised by the access they provided.

Despite the openness of my sources, I was aware of the sensitivity of the matter and conducted my interviews very carefully. Not that I am not careful when I interview any source, but I felt that my ignorance on the subject could have led to many mistakes—and you don't want to be appear a fool when you enter people's lives. My sources trusted me with their stories; I couldn't mess it up. In the end, my ignorance became my strength. I asked all of them the most sincere questions I had so that I could understand how they deal with disability when it comes to intimacy.

After I conducted all the interviews, I went through the transcripts one by one to highlight the key points of each character. To make the writing process smoother, I wrote the story in different chapters. Not only did it help me organize what I had to say and convey, but it also made the story more digestible. I wanted each chapter to show a unique scene of my source's life.

I have always written stories that pertain to the realm of social justice. Spending time with Lewis and the others helped me grow as a journalist, but it also taught me a lot about life. It made me realize that despite hardship there is always a reason to smile. It made me more aware of the discrimination people with disability face on a daily basis. Finally, it made me believe in the work of the journalists even more.

Since then, I have read a lot about the rights of people with disabilities in this country, and I have realized that there is so little discussed in the mainstream media. When I interned at Al Jazeera America during my last semester of graduate school, I emailed Lewis about a woman with Down syndrome who was fighting a law that discriminated against people with disabilities. To get people to talk to me about the issue, I sent the story I had written about Lewis and the others.

A PERSISTENT CULTURE OF POVERTY

Simina Mistreanu

There was a party at the dorm Friday night. The kids got together, had some drinks and then went off to join the West Plains night scene. They danced at the club and came back to the dorms after 1 a.m. Some of them went to bed. Others had more drinks and talked the night away. They ended up in rooms other than their own, on couches, in restrooms, in showers, in beds. When they finally woke up Saturday around noon, they showered, grabbed lunch at the cafeteria and updated each other on the previous night's events. They lingered over cigarettes and stories. Then they went back to their rooms to kill a few hours until Saturday night and the next party.

Among the partiers: Katie Castello, Tacompsy Rawson, Samantha Price and Heather Hopkins, a tight clutch of friends at Missouri State University's West Plains campus, a two-year junior college in the heart of the Ozarks. All are caught up in the drama of dorm life and the distraction of college classes. All are trying to find a way out of West Plains and into their dreams of well-paying jobs, loving families and bigger cities.

Katie wants to graduate from college, then work at something she's passionate about while she builds a family. What that something is—she's not sure yet.

Tacompsy wants to move to a big city—maybe Atlanta, where there are plenty of professional black men to meet—attend beauty school and have her own nail salon one day.

Samantha wants to become a paramedic with a fire department and someday own a restaurant.

And Heather wants to become a psychologist somewhere far away from south-central Missouri.

These are the kind of goals—vague, romantic, idealistic and unformed—common to college-aged kids everywhere. But for these four, dreams of the future play out against the realities of the past and are underscored by a background etched in profuse poverty, indifference to education and lack of discipline or ambition. These four young women typify a demographic handicapped to fail: Millennials who grew up in the central Ozarks, an area with high rates of unemployment and meth addiction and low rates of advanced degrees. They were raised in families where welfare was more common than steady work.

Now it's their turn, their time to try to shake off the inheritance of poverty and inertia to build happy, independent lives for themselves.

On a Saturday in early March, the four friends sprawl on blue couches in the dorm apartment Katie and Tacompsy share. They tell their stories, interrupting one another with laughter, encouragement and bursts of Facebook news. They are sweet and sassy, funny and frustrating, maddening and, at times, tragic.

They believe in one another and support each other's dreams of better lives. It's what they all say they want. But none of them are sure they know how to make that happen. Over the next three months, as they try to make it through the school semester with passing grades and the promise of decent jobs, those hopes will repeatedly be challenged and re-tailored by an environment of low expectations.

March

Samantha, 17, is the youngest of the four and the only one who didn't grow up in Missouri. Her family moved from Yucca Valley in southern California a few months ago when they bought a house in Alton. They saw it online and decided they could afford to buy, after renting in California. Her stepfather was disabled after a forklift broke his back years ago, and her mother stays at home and, with the help of government assistance, cares for the four youngest of the couple's 10 children.

Missouri still feels strange to Samantha.

"Everybody waves to you, but they won't talk to you in stores," she says. "In California they won't wave to you on the street, but they'll talk to you in the store. You talk, and you're best friends. And you exchange numbers, and you hang out later that night."

Everything feels new to Samantha. She is dealing with her first semester in college, her first time away from her parents and her first time getting close to a boy, who'll later act like nothing happened. She has found an anchor in the other girls, especially Tacompsy, who has her back.

But moving here didn't change Samantha's goal: To become a paramedic and, eventually, run a restaurant. She hopes to join the Missouri National Guard to help pay for college, and expects to enlist in late March.

Samantha is trying to figure out who she is, Tacompsy says.

As for herself, Tacompsy drawls: "I was born a poor black child." Her send-up of Steve Martin in "The Jerk" sends her friends into peels of laughter. But the truth is, Tacompsy was born poor and black, to a 14-year-old in St. Louis. She was adopted by a white couple from Mountain View, a town 30 minutes north of West Plains. A few years later, the couple adopted Tacompsy's biological younger brother.

Tacompsy was the only black girl at her high school in Mountain View. Heather and Katie went to the same school, but they didn't hang out together back then. Tacompsy's father was a detention teacher at her high school; he kept a close eye on her at school and didn't let her go out much at night. Her mother had a job in Springfield during the week, and commuted the two hours home on weekends. Tacompsy recalls often being left in charge of her brother, having to cook and do laundry. She left home when she was 17, first living with a boyfriend, then with several other friends until she started college a year later. She says she hasn't been home since she first left.

Earlier this year, Tacompsy found out she was pregnant. She had spent a night with a young man during Christmas break. He freaked out at the news, and she hasn't decided what she'll do. She says she wants to keep the baby, but being a parent would make it harder to strike out on her own. She has her sights set on beauty school and then Atlanta, where there are more young black people.

"That has been my dream since I was little," she says. "I don't really know what's going to happen, but I do know that I'm going to make it there sometime."

Katie, 20, lacks that certitude. She also grew up in Mountain View, after her family moved from St. Louis to take care of her grandfather. She had hoped to go to college in Springfield, but her ACT scores were too low. Now she does her general studies at MSU-West Plains, just like the other girls. She is supposed to graduate in May but doubts she'll make it. She dropped credits because she had a hard time adjusting to college, then an uncle died, and then she fell further behind. She considers graduating next year or the year after.

Katie wants traditional things—good job, money, relationship, house— but has no idea how to make that happen. She would like to travel the world but doesn't know what kind of job would pay her for that. She considers event planning because she likes to shop. She wonders about being a flight attendant, but she is afraid the plane might crash. She likes baking cakes, so she might go into culinary arts.

"Everyone keeps telling me that I need to know what to do with my life, but I don't know how I'm supposed to know, or how I'm supposed to decide," Katie says. "I've taken those career quizzes, and they don't tell me anything. So I don't know."

She says she's dating a 27-year-old man.

"No," the other girls interrupt. "Not dating. No!"

Anyway, the man told Katie to Google it. Google life. It wasn't very helpful.

She has worked at fast food restaurants in Mountain View and as a sewing operator for a Nike manufacturer in Winona. But now her family is pressuring her to choose a stable career, even though neither of her parents were much interested in advanced education. Lately, Katie has had anxiety attacks and doesn't leave her room very often.

Heather often keeps Katie company. The two have been friends since childhood. Although Heather doesn't officially live in the dorm, she's always there, often sleeping on the couch in Katie's living room. Heather spent her early childhood in Springfield, until her parents got divorced when she was 4 and her mother moved to West Plains with her three children. A few years later, they moved to Mountain View, where Heather finished school. Her mother, a single mom who for long time raised the children largely with the help of government assistance programs, didn't impose many rules—Heather could stay out as long as she wanted and sleep over at friends' houses. So when Heather was a teenager and her mother married a man who set an 8 p.m. curfew, Heather rebelled.

"I would always go to my friends' house because they weren't allowed to come over, so that's how it started out," she says. "I always wanted to be with my friends. I didn't want to be stuck at home."

Friends' parents took her in. In middle school, she went on a trip to Florida with a friend's family. Her track coach became a sort of a mother figure and helped Heather get a scholarship at Hannibal-LaGrange University. She went there for a year but lost her scholarship when she was caught smoking weed. So last fall, her coach arranged for her to go to a college in Humboldt, Tenn., and play basketball. Because she enrolled too late, she wasn't allowed to play basketball the first season and soon lost interest in school. She left after a couple of months and came back to live with her mother. She enrolled at MSU in January but can't wait to move away and be on her own.

Heather, now 20, is interested in a career in psychology and raising a family. She says she knows she could be a good mom, but she is not sure how she would provide for them.

"My mom kind of settles, and she doesn't push herself very much. We lived paycheck by paycheck, and we didn't get to do much of anything," Heather says. "That's my biggest fear. I don't want to end up like that."

All four friends separately echoed some version of that perspective. Tacompsy said she thinks that if you didn't have a great family growing up, it will make you want your own family even more, to be the best mom you can be.

Katie's parents always told her school was important but didn't model that in their own lives.

Samantha's family is the most important thing in the world to her, she says, but, also an example of what not to do. She needs to know that "I'm doing something with my life and not just sitting around, being a bum."

"A lot of my family is like that. They depend on the government. I don't want to be like that," she says. "I want to do something with my life and make a difference in somebody's life, anybody's life. One of my fears is actually to die without making a difference."

Living down to expectations

Heather has class at 8 a.m. on Tuesdays and Thursdays. Waking up is not fun, especially after a late-night party, so she easily talks herself out of it. Then she wakes up at 10 a.m. and hates herself for not going to class. Sometimes, when she's sleeping over at the dorm, the girls lure one another back to sleep in the morning, only to feel bad a few hours later because they missed class again.

The work ethic of Millennials—people born between 1980 and 2000, give or take a few years—has been studied, debated, dissected and judged. They have been portrayed in the media as the trophy children of baby boomers, a demanding nightmare for employers, the entitled members of a lost generation.

In a 2008 survey by CareerBuilder.com, 85 percent of hiring managers said that Millennials had a stronger sense of entitlement than older workers. They wanted higher pay, flexible work schedules, a promotion within a year and more vacation and personal time. Back when the economy was booming, the dark joke among employers was that Millennials expected to become CEO in a day.

Now young people's expectations have slumped with the economy, but the discussion continues about their values. Work ethic, by most measures, is not at the top of the list. According to a 2010 Pew Research Center study, Millennials were the only age group that didn't cite work ethic as a trait that identifies their generation. What they did list: technology use, music/pop culture, liberal/tolerant and smarter technological savvy, importance of music and pop culture, liberality and tolerance, and intelligence. Only 5 percent mentioned work ethic as a core trait of their generation; that's almost four times fewer than Baby Boomers and half as many as Gen Xers.

Heather echoes the surveys: "I lived my life always doing what I want, and now I want to be successful, and I don't want to be struggling. But it's really, really, really hard to make myself do stuff. I have no willpower. It takes everything I got to wake up in the morning."

Tacompsy shrugs at her lackluster performance in school. She's only "bullshitting around here," she says; none of the classes at MSU interest her or will set her up for beauty school. Yet she has strong opinions about education.

"Growing up in Mountain View, Missouri, we are screwed from the very beginning," she says. "For the whole time you go from elementary school to high school, you really don't have to do anything. To pass high school, you just show up and you're good." But all of a sudden you're in college and expectations increase tenfold. You don't know how to meet those expectations because you never had to before.

MSU tries to address that reality in part by offering remedial classes in subjects such as English, math and reading to help students perform at college level. Nationally, 58 percent of two-year college students enroll in at least one remedial class, according to researchers at the City University of New York. At MSU-West Plains, about 70 percent of freshmen, including returning adults, take at least one remedial class, said Mirra Anson, director of developmental education.

Katie, on the other hand, hasn't found college expectations to be very challenging. She turned in an English paper three weeks late, and it was accepted. The lesson she took away: That's the way things work.

Samantha doesn't reflect much on the rigors or failings of her college education. She started only two months ago, and it's as new and strange as everything else in this state and in this dormitory. But Heather, who is on her third college experience, offers a blunt solution: "Government should cut people off." Her theory is that because of welfare programs her mother wasn't forced to go out and get a job. If her mother had been forced to work, Heather would have grown up seeing someone work hard and understanding the benefits of that work. Now she sees the downfalls of not working—but she admits she doesn't know how to prevent them for herself.

Geography and poverty

South-central Missouri is one of the most beautiful regions of the state. The Mark Twain National Forest covers much of the area, and the locals take pride in the clear swift rivers, perfect for canoeing and fishing.

It is also the poorest region of the state, with an average wage of $510 per week in the first quarter of 2011, according to the Missouri Department of Economic Development. Even the residents of southeast Missouri, called the "Bootheel" and known for its striking poverty, earned on average $100 more per week; workers in St. Louis made nearly double.

The unemployment rate in south-central Missouri was 9.2 percent in February 2012, compared with a state average of 8.4 percent.

A national study published in 2002 listed south-central Missouri as one of the regions defined by persistent poverty since 1959. Wendell Bailey, a former Republican congressman from Willow Springs and former state treasurer, said he thinks nothing has changed. Last year, Bailey launched a program aimed at fighting poverty and increasing the quality of education and prospect of jobs for young people in a 10-county area in the region. He gathered leaders from 31 communities, set up a nonprofit and a 10-year plan to chip away at the underlying problems.

Bailey's aim is to change the "culture of poverty" in the Ozarks. "When you are immersed in poverty, it's generational," he says. "The parents are on food stamp programs, and children are on food stamp programs. The same way with education: When parents drop out and children drop out, it becomes a culture that's accepted to drop out of school. In fact, it's expected."

It's also likely that a 17-year-old girl who drops out of high school and gets a job at a fast food restaurant will still be working there when she is 27, because her employment options are limited by her lack of a high school diploma, Bailey says. "That creates its own expectation of failure because that's where you come from and that's where you remain."

Bailey's efforts may offer some new hope to children born during the next decade. But for those already here, the effects of being born in poverty will haunt them into adulthood. It all starts at birth, says Laura Speer, associate director for policy, research and data at the Annie E. Casey Foundation, a Baltimore-based nonprofit that supports disadvantaged children across the country. A child born into poverty is more likely to be born early, have a low birth weight and have developmental delays—and less likely to have access to quality health care. By kindergarten, the child is already behind the curve and likely to remain there throughout the first years in school.

The effects of poverty compound over time, Speer says. The child is more likely to drop out of high school and become a teen parent, and less likely to go to college, get a good job and raise children who have the skills to succeed.

Growing up in poverty weighs heavily against young people's motivation, she says, adding that it's difficult to believe that you will be successful if nobody around you is. "Even for the ones who are motivated, there are always barriers that people have to overcome. The ability to overcome those barriers a lot of times has to do with people in your support system," Speer says. "So it's easy to give up if you don't have adults around you who can help you move past those barriers that come up in front of everyone."

Early April

Another Friday night. Another party at the dorm. Someone brought alcohol, which all the kids drank with Coke. Then they started doing stupid stuff, like writing all over a guy's arms and legs because he fell asleep with his shoes on. Then they went to the club. On the way there, the young man who Samantha had hooked up with got arrested for an unpaid ticket. The others made fun of him, wondering if the cops would let him go on Facebook at jail.

Heather, Tacompsy, Samantha and Katie typically hang out with maybe 10 or 15 people from the dorm, all of whom they consider friends. In total, there are about 60 students living at the dorm, all in their own little universes. There are the volleyball girls, who mostly hang out with one another or with the basketball boys; they have their own table at the cafeteria. There are the people who don't live in the dorms but might as well because they are there 24/7; Heather is an example. Then there are the good girls, who party sometimes but not too much, go to church but not all the time and have sex but not too often. A minority of the good girls are the good Christian girls, who don't drink alcohol and don't hang out with boys. There are the shy girls, who never leave their rooms except to go to class or the cafeteria; they spend their days playing cards and watching anime movies. Then there are the weird boys, who look and act creepy and are avoided by girls. Heather, Tacompsy, Samantha and Katie would fall into the category of bitches because they tell it to people straight and like to have fun. Except maybe not Samantha, who until recently was a good Christian girl.

Losing your virginity is a dorm event. When that happened to Samantha and everybody found out, she cried for two weeks straight. Then she got used to it. It's part of dorm life.

On this Saturday in early April, Tacompsy wakes up around noon, her eyes smeared with last night's makeup. A couple of weeks ago she had a miscarriage, which made her sad but also answered the question about keeping the baby. She doesn't know what caused the miscarriage, but she suspects the stress and panic attacks that she's had recently.

About the same time, she got a message on Facebook saying: "Hey, you can be a model!"

"Dude, are you legit?" she wrote back.

Turns out he was working in the porn film industry. His offer: $1,500 for three hours of shooting. Tacompsy asked for some time to think. The man referred her to another agent. This one worked for Ordinary World Models, an agency in New York that, according to its website and job postings, supplies fashion models for print and TV commercials but also for soft and hard porn magazines, such as Playboy and Hustler, and for websites. He invited Tacompsy for a two-day shoot in Boston in mid-April.

She posted on Facebook that she might have a shot at Black Entertainment Television (BET). When friends asked, she said she had lost the baby, so was in shape to model. She wasn't sure what she should do. "I was really considering doing the porn," she says. "I mean, $1,500, that's a lot of money. But $1,500 for three hours of humiliation that other people are going to see—I don't know if that's worth it. But with $1,500 I could get out of here, I could go out and maybe get a car, I could go out and I could go to another city as soon as I wanted to."

What she had to decide was how far she would go to get away from West Plains and out of the trap she feels she's in. "Around here you grow up in one of the small towns, and then you either get stuck in that small town, you get married, you have kids, and you stay here for the rest of your life, or you go to Springfield, and you stay there for the rest of your life," she says. "You look around and it's just like, wow. Some people haven't noticed that they've been here their whole lives and have never left this part of Missouri and probably never will."

Tacompsy didn't follow up on the modeling offer. But when she pictures herself five or 10 years from now, she doesn't see herself in south-central Missouri. She imagines herself enjoying life in a big city, grasping new opportunities, going to beauty school and finding a good black man in Atlanta. That's why she's decided to drop out of school come May.

Samantha has her own things to figure out. In late March, she went to St. Louis to enlist in the National Guard. She took the drug test and the breathalyzer and everything went fine until they weighed her, measured her body mass index and told her she was three pounds over qualifying weight.

Samantha went to the bathroom and cried and tried to vomit. She came back and got weighed again. She was told to come back in late April and try again. Back in West Plains, she is on a diet, which consists mainly of avoiding junk food.

Between the National Guard experience and the last month in the dorm, Samantha grew discouraged. She stopped going to class, earning mostly Ds and one C. She got carried away by college life and her first experiences with boys and alcohol. One night she got drunk and told Tacompsy she hated black people. Tacompsy wanted to jump at her throat, but she understood Samantha didn't mean it, so instead she took care of her through the night. "Since my mom and dad aren't here anymore, I started to rebel," Samantha says. "They are not here holding the umbrella. I'm going to put the umbrella away for a little while."

Samantha says she wasn't pressured to start drinking or experimenting with boys. Actually, the other girls warned her against that. But it looked like fun, and she wanted to try it. "Sam was a really good person when she came here," Heather says in a separate conversation. "And I'm not saying she's a bad person. But she saw the way that we lived and all of the mistakes that we've made, and she kind of felt like it would be cool to do some of the stuff that we did. And it's not. And I tried to tell her a million times."

As Samantha's morals dropped, so did her confidence in her dreams. She doesn't want to open a restaurant anymore—someone told her it's hard and most restaurants die within five or 10 years. She still wants to become a firefighter and paramedic. Maybe.

Most students come to college with their dreams intact, says Dennis Lancaster, an assistant professor of letters at MSU-West Plains and Samantha's favorite teacher. Somewhere along the way they realize it's a lot of work, it's going to cost a lot of money and they might need to leave the comfort of what they know. "They feel limited. They put the limits on themselves," Lancaster says. "They might not be ready to leave this area."

Early April, continued

It's Saturday night, and the girls are going out. Katie is not with them. She just got back together with one of her ex-boyfriends, and she's with him in Mountain View. She stopped talking to the 27-year-old guy friend who wanted her to Google life.

In the last month, Katie's plans have turned upside down. While she was planning on graduating in a year or two, now she wants to speed it up and be done with school this summer. She needs one more credit to graduate and plans to take a one-week art class in the summer. She also needs to pass history this semester, where she is facing an F for not showing up.

Back in March, she had no idea what she was going to do. Now she's decided to go to culinary school in Springfield and live with her boyfriend. She got a job waiting tables at Colton's Steakhouse in West Plains, and hopes to transfer to their restaurant in Springfield. Things seem to be lining up for her. Except for one credit in the summer and that F in history.

Back at the dorm, the girls are getting dressed for the club. Tacompsy changes from her leopard print top into a simple, black one and freshens her makeup. She keeps on her silver-colored necklace, which reads "I love Boys." Heather puts on jeans and a flowered top. Samantha doesn't dress up because she is underage and won't be allowed in the club.

Heather's phone rings. It's her boyfriend, Tommy.

"Where are you at?"

"I'm at the college."

"Stay there, I'm coming to pick you up."

Heather leaves with him. The girls comment on how possessive Tommy is. Tacompsy goes to the club with another friend. It's fairly quiet. The volleyball girls hang out with the basketball boys at the bar and a few people dance to rap music. Tacompsy goes back to the dorm after about an hour.

The next morning, Heather comes down hard on herself for not standing up to Tommy the night before. They had been together for about three months. It was all good at the beginning; they were best friends. But then Tommy started having trust issues, so Heather decided to make their relationship official and declare publicly they were a couple—the first time she's done that with a boy. It only made things worse. Tommy started suspecting Heather of cheating on him every time she went out without him. "I don't know how to make the kid trust me," Heather says. "I don't even know why I want to be with him, honestly."

On top of that, Heather has been kicked out of the house in West Plains where she was living with a friend. In Heather's version, the friend got upset that Heather was never home, hanging out at the college all the time.

Now she has no clue where she will stay. She considers moving in with her father, but that would be weird because they haven't lived in the same house since she was a toddler, before her parents divorced. "Right now sucks," Heather says. "Eventually it will be OK but right now sucks really bad. Money is a big deal, and I hate it because my family is not rich. Whenever you're a child or an individual going out into the world trying to do something for yourself, whenever you start out it's not easy, especially if your family doesn't help you at all. I don't have any support to fall back on. If I fall it's all on me, and it's a million pounds, and it sucks."

She wants to leave, go to a four-year college and mostly go far away from home, to a place where nobody knows her and nobody judges her. But ever since she got suspended from the college in Hannibal, Heather feels she started digging a hole into which she sinks deeper and deeper. "I feel like I'm making a huge leap because we are really low class, and I have this expectation from myself way higher than that, and for my family way higher than that, and so it's really, really, really frustrating because I'm 20 years old, I want to get this going," Heather says. "But I'm stuck, and I feel like I'm stuck forever."

The ways out

It would be easy to watch how these girls party, skip classes and make random, questionable decisions and not see much beyond that. It would be easy to chalk them up as irresponsible members of a "lost" generation. It would be easy to miss their warmth and their kindness, how they take care of each other, how conscious they are of the effects of their decisions and how terribly they struggle.

What would be harder would be to ask how the lives of these girls, and others like them, might have been different had they been born in a different family, in a different place or in a different culture.

Grown-ups and officials offer their solutions.

For Sheila Orchard, who worked for 25 years as a middle school and high school counselor in the local school district until she retired two years ago, it's making tiny steps in helping students define their goals and the path to achieve them. The first step is to convince them to get up and go to school every morning as part of the "big life plan." Programs such as the Missouri A+ Schools Program will pay for students to attend certain colleges if they graduate high school with a minimum 2.5 GPA and 95 percent attendance rate.

For Dennis Lancaster, the MSU-West Plains professor, it's engaging students in one-on-one mentoring, sharing his own experiences and showing them that somebody cares about their struggles.

For Wendell Bailey, the ex-congressman, it's a strategic plan to increase the quality of education and convince businesses to offer more and better jobs for students and parents.

For Laura Speer at the Casey Foundation, it's early education and mentorship—finding successful individuals to serve as role models for the young and help them overcome barriers. At a more macro level, parents need access to better-paying jobs, even if that means going back to school or, in the case of immigrants, learning better English. "Unless there's real commitment to the next generation there's no telling what's going to happen," Speer says. "It won't be good, though."

Early May

There was a party at the dorm Friday night. The kids reveled in the early summer weather and the approaching end of the semester. Some of them stayed in their rooms and prepared for finals week. Others had already given up, walking away from college life. Still others counted the remaining hours until they could be out of here.

One Sunday morning, a young man swung by to pick up Tacompsy and her things. She was finally getting out of West Plains. But her destination was not Atlanta or some big city. It was Springfield, where she would live with the young man and another roommate. She gave up the modeling idea and now she needed another plan.

Tacompsy's early departure fits the predominant trend at MSU-West Plains, where only 27 percent of the students graduate from the two-year program within four years. Another 23 percent end up transferring to other colleges before they finish their degree here.

Katie also left, in April—not to Springfield, as planned, but to Birch Tree, a town 45 minutes northeast of West Plains. Her boyfriend, Michael, has a house there, which he received as a graduation present from his parents and where he moved after he got a job as a McDonald's manager in nearby Mountain View. Katie moved in with him, giving up her plans of attending culinary school in Springfield and graduating from MSU-West Plains in May. She failed several classes toward the end of the semester because it was hard to keep up with school on top of moving and going to work. She quit her job at Colton's Steakhouse after two weeks, instead taking a job as a cashier at the Walmart in West Plains. But she quit that because commuting was exhausting and expensive. Now she has a job at a Mexican restaurant in Mountain View. She doesn't like it very much, but it pays the bills. She and Michael are discussing marriage.

Samantha was sworn into the National Guard in late April. She also got a job, as a cashier at McDonald's in West Plains. She starts mid-May and will work there until mid-August, when she goes on a 10-week boot camp with the National Guard at Fort Leonard Wood. She will then spend the rest of the fall and winter in South Carolina, where she'll get her training as a mechanic with the National Guard. She failed all of her classes this semester, and she doesn't know if she'll come back to MSU. She plans to get her training as a paramedic and become a firefighter, her long-time dream. The complication is that she will need to return to Missouri because her family is here and she doesn't want to live apart from them for too long.

Heather also has decided to try to enlist in the National Guard. "I've been going to college for two years, and it didn't work out so well, so I need a plan B," she says. Meanwhile, she'll be in West Plains for finals week. And before finals week, there are parties.

Sunday is usually Sober Day among the girls' friends (after Margarita Monday, Tequila Tuesday, Wine Wednesday, Thirsty Thursday, Fun Friday and Super-fun Saturday). But on this Sunday in early May, they use the S for Single and find a theme for their party. On Friday, Heather's boyfriend, Tommy, broke up with her, so she joined the others at a friend's house. They played beer pong, a game in which each team tries to throw a Ping Pong ball into the other team's plastic cups. Usually, if the ball gets inside, the members of the opposing team drink from the cup. In this case, the garage floor where they were playing was too dirty, so they used cups with water and kept their drinks on the side.

The party started in the early afternoon. By 9 p.m. the game was old and the girls were tired. Heather and Samantha dozed off on a large couch in the garage, covered by a patchy blanket, in a tight embrace. ▨

Simina Mistreanu on mentors and influences

I know of three things that have contributed to my writing during college, grad school, and my work: reading, writing, and being edited. Reading other people's work and analyzing it is the best way I know to become a better writer. You see what makes you tick as a reader, and then you deconstruct it with a writer's eye. Secondly, reporting and writing stories is crucial because it puts you out there and gives you experience. Editing is also helpful (when you have a good editor) because you can see how your work can transform and improve before your eyes.

This paragraph I just wrote is fine. But my Romanian editor would tell you that my writing is great when I let my guard down. That means caring about the people and the situation I'm writing about and letting that transpire in my writing. Stepping up to your subject with an open heart will make good writing great.

With that, two writers have influenced me more than anyone. The first is Jacqui Banaszynski, a Pulitzer-Prize-winning journalist and professor at the University of Missouri School of Journalism. The second is David Finkel, writer and editor at the *Washington Post*.

My first "Jacqui experience" happened when I was a twenty-year-old journalism student in Bucharest, Romania. I took a narrative journalism class, and all the participants in that class received a copy of *Telling True Stories*, a nonfiction guide to writing. I went home and began reading the first chapter—"Stories Matter," by Jacqui Banaszynski. I had no idea who the author was, but she was writing about reporting in Ethiopia and listening to people sing their stories around the campfire, despite the hunger, disease, and misery they had faced during the day. She said we need stories in order to derive meaning from our lives. She said they make us human—they are our prayers, our parables, our history, our music, and our soul. I read that chapter about thirty times, with a racing heart and a big smile. It explained everything.

Jacqui became my professor, mentor, and friend at Missouri. She will forever be my biggest reminder that stories matter and that I need to trust myself to tell them.

I discovered David Finkel through his books, *The Good Soldiers* and *Thank You for Your Service*, and subsequently through his stories. His books present people's personal experiences up close, while also explaining the systems that influenced them. He transitions seamlessly from micro to macro, from present to past, from rational to emotional. Stories written with this combo are powerful enough to change the world.

THE BIG PAYBACK

Pate McMichael

May 23, 1998

It was already late by the time Ricardo Meza left work at Barnacles, the sports bar near Gwinnett Place Mall. But it was Saturday night, and the 19-year-old had plenty of energy, and regardless of the hour, 11 p.m., he wanted to see his girlfriend, Brenda. She'd told him she had a secret to share.

Ricardo drove from his Norcross apartment to wash up. He lived with his two brothers and his sister—a close family. He took out a nice blue shirt, some Menace jeans he paid too much for, and a clean pair of green-and-black Nikes. The shirt covered most of his tattoos—he had MEZA inked across his light-skinned shoulders and a crucifix at the center of his chest. LOVED ran across his stomach, and the Virgin of Guadalupe with the inscription "Cuída mi Vida"—care for my life—decorated his right shoulder. All that showed was the spiderweb inked on his left elbow. He put double-loop earrings in his left ear and a single hoop in his right and stuffed some pay stubs, two beepers, and $91 in his pockets, then slid into the badass, twodoor, blood-red Honda Civic everyone envied. The car had been lowered and outfitted with wide chrome wheels and window tint. A Mexican flag license plate faced the open road. Old English lettering on the windshield read "La Ley." The law.

Brenda, 17, was staying at the Motel 6 because the power had been turned off at her family's apartment. When Ricardo arrived, he found the family—mother, aunt, uncle, brothers, sisters, cousins—crowded in two rooms with the doors open to let in the cool spring air. Ricardo started horsing around with the little ones right away—he loved children. Brenda's mother, Lucy, took note of that. The boy had a good heart. He worked so hard. He believed in God. He didn't mess with the gangs, although be could pass for a banger with his tattoos, earrings, and goatee.

Lucy had been there the day, three months ago, that Ricardo and Brenda met at the car wash. He was primping the Civic, and Brenda's family was washing her aunt's car. Brenda couldn't take her eyes off Ricardo or his ride. They chatted and exchanged beeper numbers.

Soon Ricardo started visiting their apartment. He took Brenda's little brothers out to eat. He would even help bathe the wormy little devils. Tonight Brenda's mother needed another favor from Ricardo. Would he please take her nephew Joseph home? It was just a few miles away, on Winters Chapel Road.

Ricardo looked like he wanted to say no, but he didn't. Brenda, Joseph, and Brenda's sister's boyfriend, Frog—who claimed to have recently left the gang SUR-13, known by their blue bandana hopped into the Civic.

"We'll be right back." Ricardo said.

At the Waffle House down from the Motel 6, Joker looked through the dark tint of a 1966 Chevrolet Impala. He wore a khaki bandana around his neck. He was high and drunk. Two of his fellow Brownside Locos gang members, Boxer and Turtle, had gone inside to purchase cigarettes from the vending machine, leaving him with the driver. None of the four had turned 18.

Ricardo Meza's red Civic pulled in a few spaces away, near the pay phone. Joker had seen the car before. Members of the gang had even hurled a beer bottle at it and thrown threatening gang signs Ricardo's way. He was always over at Forest Vale Apartments visiting Brenda, whom gang members wanted as a homegirl. And now Ricardo Meza had the nerve to hang a blue bandana—the color of rival gang SUR-13—from the mirror of the tricked-out Civic.

Boxer returned with the cigarettes, incredulous at the sight of the blue bandana.

"Be quiet, just calm down," Joker told him. "Don't act. Don't get crazy. Just don't look at 'em. We're gonna follow 'em. We're gonna follow these guys."

To the driver he said, "Hey, follow these guys now. We're gonna get 'em."

Joker and Boxer were cousins. Their parents had moved to Atlanta from Fresno before the pre-Olympics construction boom. After dropping out in ninth grade, the two spent their time making the Brownside Locos one of the biggest street gangs in Gwinnett County. Brownside sold drugs and committed petty thefts, armed robberies, and, increasingly, drive-by shootings. There was a warrant for Joker's arrest because he'd sprayed a round of bullets outside Selena's nightclub a few weeks back, an event that boosted his confidence.

As the Impala eased out of the parking lot behind the Civic, Joker reached inside his CD case and grabbed an album by the Psycho Realm, a gangster-rap group from Los Angeles. He called up "The Big Payback," the Brownside Locos' war chant.

I'm looking for you,
I'm gonna get you back
when I catch you on the streets slippin',
And that ass is mine

The Impala followed the Civic for about 10 minutes, down Jimmy Carter Boulevard, past I-85, past Buford Highway, to the Peachtree Industrial Boulevard access road, where the Civic stopped at a red light. Joker took out the .45-caliber Springfield 1911 he kept in his waistband at all times.

"Stay close, stay close man," Joker kept barking at his driver. "Don't lose them."

The light turned green. The night of May 23 had become the Sunday morning of May 24. The cars passed Peachtree Corners Circle. No others were around.

"Get beside him now, now!" Joker told the driver.

The Impala pulled into the left lane alongside the Civic. Boxer, who was in the back seat, had his 9 mm locked and loaded, a khaki bandana covering his face. Just then Joker and Boxer slid out of the passenger side window, balancing themselves on the roof of the car.

Before emptying his clip, Joker looked directly at Meza and yelled, "Brownside, motherfucker!"

In the backseat of the Civic, Joseph and Frog had been scheming how to sneak out on the town after Ricardo and Brenda dropped them off. Then, chaos: Flashes of fire, a blown tire, Brenda leaning forward to help Ricardo duck. Brenda pushing the steering wheel, steering the car toward a median and saying, "Is everyone all right? Is anyone hit?"

"Sí," Ricardo groaned. Brenda didn't hear him for the noise. She watched him lean back in his seat. Then blood poured from his nose and mouth. Brenda screamed.

Ahead, Boxer continued to fire at the Civic. "You know you probably killed that guy, man!" the Impala's driver said.

A short silence, then an eruption of laughter.

"We got 'em, we got 'em, we got one," Joker said, embracing the driver as the Impala sped away.

Brenda jumped out of the Civic in a panic. She finally flagged someone down, got a ride to the nearby QuikTrip, and found a police officer, who took her back to the crime scene. There, a man was talking frantically to a 911 operator and trying to resuscitate Meza. Blood had caked on his face and neck like a mask. Only one of about a dozen rounds had hit him, but it entered under his left armpit and tore straight across his chest and lungs, exiting near his right shoulder.

The bullet was nowhere to be found.

And Ricardo Meza was dead.

The Impala left the scene so fast a cop on I-85 flashed blue lights at it just minutes after the shooting. The Impala's driver slowed down and headed to Selena's, near the Chamblee-Tucker exit, where a parade of aligned gangsters cruised the entrance and where Joker sprayed a round of bullets several weeks earlier. When a bouncer saw that Joker was back—hanging out of the window, flashing his Springfield—he ran inside and called the cops. The Impala fled toward I-85 South.

The police immediately set up roadblocks, but the Impala's driver saw a thicket of blue flashing lights in the distance and turned off the interstate at the last minute. A convoy of cars full of young men who'd been following the Impala from Selena's were stopped, and the drivers and passengers questioned by the police.

Sunday, May 24, 1998

At 3:26 a.m., investigators arrived at the Motel 6. Brenda's mother and younger sister, who had heard that "something happened" and went looking for Brenda, returned a few minutes later. Together they began telling

Detective J.W. Mashburn about the Brownside people who lived in their apartment complex—how they drove a white Impala and had been threatening Brenda and Ricardo with gang signs. They told the detective about the bottle that had been thrown at Ricardo's Civic.

Then Ricardo's brother, Gonstalo, arrived, looking for his brother. An officer took Gonstalo into one of the motel rooms and told him the news, then gave him a card and told him where his brother's body would be available for identification and pickup. Later that night, Gonstalo called Mexico and told his mother that her son was dead.

Though scared, Brenda dropped the name "Joker" to a detective on the scene. After that, she and her family left the Motel 6 and went underground. The cops were able to communicate with Brenda through a friend in Stone Mountain even after Brenda moved on to Texas.

Gwinnett County issued a warrant for the arrest of Joker—real name Oscar Flores Lopez—but when cops arrived at his apartment, he had vanished. They located the Impala, but the driver cleaned it the day after the shooting, at a car wash. He threw out the shell casings and wiped the glass dean of fingerprints.

June 3, 1998

Nine days after Ricardo Meza's murder, the phone rang at the Gwinnett County police station. A detective took the collect call. A young Hispanic female cut right to it: She said she wanted out of Brownside and figured the best way would be to have the leaders arrested—then the gang would disintegrate. She refused to identify herself but said she knew where to find Joker.

The detective listened.

The caller said Joker and his cousin Boxer—real name Rubin Flores Hernandez—boarded a Greyhound bus in Atlanta the Tuesday after Meza's murder and arrived in Huron, California, on Thursday at 2 or 3 in the morning. She provided the telephone number and address at which the two cousins were staying.

The detective quickly approved extradition through the Gwinnett County sheriff's office. The next day, a sergeant in California called. He had Boxer and Joker in custody, but neither would talk, and they had to let Boxer go. But Joker would be sent back to Georgia, and the detective asked to be contacted when he arrived so the state could seek a confession. Somebody didn't get the memo. By the time the detective heard of Joker's arrival, the triggerman had an attorney.

That left Gwinnett with no evidence, no indictment. So the case went cold.

October 2000

Brownside Locos operated like any other gang—of any ethnicity—in America. It was made up of troubled teenagers. It existed to preserve and flaunt its heritage, to expand its turf in a given neighborhood, to remain in a constant, escalating state of war, and to prove that its members can and will take lives. Regular Brownside meetings took place at the will of the leaders. Nothing was formal. Members took initiative, proving themselves and rising in power by selling drugs and confronting rival gangs. Murder often separates a weak gang from a strong one. Brownside was not weak.

Nor was it immune. Brownside members lived in fear. They were constantly being shot at, assaulted, and pursued by other gangs. They expressed solidarity by inking the BSL [Brownside Locos] tattoo on their forearms, by wearing khaki bandanas and clothing, by spraying graffiti on neighboring turf. Brownside considered itself autonomous but also part of a loose confederation of five Hispanic gangs known collectively as La Gran Familia. The "family" would occasionally have formal meetings at locations such as Lake Lanier to discuss problems like who should wear what color bandana, what gangs should be targeted, which streets each gang should own. Meetings were usually called when gangs within the family were feuding or when a member was killed in action.

From 1998 to 2002, Brownside expanded its turf in Gwinnett County and took over Norcross. Murders and assaults started spilling into DeKalb and Cobb. It continued until October 2002, when a running gun battle down Sugarloaf Parkway led to a double homicide. It was a Sunday afternoon, the last murder attributed to the Brownside Locos.

September 5, 2002

A month before that gun battle on Sugarloaf Parkway and four years after Ricardo Meza's murder, a fax rolled into the clerk of court's office in Lawrenceville. The request came from the FBI's Gang Task Force, which was demanding certified copies of criminal files for 25 suspected gang members. Earlier that year, the U.S. government had indicted 15 members of Brownside on racketeering laws once used against the mafia. Those laws provide advantages local authorities do not have: People can be charged with guilt by association and held for years pending trial. It leads to snitching, cutting deals, and generally betraying the gang for which gangsters were once willing to die.

Oscar Lopez's name and alias, Joker, were not on the fax, but the name Rubin Hernandez, aka Boxer, was. The Feds simply couldn't prove that Joker stayed in the gang after his eighteenth birthday. Boxer was indicted in Meza's murder, as well as another gang-related shooting. If convicted, the racketeering law would put him away for up to 20 years without parole.

June 2004

Detective David Henry received a tip regarding Ricardo Meza's murder. It came from an FBI agent working the Brownside case. The agent told Henry to drive to Hays State Prison and interview "Crazy," a former Brownside member who had been put away for child molestation.

Henry was the investigator who six years earlier had interviewed Brenda next to the bullet-riddled Civic that contained Meza's corpse. Henry was among the group that later stopped the post-Selena's convoy of gang members. He had interviewed another confidential witness the following afternoon, a witness who claimed to have heard Joker bragging about the shooting hours after the crime.

At the prison, Henry learned that Crazy had been the Impala's driver. Crazy—real name Amado Osorio, also known as "Lil Crazy"—told Henry the whole story and agreed to testify against Joker. So the FBI let Detective Henry interview Turtle, the fourth person in the car that night. Turtle—real name Jose Ivan Quiroz—also identified Joker (Lopez) and Boxer (Hernandez) as the shooters. With that information, Henry secured a warrant for Joker's arrest.

Oscar Lopez, the 16-year-old triggerman, had become a 23-year-old father with no gang affiliation. He lived with his girlfriend in a Post Apartments complex in Gwinnett County. He still had "Joker" tattooed on his neck and "BSL" on the inside of his left forearm. He answered Henry's knock.

After booking Joker, Detective Henry returned to the apartment with a search warrant. He knew that former gangsters suffer from chronic nostalgia. They keep photographs and writings that can be used as evidence in trials. It proved true once more. In the back of a closet in the kids' bedroom, police found what they were looking for: A box containing a stash of porn magazines under which was hidden a picture of Joker in a tank top, holding an AK-47 in one hand, a pump-action shotgun in the other, and a smaller piece tucked in his waistband. That smaller piece, a Springfield 1911, was the murder weapon.

The Thursday before the trial's Monday start, Joker pleaded guilty to killing Ricardo Meza. He apologized to Meza's brother Gonstalo and wept.

January 4, 2007

That left Boxer, Joker's cousin, to face trial.

Brenda came to the courtroom. She had come to remember and redeem Ricardo Meza, the man she had loved for three months then spent eight years mourning.

And now, today, in the 23rd-floor courtroom of U.S. District Judge Beverly Martin, Brenda would address the court at Boxer's sentencing. She would tell them about that horrible night in 1998, and about the man she had loved for such a short amount of time. She wanted to clear any suspicion about Ricardo's blue bandana, the two pagers in his pocket, the spider web tattoo. Kim Dammers, of the U.S. attorney's office, introduced her to the court. A burly FBI agent kept looking back at her and smiling reassuringly.

Brenda walked up to the microphone.

"All he did was work," she said, then started to cry.

Boxer asked for permission to respond. He had recently carved the Brownside tattoo off his right arm with a razor blade, a crime punishable by death in the Brownside code. Years of pretrial detention had changed his mind about gang life.

Turning his back to the judge, Boxer addressed Brenda. He switched from good English to perfect Spanish. He spoke in a formal tone, as people do when greeting mourners at a funeral home. She looked him straight in the eye. "I thank God every day that I am still able to ask for forgiveness for what I was involved in," he said.

As he spoke, two 8-year-old U.S. citizens rubbed their heads against Brenda's arm. She stroked them calmly but never took her eyes off Boxer. The twins giggled and squirmed in the bench as the man who helped kill their 19-year-old father apologized for what he had done. They were the secret Brenda shared with Ricardo Meza the night he died. ▨

Pate McMichael on finding the right vehicle for a story

I always had the ambition to write but not the talent. I taught myself to write by reading great writers and throwing first drafts in the trash. That's right. Put it down on paper and throw it away. Very often you can't fix a first draft. And if you get in the habit of trying to fix a first draft, then you're in for a short career. Modern editors are usually writers in drag, and they don't really care for the art of encouraging writers. You're expendable. So ego is not good for a narrative journalist. Discipline, humility, patience, and resilience are better.

I write to entertain, educate, and—I hope—advance the best ascertainable version of a forgotten or disputed truth. The mystery of our existence is the reason why true stories about real human beings will always fascinate and entertain other humans.

I don't think that I've written a great story yet. I'm always in pursuit of a great story. Touching all the reader's emotional and intellectual sensors with words alone is very difficult. Hollywood has made this harder by simplifying true stories in dishonest ways. Most great true stories are pumped up with performance-enhancing lies. Our challenge as journalists is to tell them without cheating.

I developed my style by working extremely hard on structure and plot. I believe the best narrative journalism should read like a short story. You have to show more than tell. Where other writers might try to develop a style with rhetorical questions or excessive figurative language, I try to master the art of plot through dramatic techniques like complication-resolution structure. Plot allows you to build suspense and willful disbelief, two key ingredients to keeping a reader on the hook. The quality of your plots helps to illuminate your voice and, over time, build a brand.

I don't think in themes but rather vehicles or scenes. In this story, the vehicle was a gang-related, drive-by shooting. In others it has been a plane crash, an assassination attempt, a medical evacuation from a war zone, and an unfaithful handshake. I try to use these vehicles to sell the reader a much bigger story. I'm a big believer that long-form stories and book-length works of narrative journalism should have a soul. Readers should take something away.

WHEN DADDY COMES HOME

Walt Harrington

Georgia had never seen her father naked.

Certainly not when he was young and prideful, walking with a bantam swagger that she and her sisters called "the strut"—a walk at once jaunty and commanding, with an unforgiving posture softened by a long, friendly gait and made theatrical by arms that pumped confidently from rolling shoulders. *Make a path, folks, here comes the reverend, the Reverend James A. Holman.* Georgia's older sister, Leila, when she was a girl, would feign exhaustion just so Daddy would hoist her onto his chest and shoulder, where she'd pretend to be asleep, all the while watching with fascination over his back as his legs, like tiny rockets, launched him and her off the sidewalk with each dancing, prancing step.

That legendary strut, where was it now? When Georgia first touched his skin in the hospital, helped turn his body in bed or helped change his diaper, she nearly recoiled, as if meeting these intimate needs for her sick 80-year-old father were unnatural acts, a violation of all human hierarchy. She thought to herself: *This is not my father.*

It was not the father who had mesmerized huge revival crowds with his stunning "Take Up the Cross" sermon. It was not the father who had signed men out of jail on his word alone. It was not the father who had always arrived with pennies for her piggy bank. And, surely, it was not the father who had sat on the front porch rocking her on hot summer nights while he recited poetry.

This frail man's bones poked at his skin like sticks prodding soft leather. The man didn't recognize her, called her "Cat," the nickname for her dead sister, Catherine. This man rambled deliriously about a Reverend Johnson, asked the name of the street where his own former church stood and insisted that one of the nurses was his dead wife, Anna Pearl. The man seemed afraid. All hours, Georgia and Leila sat beside him, his body as light and fragile as settled dust, his skin dark against the ocean of white sheets into which Georgia was sure he was about to disappear.

She wondered, "Where are his dreams taking him tonight?" She wrote in her diary: "This, the man who held my hand."

But Daddy didn't die. . . .

For months, Georgia Kaiser, who is now 50, and Leila Davies, who is now 58, took turns driving or riding the bus back and forth from their homes in Silver Spring and Chevy Chase, Maryland, to Augusta, Georgia, where Daddy had left the hospital and was staying with a friend. The commuting was exhausting and expensive. Georgia and Leila were schoolteachers with only so many days off, and they had children and husbands who needed their time. In theory, they had two choices: Put Daddy in a nursing home or take him into their own homes. But like many elderly people, their father had let it be known that he'd rather die than go into a nursing home. In a sermon, Georgia remembered him preaching when she was a girl, he said, "Some people marry their cross. Some people give birth to their cross. And some people put their cross in a nursing home." The sisters really had only one choice.

That was four years ago, just before Georgia cleaned out a room and Daddy moved into her house. When he was strong enough, he began splitting his time between Georgia's and Leila's, only a few miles away. The women's decision to take their father into their homes seemed to Georgia a private choice. But such private choices will be occurring more and more often in the years to come. By 2025, nearly 20 percent of the population will be 65 or older. In 1900, only an estimated one in 10 married couples between the ages of 40 and 60 had two or more parents alive. Today, thanks to U.S. life expectancy that has risen by about 25 years in the 20th century, more than half of America's middle-age couples are estimated to have two or more parents living. Despite the myth that modern children dump their parents into nursing homes, only 5 percent of people over 65 are in such facilities, and nearly three-quarters of the nation's frail elderly are cared for by family members who live in the same residence. The numbers are daunting: In 1985, there were about 6.5 million dependent elderly in various living arrangements. By 2020, there will be an estimated 14.3 million. Hardly a family in America will be untouched.

But Georgia wasn't thinking about other families. First came her duty to her father. Beyond that, she worried how her own life and her own family would be changed. Deep down, she childishly wished her father hadn't gotten feeble. Then she felt guilty for feeling this. As Georgia packed his things for the move to Washington, she stuffed her father's old family photos and memorabilia in a brown box and put it all away, unable to even look. She thought, *This is all that's left of him.* In her diary, she wrote: "If you should go and I remain, whatever shall I do?"

Looking back now, looking at her family as a human laboratory for what is about to touch so many lives, Georgia believes life with Daddy has turned out to be a bittersweet blessing for her, Leila, their children, their husbands—and for Daddy. Don't get Georgia wrong, it has been no picnic for any of them. But it has been no horror show either. It has made her feel good to know she has returned what was given her as a child, and it has created a time tunnel through which she, her family, even her father have looked back and ahead at their own lives. She puts it simply: "I feel more grown up."

They are brother relics: the reverend and the curio. He is 84. The curio—a dark wooden cabinet with a curving glass front, three shelves, feet that are carved into animal paws and a horizontal mirror that rests on a warping top—is probably that old too. The reverend was only 15, working as a delivery boy at a dry goods store in his hometown of Americus, Georgia, when he heard two sisters from the family that owned the store mention that they were selling the curio to make room for a new piece of furniture. The boy spoke up, saying he'd love to buy it as a gift for his mother, the deal was struck: 50 cents from the boy's $3 weekly wage for 40 weeks—$20, a lot of money in 1925. The boy borrowed a truck and delivered the prize to his mother, who was elated. Sixty-four years passed. And when Georgia was packing her father's books and roll-top desk and a few belongings, the curio was the only item he asked her to bring along.

"If you can," he said.

The curio and the boy, now antiques.

The reverend sits in a tall, flowered wing chair to the left of the curio. He is a militantly dignified man, his shoulders still erect, his head bald and buffed on top, his remaining hair short and snowy white against his skin. He shaves himself and does a good job, leaving only a few patches of gray beard. His face, like his body, is taut and lean, his cheeks high and hollow, his forehead remarkably unwrinkled. As always, he wears a white shirt and tie, this day dark blue with diagonal gray stripe and held in place with a gold tie bar. When he was young, he required two starched and ironed white shirts a day, which his wife, Anna Pearl, delivered without fail. He crosses his thin left leg over his right leg at the knee, adjusts his wooden cane against his side, plants his elbows on the chair's armrests and steeples his fingers. He rubs his palms together softly, barely touching, then plays with the change in his pocket. For a moment, he taps his cane with the nail of his finger, then lightly rubs his thigh with his right palm.

He does not squirm, but rather makes each move with a methodical, self-conscious elegance. He holds his hands at his chest and rubs them together slowly, as if working lotion into his skin. The hands are large, with long, expressive fingers that curl upward after their middle joints. On the bridge of each hand is a spider web of wrinkles that record his many years like the rings of an old tree. But his palms are as smooth and glassy as pebbles drawn from a running creek. Unlike a laboring man's, his hands were not his most precious tool.

"Let me tell you a story," he always says, his coarse, gravel voice animated by an array of rising and falling volumes and pitches and a masterful range of poetic rhythms, hesitations and inflections. "I was sitting in the house, the telephone rang and it was a young lady whose husband was a Pullman redcap. . ."

This is not the man who moved into Georgia's house four years ago. After what doctors called a seizure, that man's memory was wrecked and he had to be taught to walk again. That man was so frail and confused, he spent the early days at Georgia's house in bed, not knowing where he was. He constantly apologized for being in the way. At night, he rambled about the house knocking on doors, saying, "Time to go, anybody taking me to work?" One night he got up and packed his bag for a trip he'd gone on years

before. He couldn't take himself to the bathroom. He had to be reminded
to eat. He had to be told, "Daddy, here's your shirt, put this on." Night after night, he asked, "Where am I?" And Georgia answered, "Daddy, you're
with me." And he asked, "Now, who are you?" When Georgia returned
from a brief trip, he told her that the man and the girls in the house had
been very nice to him.

"Daddy, that's my husband."

"Your husband?"

"Daddy, that's Carl and those are my children."

"Those two girls? Well, they certainly were nice to me." It was almost
more than Georgia could bear. "This is my father!" She couldn't get past
her perception that he was now the child, she the parent. She remembered
her mother nursing her 93-year-old father. "I'm taking care of Papa," her
mother would say. She remembered her father's mother, who lived to be
104, sitting on the porch of the family home in Americus, where she lived
with two daughters. She remembered Uncle Willie, crazy with dementia
and sick with cancer, who lived with his wife until he finally died. She remembered Uncle Robert, never quite right after returning from World War
II, who lived with his sisters for the rest of his life.

Georgia was a grown woman, but she couldn't accept that it was now
her turn. "I was in charge of him," she says. "I've got to tell this man what
to do. . . . This is my father, who would tell me." She balked at the profound
gap between saying, "Daddy, dinner's ready," and saying, "Daddy, come eat
dinner now."

"I just hadn't grown up to that."

Her father's illness also threw Georgia into renewed mourning for her
mother, who had died three years earlier. "It just made a microscopic image of the fact that she's dead, and he's alone. . . . All the things that had
been, never would be again." Then, in the midst of it all, her father angri-
ly accused her of trying to steal his money. "It hurt me," she says. "I was
angry. How dare he!" She sometimes thought: "I wish he were not here. I
don't mean dead . . . I don't wish he were in a nursing home. But I wish it
hadn't happened. That's what I wish. I wish it hadn't happened." Georgia
even found herself wondering if her enfeebled father wouldn't be better
off dead. But each morning, when she went to awaken him, she worried
he might actually be dead. Then it hit her: What if Karen or Lisa finds him

dead? From then on, she made sure waking up Grandpa wasn't one of her daughters' chores.

The oddest things irritated her. On the first evening that her father was well enough to eat at the dining room table, he happened to sit in Georgia's chair. "That night I let him," Georgia says. But she was astounded how much his sitting in her chair annoyed her. It was silly, irrational. She knew that. But she couldn't help herself. Then she remembered something her father had told families he counseled as a minister: "People argue about what they're not angry about." Of course. It wasn't the chair: Daddy was here and her life was forever changed. She wasn't angry at him but at her helplessness in the face of it all. After about a week of stewing, Georgia politely said, "Daddy, you're going to sit here now." Daddy did, never knowing the little psychodrama that had unfolded, and Georgia reclaimed her place at the table.

Summer 1954, Georgia is a little girl. . . . It's hot and dusty in rural north Georgia, in the towns of Gainesville and Dahlonega, before air conditioning, a time of straw hats and cardboard fans, a time when sweaty shirts drew no disapprobation. Little Georgia, with her pretty cotton dress, is the apple of everyone's eye—the Reverend Holman's daughter, the youngest by eight years, spoiled by his undivided attention, the daughter who most takes after his outgoing manner, who, like him, loves books and poetry, a good speaker too, and polite to a fault. When the reverend comes to town on the dirt-road revival circuit, often carrying little Georgia along, the church women pretend to bicker over who'll get her for the day—for sewing or fishing or, just for fun, a stint picking cotton. She is a princess because Daddy is a king.

Every night, Georgia takes her place in the front pew. If Daddy's revival is set to start at 7 p.m., it starts at 7 p.m., not a minute or 30 minutes after. In a world of dynamic Southern preachers, the Reverend James A. Holman always held his own. He'd graduated from Atlanta's Gammon Theological Seminary and in 58 years of ministering rose to become presiding elder in the Christian Methodist Episcopal Church. He ran his churches like a benevolent dictator, not only giving the sermon but picking the choir music too. And no chatter in the pews, no droning on about fundraising picnics. No, Daddy was a choreographer of spiritual emotion. To

Georgia, it was as if the whole congregation went into Daddy's magical trance, left themselves behind and entered a realm of Daddy's making. He could "line a hymn" like nobody—prayerfully announce or echo each line, turning a hymn into a sermon in itself.

Says Georgia now, "It was a big life."

But three decades later, living in her home, he shuffled along the walls, his hand bracing him as he went. He stuffed bread into his pockets at the dinner table and was terrified to be alone, afraid an intruder would kill him. He picked up schoolbooks, magazines, pens, pencils and hoarded them. He hid soiled and stinking clothing in the corners of his room. When Georgia read him their favorite poem from her childhood, Rosa Hartwick Thorpe's "Curfew Must Not Ring Tonight," he did not recall it.

Again, Georgia is a girl. . . . It is 1 a.m. and she wakes up instinctively, waiting for her father to return from his weeknight job as a waiter at the Buckhead Elks Club. She hears the door open and close and, as footsteps come down the hall. "Where's my baby?" Then, predictable as dawn, she hears her mother say, "James, don't wake her up." When the bedroom door opens, Georgia feigns sleep under her daddy says, "Here's some pennies I brought you. Put them in your bank and get back in bed."

Another time. . . . Georgia comes home from junior high school three days in a row and thoughtlessly lets the screen door slam. Each day, her father tells her not to let it slam. After the third day, he stops her and she's in trouble. Then he makes her go in and out the door five times without slamming the screen.

Sunday night, suitor night. . . . Georgia's teenage boyfriend comes to the house and sits in the parlor with his beloved and they watch television. At 10 o'clock Daddy comes in to watch his favorite half-hour of TV, *The Loretta Young Show*, and sees the boy give Georgia a little kiss on his way out the door. Daddy says nothing, but the next morning tells Georgia that for a boy to kiss her in her father's home is an act of disrespect. She is not to see the boy again. Every day, Georgia sneaks around the corner and calls the boy on a pay phone. After a week, her father says, "You don't have to call on the phone around there. We've got a phone, and he can come back."

But three decades later, living in Georgia's home, her father didn't always recognize her. She wrote in her diary: "Not the man that I remember."

Sitting in the tall, flowered wing chair to the left of his curio, the reverend tells his story about the phone call from a young lady whose husband was a Pullman redcap. She asked the reverend to do an anniversary service, and he agreed. He says he got down on his knees and asked God for guidance with his sermon. He thought of the Bible story about a man on his way to Jericho who fell among thieves and was left for dead. The man was passed by a priest and a Levite, before a Samaritan took pity on him, bound up his wounds, took him to an inn and paid his way. Jesus said, "Go, and do thou likewise." In this Bible story, the reverend found a good message for train porters, who, like the Samaritan, had many chances to do a traveler good. "When I preach, the reverend says, "I aim at something just like I'm shooting at a bird." He says he didn't just preach God is love. He always laid down a challenge, a tough challenge. He pauses, leans forward, cocks his head and smiles. "I'm sorry if I bored you."

The reverend sits on the edge of the piano bench. In movements so deliberate they seem sculpted, he shifts his cane from his right hand to his left, turns to his right and lowers the arm of the record player onto Frankie Laine's version of "I Believe." Behind him on the chalkboard is printed, "God Is Our Refuge." At the Holy Cross Hospital Adult Day Care Center, where he and about 30 others go every weekday, the reverend's Tuesday morning prayer meeting is about to begin. The congregants arrive slowly—two in wheelchairs, four with canes, one who is blind, one who is nearly blind, one with her chin bent violently to her chest, one to a conversation only she can hear, one elegant old woman dressed in a bright green jacket and looking a if she's about to play golf at the country club.

The reverend, still the choreographer of spiritual emotion, intones, "We humbly ask you to give us your attention for these few minutes." His voice is tranquil, soothing, confident. He stands, leans on his cane with his right hand. With his left hand, he gestures in a half moon, his long, dexterous fingers wide and open and seeming to trail behind the sweep of his palm like the spreading tail of a comet. "Whatever else you have to discuss, social matters, jokes, let's forget them now.... Our theme here is 'God is Our Refuge.'... This is a prayer meeting."

An old woman begins to read the 91st Psalm from her Bible, and the reverend gently touches her shoulder and whispers, "Not now," as Frankie Laine sings: "I believe that somewhere in the darkest night, a candle glows...." And the reverend, conjuring the magical trance Georgia remembers from childhood, lines the hymn.

I believe above the storm the smallest prayer...
"Above the storm..."
Will still be heard?
"Do you believe that?"
Every time I hear a newborn baby cry...
"You believe it..."
Or touch a leaf...
"Touch a leaf..."
Or see the sky...
"That's belief..."
Then I know why, I believe.
"You hear those words? You know why you believe."

The reverend pauses for a long moment. Everyone is silent. One woman has tears in her eyes; two other women hold hands. He switches his cane from his right hand to his left, reaches out and again touches the shoulder of the old woman with her Bible open to the 91st psalm. He nods to her and says, "Now."

It took about six months after Daddy moved into Georgia's house before she realized she had her father back. After the first few months, he began spending half his time at Leila's, which gave Georgia a respite. His memory was much clearer, he bathed and dressed himself, although even today his clothes must be laid out every morning or he might put on yesterday's dirty clothes. Eventually, he agreed to wear Depends, which made his occasional accidents only a nuisance. His sharp humor returned, and he and Georgia spent many evenings reminiscing, he telling her stories she did not recall and she telling him stories he did not recall. Georgia was once more able to think of those childhood moments with her father—when he made her go in and out the screen door five times or brought her those pennies or banished her boyfriend—without mourning that he was no longer the same man. She took out the brown box filled with her father's old pictures and memorabilia, the box she had put away, and pored over the material, laughing and crying joyful tears as she went.

Daddy was the same man but only in flashes. When he cracked a joke about Georgia's driving: "Too bad the brakes on my ride didn't work." When he asked to be taken to Metro's Kiss and Ride so he too could get a kiss. When he got sad after reading that a stray bullet had killed a child. When he put on his black fedora at that certain rakish angle, stopped, glanced back over his shoulder, touched the brim and smiled. When Georgia took a different route to Holy Cross and he asked, "Where are you going?" And she said, "I couldn't lose you, could I?" And he beamed. "It makes me feel that, yes, family and love and care will make a difference," Georgia says. "He's so much better." And, "I'm definitely a better person. I'm a more tolerant person . . . The change in me that I didn't think I needed to have."

Daddy had always been a hard man to live with. As a minister, he was accustomed to the spotlight, craved and demanded it. His wife, Anna Pearl, also had spoiled him rotten—not only supplying his starched shirts but getting up to fetch him a glass of water or a snack whenever he asked. Decades ago, when he smoked Camel cigarettes, no ashtray was ever so close that he wouldn't summon Anna to move it closer. Once, just after the reverend had left home for a tour of the Holy Land with a group of ministers, she hopped in the car, sped after the bus, beeped her horn and motioned the driver to the roadside: The reverend had forgotten his favorite hat.

But Georgia soon realized that if she had changed her life to accommodate Daddy, he too had changed. For instance, he'd always been a finicky eater. A woman on the revival circuit had once packed him a lunch and later found him down the road feeding it to the hogs. But now daddy ate everything without complaint. All his life, daddy had a refused to eat garlic, but now he did. All his life, daddy had refused to eat chicken. Now he did. Leila even believed he'd come to like chicken. Privately, the reverend still detests it. He laughs. "I am looking to be as easy as I can."

The changes went beyond food. Growing up in the old South, Daddy always had a deep fear and distrust of white people, but he went to the integrated Holy Cross Center and became good friends with many whites, even deferring to one white woman's insistent requests for an occasional peck on the lips. Daddy had a temper as a young man, but he had almost no temper now. He also had an opinion about everything. So when he arrived, Georgia never yelled at her daughters in front of him, sometimes took them out to the car for scolding, afraid her father would judge her a bad mother. But he never said a critical word about how she and Carl raise the girls, and he never said a bad word about the girls either, only praised them. When Georgia was embarrassed by one daughter's temper tantrum, he said calmly, "We all get angry . . . They're doing fine." Daddy also had always hated cats, but now he loved Georgia's cat, sat petting it, even let it sleep on his bed. In his own way, Georgia realized, her father was trying hard to fit into the family. At his age, over the hill, he was still growing.

Even Carl, Georgia's husband, who hadn't felt close to Georgia's father and who believed he was too domineering and self-centered, came to admire him. He loved the wise aphorisms the reverend dropped from time to time. Carl's favorite: "Just because you didn't mean to step on my toe, doesn't mean it didn't hurt." Carl had always cooked most of the family meals, and he quickly added softer fare to accommodate the reverend. He cooked the reverend's breakfast and freely pitched in to help Georgia with the new workload. That made life easier for her, but it also had an unexpected benefit: It deepened Georgia's already deep affection for her husband of 21 years.

Georgia's and Leila's greatest fear was what Daddy would do with his time while they and their husbands were at work. Then a neighbor told Georgia about the Holy Cross day care center, which saved the day. Because the reverend's only income was $568 a month in Social Security, he qualified for Medicaid to pay the center's $51-a-day cost. Georgia and Leila worried that Daddy wouldn't go—he had always refused to socialize with old people and was still nervous around whites. But again, he surprised them. He said, "The people there, I could be a morale builder for them." Soon, the reverend was center stage at the center, eager to arrive before 8:30 a.m., so he could greet everyone in the morning, always inviting one of the women to dip a finger in his coffee to sweeten it up, always asking at the morning gathering, "What's for lunch?" And when he began his Tuesday morning prayer meetings, he was again able to do his life's work. Having people pay attention to him and listen to him, making a contribution again, being accorded special respect and status enlivened him.

The reverend's condition improved, but Georgia still struggled with her grief at her father's decline, still felt the shame that she wished he didn't need her care, still felt guilty that his presence in the house grated on her. He's not doing anything to bother me, she thought, but he's still getting on my nerves doing it. She began attending the center's group counseling sessions, where she saw that her emotions were downright mundane, as she heard others caring for elderly loved ones gripe about the same kind of irritations. She thought, hallelujah, somebody feels the same way! She saw that her burden was neither unique nor the heaviest to bear. At her last session, a man explained that his wife couldn't remember where anything went in the house they lived in for 50 years. Another man said his elderly wife had become so incontinent that even with adult diapers, the church choir head finally asked that she retire. A woman said of her stroke-victim husband, "He's like a dummy sitting there . . . I don't know how to do it. It's getting harder and harder."

When the center's director, Bob Grossman, said that as many as half the people over age 85 have some form of dementia, Georgia felt suddenly blessed by the clarity of her father's memory. When he explained that people caring for the elderly often suspect that their charges are pretending frailty to get more attention, Georgia felt relief: She was not an ungrateful daughter, she was only human. Georgia learned that beyond the confines of the center was full spectrum of elderly life—elderly people living independently, those living in group homes with special assistance, those living bedridden in relatives' homes with help of professional aides and nurses, those living in nursing homes. The sad truth is, few elderly people die today without some period of dependency. Georgia's father could be in better health, but he could also be in worse health. For that, Georgia was grateful.

And she realized she been wrong: She had not become the parent, her father the child. The needful child will become less needful, grow in strength and self-mastery, and a parent burdened with the demands and irritations of constant care knows this, anticipates it. This anticipated future is part of the joy. In Daddy's case, the joy was strictly in the here and now, because the longer he lives the more he will decline. The more jokes he will be unable to finish, the more often he will repeatedly ask Georgia what time a favorite TV show starts, the more often he will hang his dirty clothes in the closet, the more often he will apologize for boring his listeners. But there will be satisfaction later, after his death, in knowing she was a good daughter. "When I look into his casket," Georgia says. "I want to know my mother is looking here, saying that I did a good job. And I want to be able to say, 'I did a good job.'"

Leila never attended the counseling sessions, and it amazes Georgia that her sister didn't agonize over their father moving in. Leila is a practical-minded, matter-of-fact woman. "We have little things that bother us, but so what?" she says. "This is life." Leila enjoyed hearing daddy stories about her childhood. She loved it that her husband, Langston, and Daddy would sit for hours talking about the Bible. She glowed with the pride that he always found the strength and concentration to comport himself with dignity at her church's Sunday services, a couple of times even giving a decent sermon or prayer.

Leila took her father's presence in stride, while Georgia struggled with it. Perhaps because Georgia was the youngest by so many years, had been babied and spoiled in that role, had shared a love of books and poetry, she saw more of herself in her father. Who knows? At the counseling sessions, seeing the wide range of people's ways of dealing with their aging parents and spouses, Georgia realized there was no right way to respond. She says, "It lifted a lot off my shoulders."

Back at his Tuesday morning prayer meeting, the reverend leads in reciting the 23rd Psalm—"the Lord is my shepherd . . ."—And then, his voice strong, his eyes closed, he prays: "Father in heaven. Here we are now. Our heads are white with the frost of many winters, our faces are wrinkled with the furrows of age and our bodies are bent beneath the weight of years, but in spite of all that, You have sustained us and kept us in the evening of our lives. . . ." And the voice of Frankie Laine again rises: "I believe that somewhere in the darkest night. . . ."

He is in his room at Georgia's house. It is evening. He often secludes himself here, no phone, no bother. In this room, with a blend of prayer and conversation, he talks to his wife, hears her voice when she says of their daughters, "Stand by them. They are all you have." He reads from the scores of religious books he has collected, searching for themes and passages for his Tuesday prayer meeting. For next week, he selects a stanza of poetry originally written in ancient Sanskrit: "Look to this day, for it is life, the very breath of life." He sits on his bed, a big bed covered with a brown and white quilt in a small, darkly paneled room. Around him: a picture of Jesus; a bronze relief of the Last Supper; a sepia-toned photo of his father, a handsome man with mustache, white shirt, dark jacket and old-fashioned necktie; a photo of Anna Pearl; his roll-top desk, which is cluttered with pens and pencils, its top drawer holding the false teeth he no longer wears; his last automobile license plate—DDR 207—posted on the wall; and two ties already tied hanging from a hanger on a hook in the closet. Everything washed with light turned a vague amber through a tan shade.

The reverend studies and then presses a button on the tape recorder next to him on the bed, inserts a tape, to do what he enjoys so much: listening to his old sermons, some dating back 20 years. When Georgia moved away, she asked him to tape them and send them to her so she could hear them. Now it is he who hears them. Sometimes he gets ready for bed and climbs under the covers to listen. Sometimes he paces the room, gesturing along, moving his lips to his own words. Sometimes he lines the hymns out loud. He thinks of himself as an old preacher listening to young preacher. He is not that man anymore, but still he is.

"I'm that preacher. I'm doing that speaking now."

"That's me."

"I haven't changed."

"I still have the same philosophy."

"I was"—he hesitates—"good."

"Something that I did that turned out to be magnificent."

"Be that it made some contribution."

The voice on the tape is more than the voice of the Tuesday prayer meeting, layers more. A deep, powerful, chest-rumbling voice, preaching and singing at once, a voice somewhere between that of a whispering prayergiver and that of a bellowing auctioneer: "Anybody can live good when there ain't nobody bothering ya! Anybody can live good when they got a good job! Anybody can live good when there ain't nobody picking at your wife! Anybody can live good when the money is right!" In that church decades ago, amens and laughter arose.

"But if you stand with God when the chips are down!"

"Everybody! Because it's a cross."

"Jesus, keep me near the cross."

On his bed, a white handkerchief held to his face like a mask, his dark hand silhouetted against it, the reverend cries.

Living with Grandpa has been a complicated ride for his three granddaughters. Leila's son, Paul, was 22 when he arrived, and he took the change in stride. He wasn't home much and eventually married and moved out of his folks' home. But for Leila's daughter, Ursula, then 18, and Georgia's daughters, Karen and Lisa, 15 and 14 at the time, their grandfather's arrival loomed larger. Politeness is an enforced virtue in both families, and the girls were never rude to the grandfather, but inside they often fumed as they struggled to understand his place in their lives.

"I couldn't understand why he was coming all the way here," says Ursula, now 22. "I worried about having to stay home and babysit him. I don't mean to sound selfish, but I had my life too. I couldn't understand why they didn't put him in the nursing home nearby and we could go visit him."

It was Ursula's job to clean the downstairs bathroom and it irked her that her grandfather didn't always hit the mark. The idea of sharing the same bathtub with an old man also annoyed her, and she always sanitized the tub before she bathed. He put half-consumed cans of soda back in the fridge. He sometimes used Ursula's drinking cup. He interrupted conversations and told the same jokes repeatedly. He asked, "Ursula, you heard this one?" She answered, "Yes, Granddaddy." Then he told the joke anyway. And worst of all, Ursula was embarrassed for her friends to meet him. He was so, well, so old.

"It was just not cool," Ursula says. "Only in the last year have I started to pay attention to him." She has learned to put away her drinking cup so he won't use it by mistake. She has learned to say, "That's a good one, Granddaddy," when he interrupts with a joke that she has heard before, and then go back to her conversation. She has tried to imagine what it will be like to someday ask her own father, "Daddy, did you go to the bathroom?" before they walk out the door. She has listened to her grandfather tell horrible stories of life for blacks in the Old South, and she has resolved to complain less and appreciate more the opportunities open to her today. From her grandfather, she has taken this lesson: "Even though he has aches and pains and can be forgetful and had his wife die, he still seems to enjoy life."

Sometimes, Ursula will be in a hurry in the morning, running out the door, trying to get her grandfather off to the day-care center and herself off to Howard University, and he will step outside and say, "Look at the sky, not a cloud! And the grass is so green." That makes Ursula stop in her rush, look at the sky and the grass and see that he is exactly right. She says, "It's an inspiration."

Karen and Lisa, 19 and 18 today, tell of similar journeys. In the early days, Karen couldn't help but be amused when her grandfather got up in the middle of the night and knocked on doors—it was just so weird! It bugged Lisa that he claimed a chair in the TV room as his own, when nobody had ever had assigned chairs in the TV room. When she sat in it, he shuffled around nearby, hoping she'd get up. But she didn't. Not unless he asked, which he rarely did.

Georgia didn't have as much time for the girls and that bothered them. But once again, it was the trivial irritants that irked them the most. New, unpleasant odors filled the house. Grandpa left the toilet seat up. He tilted lamp shades to read and left them crooked. It angered Karen terribly that she and her sister had to squeeze their chairs on one side of the dinner table. He went up and down the stairs so slowly when Lisa was behind him that she became convinced he did it to annoy her. Both girls believed their grandfather acted more feeble than he was so they'd wait on him—get him a drink, a snack, a newspaper—just as Grandma had always done.

Karen harbored the deepest resentment, which she kept to herself until just last year, when she talked with Georgia about what she had come to see as her irrational anger at her grandfather. "He didn't do anything, really," Karen says. "It was me."

Karen felt gypped. "I wanted grandparents like my friends' who took them shopping and on trips and to a play." She believed her grandfather's infirmity was something he'd done to himself. "I couldn't see that he was just old," she says. Karen also was angered by stories that her grandmother had waited on her grandfather hand and foot. Unlike her mother, Karen saw nothing quaint in this. She thought, "Why should a woman have to do that?" When her grandfather seemed to expect Karen to do him small favors, she couldn't help but think he was treating her the same way, like a servant. "It disturbed me for so long," she says. "I didn't know the context.

"Looking back, I just wasn't at all compassionate. . . . Now I realize he didn't like being so dependent. That's something I've thought about: What if I couldn't do anything by myself? I wouldn't feel good about it, and I'm sure he didn't either. What if I were paralyzed in a car accident? I realized that's how he must feel."

Last year, Karen began to sit in the yard and talk with her grandfather. Without being asked, she did his laundry occasionally and was surprised at how the smell of the soiled clothing no longer sickened her. She found herself listening intently as her mother and grandfather told old stories on each other and found herself imagining her own children and grandchildren someday sitting with her, an old woman, talking about the life she was living right now.

And she saw herself in their stories, realized that her grandfather had seemed to act so strict when her mother was a girl but was actually quite indulgent—a carbon copy of how Georgia had raised her and her sister.

"We're all pretty much alike, as much as I'd like to think I'm different," Karen says. "But pretty much I'm not." Lisa's resentment of her grandfather was never as deep as Karen's, and she says only that she has learned patience from living with him. But Karen's silent anger was once so fierce that she still sometimes asks God to forgive her for it. She has had long talks with the man she dates about how when her parents get old, she will expect to take them into her home. Like her cousin Ursula, when her grandfather moved in, Karen couldn't understand why they didn't just put him in a nursing home. Now Karen understands. "I know it would hurt him to know we put him out. . . . I also wouldn't want him to think I was the kind of person to put him out.

"I'm glad I grew up."

The reverend's room at Leila's house is larger and brighter, though it is still cluttered with his books. He sits on the stiff-backed chair, stiff-backed himself, rubs the palm of one hand lightly along his thigh and with his other hand plays with the change in his pants pocket. A person has to understand: The feeling the reverend got while preaching was the most powerful emotion of his life. More powerful even than his love of his wife or his children. That's why listening to his old sermons and conducting his prayer meeting at the center mean so much to him. They touch the old emotion—the power, the joy, the intimacy with God—that he felt every Sunday and every revival for half a century. Like an aging athlete, he still feels as if he should be able to make the mark but cannot get his body to cooperate, the reverend still feels like a young man, although his mind and body won't cooperate.

"I feel like I have something to offer. . . . I'm afraid people don't want to hear it. . . . It's difficult for me to come to that place, but the only way not to come to that place is to die. . . . You adjust. You wake up on Sunday morning and say, now if I was in Americus, I would have a place to preach this morning. I don't have a place. So I put on my clothes and go to church."

The reverend, in his deliberate way, brushing his face lightly with one hand, tapping his cane with the nail of his finger, says it has been a joy to live with his daughters and their families, seeing his grandkids grow up, seeing how competent his daughters are as mothers and wives, seeing how decent are their husbands. "I had a wife who was almost a mother to me," he says. "I was known as a spoiled brat." But as an old man, living with his daughters, he has learned something about compromise, about not always getting his own way. It may have been a long time coming, but the reverend says, "I learned how to get along with people." He acknowledges that, yes, he does make little demands on his family just to get attention. He asks for juice or cookies, asks someone to recite a poem or listen to him recite a poem. "I just abhor loneliness," he says. "I do like babies, I cry." He smiles. "I need attention. I need to feel like they need me."

When the reverend was a young minister he would go to the home of an elderly preacher he knew to help him bathe, make sure he got a haircut when he needed it. He ran errands, picked up the old man's spending money at the bank. "That man had something to offer," the reverend says, "but he needed help to do it." Once again, he tells the entire story of his sermon in honor of the Pullman redcap, which reminded the baggage handlers that they had many chances to do a traveler good. The message: "Everyone can make a contribution."

At Holy Cross, the reverend knows elderly men who say little, are perhaps locked in their loneliness or debilitations. So he talks to them, compliments them, because he believes he knows what they want and need—attention. Because if a person doesn't get attention, it's as if he or she has disappeared.

"The ones I ask," the reverend says of Georgia and Leila, "are the ones I gave glasses of water to when they couldn't get them. Reciprocity is the order of the day. I feel like my daughters are obligated. I need it done and I feel like they ought to know I need it done." It's harder to get up and get a drink, he says, than young people realize. It's harder to take a glass down from the shelf for fear of breaking it. It's harder to pour a hot cup of coffee, and it's harder to clean up the crumbs after making a sandwich. And every day, it gets harder to remember what pants and shirt he wore yesterday. "I shouldn't have to admit that I can't do at 84 what I did before. You ought to know it. Maybe when they get to be my age, they'll say, I know what he means. But I'll be molding in the grave." Maybe 25 years from now, he says, Georgia or Leila will think back on their dead dad. "And they can be more tolerant of their own children."

He tells a story: When he was a minister in Augusta, he had elderly congregants who couldn't get out of bed to eat or go to the bathroom. "If you have one on your hands," he says, "don't make them concede they have a problem. They know. Don't frown every time they call. Turnabout is fair play. Time is passing for me, but it's also passing for you. I'd hate to have Leila or Georgia put me in the bathtub when I was naked. I'd hate that. . . . I still have my pride. I don't worry about it, but I think about it. And I believe if I come to that place, they'd do it. . . . I believe this is life. You have to take it as you find it."

The reverend sits forward in his chair, straightens his back, says, "There's one thing you have to know." As he speaks, his voice goes deep and clear and his arms gesture in grand designs.

> My latest sun is sinking fast,
> My race is nearly run.
> My strongest trials now are past,
> My triumph is begun.
> I know I am nearing the holy ranks
> Of friend and kindred dear.
> I brush the dew on Jordan's banks;
> The crossing must be near.

The reverend stops, pauses for a long moment. "I may be here tomorrow. I may not." He leans forward, cocks his head and smiles.

"I'm sorry if I bored you."

Walt Harrington on the freedom of a perfect dovetail

I wrote the Reverend Holman story two decades ago. I liked it then and I like it now: nice details revealing a good observer's eye and ear, sensitive immersion reporting in the daily lives of the reverend and his family, evocative writing that doesn't go over the top into maudlin. But that's not why I like the story. Those elements of the nonfiction craft are actually the easy part.

That idea baffles young, aspiring nonfiction writers who have so many pieces of craft to juggle and master that they can't help but lose the forest for the trees. Sights, sounds, smells, tastes, the direction of the wind, style of dress, dialect, physical description, dialogue, private thoughts.

So many discreet parts to think about, they don't have time to think.

I once wrote a story about a furniture maker who told me that for many years after he started at his craft, he had to concentrate intently as he cut the scores of hand-sawed, interlocking dovetail joints that hold fine furniture together. If he didn't focus entirely on that laborious task, he would botch it and ruin a piece of expensive wood. After years and years of cutting, though, he realized one day that he no longer thought about that part of his work. In fact, as he went mindlessly through that task for hours, he now thought about the larger elements of his work—the design of the whole piece of furniture or the design of another piece he was going to be working on soon. *Esquire* magazine writer Mike Sager puts it this way for nonfiction writers: "The key is to get your tools honed to such an extent that the tools do their job without too much thought. Then your head is freed to do its job."

By the time I wrote "Daddy," my head was freed. I had been striving to do such stories for more than a decade by then, and I had learned that if I intently followed all the necessary craft steps of reporting, observing and inquiring, I would end up with something interesting and valuable. I knew that because it had happened to me many, many times by then. Like the furniture maker, I had become free to ponder the ideas that would animate my stories as I walked through the several weeks of collecting the atmospherics of scene, action, and setting. For furniture makers or nonfiction writers, there are no shortcuts to that place. But you must get there. For all the changes in technology, that hasn't changed.

For me, the best nonfiction stories aren't collections of colorful facts and details. Instead, those facts and details exist to prod readers into considering the eternal verities. As Rita Dove, then the Poet Laureate of the United States, once asked me, "How many different plots do we have in this world?" Her answer: "Not many." How many different animating ideas do we have in this world? Love, hate, fear, remorse, ambition, faith, forgiveness, creativity. Not many. Yet only when a nonfiction story goes beyond informing readers and—through the action of the telling—prods readers into reflecting on such eternal imponderables in their own lives have we done something special. That's when nonfiction stories about the fascinating particularities of *other people's lives* become mirrors that reflect readers' own lives back to them with new questions and dimensions.

I believe that on the Sunday morning "When Daddy Comes Home" appeared in the *Washington Post Magazine,* adult children all over the city and suburbs were suddenly asking themselves questions about their own parents, and parents were suddenly asking themselves questions about their own children. I believe they were reflecting not on the Reverend Holman's family but on their own families.

By then, creating that mirror had become my goal.

So what's the Reverend Holman story about? Aging? Love? Family? Empathy? Wisdom? Death?

All of the above?

It's certainly not about cutting a perfect dovetail.

THE TOWN THAT BLEW AWAY

Justin Heckert

Vaughn, Georgia, was a good place to live. Before its houses were wrecked and its trailers spit into the treetops, before its ancient oaks were uprooted and snapped in two, before its residents crawled from the ruins to see that almost nothing remained. It was a place of families, and children. It was a place of vegetable gardens and swing sets, porch lights and birdfeeders.

It was a place where old Mr. English took meticulous pride in his lawn. The neighbors knew each other: Paul Porter and his grown son and daughter, his ex-wife who lived across the street; Ms. Willis and her two foster kids; the Viera family, with old license plates nailed to the walls of their pigeon coop; the Barretos, a mother and daughter, with their dogs, in the one-room cinder block house with a teeny closet; the Briscoes in the trailer beneath a giant oak tree. There were more, but not many. They all saw each other most every day. They had parties in the aboveground pool and cooked hot dogs on the grill. Their kids played together at the top of the hill, in the woods, and down in the valley, by the street. Vaughn was so small that the people there couldn't *help* but see each other, talk to each other, maybe occasionally shout a joke from the porch steps. It was a ten-acre square of earth in unincorporated Spalding County forty miles south of Downtown Atlanta, with a thin paved road called Bendview as a divide. No one there had a lot of money, but they all made do. To a driver passing by, Vaughn could've appeared as a hamlet, a bedroom community, or a place where some rednecks parked their cars on the grass, little houses tucked into the thick of the woods. Tired vehicles slouched in the yards, yes; but the trees above them, everything around them, was beautiful.

Well, not anymore. The earth was pulled up and spread over the grass, bright as blood. The trees left behind were pitiful and thin, skeleton bones. A few houses still stood, but with holes in their windows and blue tarps flapping on their roofs. There was a propane tank that smelled like a dead animal on the top of the hillside and a line of concrete steps leading to where a trailer had completely disappeared. There was the shell of the Briscoe children's empty playhouse, a foam mattress impaled on the branch of a dead pine, stacks of cinder blocks, and uneven mounds of bricks.

In mid-August, more than three months after the community was blown away, a few of the remaining residents smoked cigarettes from beneath a tent donated by a local funeral home, drank Gatorade, and watched the people driving by on West McIntosh Road. Just about every other car slowed, someone inside pointing, occasionally taking a picture, then driving on. One of the residents, wearing aviator sunglasses, his skin dark from the sun, do-rag tied around his head beneath a ball cap—a man nicknamed "The Sheriff," who always spoke the truth—raised his voice and yelled at them to speed up and drive the hell on by.

On April 28, a few minutes past midnight, it was raining in Vaughn. There was a strange heat in the valley below the top of the hill. Mary Willis was in bed and had the two babies tucked in. John and Brenda English had been on the computer, because the satellite dish was out. The Crowders—Howard and Cathy—sat on the end of their bed, watching the weather update, which must've been a few precious minutes behind. Billy Briscoe woke, adjusted to the darkness, walked outside. He could tell something was wrong. He went out onto the porch of his single-wide and stared into the woods. The pine branches had begun to pop and dance. There was something terrible coming. There was a noise in the distance, building. The sky shivered with lightning.

He could feel it, though he could not hear the siren that had been wailing four miles away. He told his wife to get their kids, take them into the hallway. Paul Porter was dressed for bed, in pajama pants and socks, when he heard his son's footsteps on the stairwell. He did not hear his phone ring, never heard his daughter's voice message. Mike Porter had rushed to his father's bedroom doorway, having watched the window fan fly completely across his own upstairs bedroom seconds before. His hands shook on the doorframe, and his head thrust through the door. Mike yelled, "Tornado! Tornado!"

Then the house fell on top of them.

Five seconds, ten seconds, a minute, forever—no one could quite remember just how long it lasted. Across the street from the Porters, in the corner of another bedroom, a screen door rattled open and nearly broke off its hinges. The breeze had been born anew into a god-awful howl.

John English, 66—nicknamed "The Mayor" by his neighbors because he was always checking on them, and always outside in the yard, by the lemon tree, in his T-shirt and straw hat, mowing—stood by one of the wooden posts at the edge of his bed and traded shouts with his wife.

"We're going to die!" she called out, unable to see him in the dark. She was sure she could feel the house beginning to wobble on its foundation.

"Naw, we ain't!" he shouted back, standing beside the screen door. He had never been in a tornado; neither of them had, and thus the conflicting views on whether they were in one now.

"It's going to kill us!" she wailed.

John was staring through the screen at the hail, at the objects spinning above the yard, including his grandchildren's play set, the shingles of his shed. Plant pots and trees were slamming into the roof of the porch. His ears popped. A set of chairs swirled past him as he tried to pull the door closed. He asked, "Brenda, where you at?" She replied, "I'm holding on to the bed post!" then reiterated, "It's going to get us, it's going to *kill us!*" Now John, too, could feel the house start to lift.

"God a'mighty!" he said. He could not look away. He was in awe. Staring at the tornado so close was like blinking his eyes ten times, as fast as he could, and every time he opened them, seeing the pop of light and flicker of dark—that's what the middle of it looked like.

The house, which had belonged to Brenda's mother, was more than a century old, so its wood gave a desperate groan as it broke apart. Brenda had spent her childhood playing marbles in the yard and hide-and-seek and washers across the road, spin the bottle at a party within the very same walls fifty years ago, as a girl. When they'd purchased the house from her brother in 1997 and moved back in, she had told her husband, "It's wonderful to come home." They'd remodeled the porch and fixed some of the rooms up.

In pieces, the ceiling landed around them, and the home's two chimneys shattered, fleecing soot into the bedroom. Rain soaked the couple as they hung on to their bed.

"You okay?" he asked, when it seemed to be over.

"Yeah," she said.

Jesus crashed to the floor of the Crowder home. His face shattered in the frame of Cathy's picture. The tornado took the roof and sent it away, too. The tornado busted the windows, except for in the bathroom. Cathy and Howard, who had a beard like Santa Claus and dressed up as Santa for a special needs school, sat on the edge of their bed, and nothing touched them. Across West McIntosh, Mike Porter, in the doorway of his father's bedroom, was briefly pulled off his feet and whipped around like a flag at the top of a pole. Paul was crushed by the wooden door and pinned between his mattress bedsprings, his socked feet sticking out, but wasn't hurt. Mike himself survived because he was standing in the doorframe, which remained intact even though the wall surrounding it fell.

At the top of the hill, Billy and Amanda Briscoe knelt in the hallway of their trailer, holding each other's hands, at opposite ends of their three children. With their other hands, they squeezed the padded edges of the bed mattress they were kneeling under, and prayed. The giant oak tree was torn from the ground with a bang and dropped lengthwise across the entire roof of their trailer, which had been reinforced months before, bowing it down close to the tops of their heads; the tree, they decided, surely kept them from being swept away. They were able to climb out of their bedroom window and into the rain. Mary Willis hid beneath her bed, which was covered by fallen layers of the house; she was holding the children. She'd had just enough time to grab them both. She was screaming. Andrew Varela was in the county jail on a probation violation, and not in his mobile home, or he would've been a goner, because the tornado picked it up off the ground and demolished it; the pieces formed a trail. In a house on Bendview, in front of a pond, an out-of-work carpenter named Chrysostom Sullivan was impaled in the leg by a metal shard; some of his ribs were crushed under a wooden wall in the only corner of his home that wasn't completely destroyed. He pulled himself up and sat on what remained of his couch, while the rain poured on his head, for nearly thirty minutes. When it stopped, he sat bleeding and vomiting onto the floor for another hour and a half, in shock. It took paramedics the entire night to crawl through the blasted forest, find him, and maneuver him out. He remembered they pulled him, on a backboard, through a giant hole in one of the trees. Susan Barreto's daughter, Shalena, had gone outside in the storm to rescue a baby bird from a tree. She put it in their bathroom sink. They headed toward the teeny closet to hide, but didn't make it. Shalena was sucked under the bed, which broke on top of her and helped hold her down. A cinder block wall fell and killed one of their dogs. Susan looked up and saw sky. Something hit her face and knocked out a tooth. She huddled on the floor, more cinder blocks spilling around her.

No one died.

It smelled like Pine-Sol. Of all the things that night to startle the senses, that's what nearly everyone remembered. The trees smelled like that after they broke. The sky cleared. The breeze hushed up, and the stars popped out. John English found a flashlight and walked over what was left of his property. His johnboat was hanging up in a tree. Billy Briscoe helped pull Carlos Viera out from beneath the concrete slab of his family's home, which had been turned and scattered all over the Porter property. John English checked on the Porters; Mike Porter went over to see about Ms. Willis. The houses were gone. The ground was full of glass and everything else that had been inside the houses. Insulation. Piping. Toilets. Bricks. Ceiling fans. Little things that were impossible to replace, like pictures. It was difficult to walk around anywhere, there were so many damn trees—the entire woods, laid waste—yet Paul Porter did, in his socks, dripping wet, like maneuvering through a minefield, to his ex-wife's house. It was too dark to even see. Had his daughter, Amanda, not been over at her mother's house earlier, she would have been crushed by the debris of her little red house, which had been next door to her father's. Paul's truck was gone, flattened when the Vieras' house crushed it. Power lines were down like slaughtered snakes on the ground. It was the worst thing any of them had ever seen.

And it was also the weirdest: The tornado had picked up John English's lone picture of his father and placed it all the way across the road, without a scratch on the glass. It took the tomato plants but left the beans. It took most of the house but only blew over his grill and bent a side of the pool. It took away the play set but left the air-conditioner. It took some big, comfy chairs and two Bradford pear trees right out of the ground, but didn't take the porch fixture or the butterfly plant in the bowl. Next door to the Englishes, in an old house everyone thought used to be a hotel, a man named Kenneth Youngblood lost his porch, some windows, part of the roof on the back, but that was all.

John and Brenda slept that night in the back of their van and periodically looked out the windows and up at the sky, then somehow found slumber. Mike Porter would lay out a sleeping bag beside the road. The Briscoes crawled back inside their bedroom, beneath the oak tree, and tried to go to sleep.

Behind what was left of the Vieras' house, the coop was broken open and the pigeons taken away.

Fourteen other tornadoes hit Georgia on April 27 and 28. This was not the record—that would be twenty, during Tropical Storm Alberto in 1994. But it was one of the worst twenty-four-hour periods in the history of the state. Tornadoes hit Trenton, Cherokee Valley, south of LaGrange, and Covington; killed seven people in a neighborhood in Catoosa County, swept through Ringgold, and killed two more—a disabled man and his caregiver—in a double-wide trailer on the far end of Spalding County. Those tornadoes got all the attention. The Vaughn tornado didn't even warrant an article in a major newspaper. No one talked about Vaughn. The only way for a person to really find out about it was to drive past. The tornado, classified an EF3 (the largest classification is an EF5, like the one that destroyed Joplin, Missouri, in May) by the National Weather Service in Peachtree City, had winds up to 150 miles per hour, touched down near Alvaton in Meriwether County at 11:59 p.m. on April 27. It came atop the hill and popped the pine branches in front of the Briscoe trailer at 12:17 a.m. It was three-quarters of a mile wide. It followed a northeast trajectory, going down the hill, until it fizzled out near the Towaliga River, between Luella and Hampton. On the ground it moved at a little more than 40 miles per hour, taking those chairs off the Englishes' porch, scrapbooks from Amanda Briscoe's house, pigeon feathers from the Vieras' coop. It took forty-five seconds to move through Vaughn. In some of those other places there was more destruction, more devastation, more human suffering, sure. One of the reasons the police couldn't establish patrols in Vaughn immediately is because they were spread thin as it was in all the small counties, had to be in those other areas, which were getting more publicity. But in no place in the state was the destruction more centralized, more grand on a visible scale, in terms of what it did and did not leave behind.

There was a church in Vaughn. It had stood for exactly 107 years. It was a microcosm of what the town once was, and what it had become. It was nothing much from the outside. It had fallen into disrepair. The interior looked about as smooth as the Cherokee arrowheads often found in the woods behind it. The pews used to be full, but the congregation had dwindled to thirteen or fourteen people, in a sanctuary that could hold up to 100. Several of its elderly members had recently died, in succession. It did not have a driveway. The walls needed paint. The floor needed to be redone. There were few spots to park in the grass surrounding it and on the edge of the road, not that it needed them. Hardly anyone in the neighborhood even went there. But the church, Vaughn United Methodist, and its pastor, a woman named Sandra Fendley, considered the squat building to be the hub of the community and did not want it to wither and die. There were oak trees behind it, on the hillside, with muscular branches that shadowed the church, which no one could even see from West McIntosh; but it lent Bendview a sense of protection, as if the church would always be there, as persistent as nature. So this past January, Fendley and other members went door-to-door in the surrounding area, spreading word about Vaughn United. They drove out beyond the abandoned Varnadoe's store, past horse farms and the ponds, to houses a couple miles away in Rio and Griffin; threw a picnic for people who wanted to come. They had been able to procure $20,000 to revitalize the little old building. This included a new floor, more lighting, and a new paint job. New pews. Before the tornado hit the church, it was almost thriving. When the tornado hit the church, it tore out its entire rear wall, facing the woods; the roof was ripped off, flew away, and the stained-glass windows were smashed. Those protective trees were completely obliterated. Some angel figurines, light as paper, were left undisturbed on a piano in the fellowship hall.

"To have the storm take everything away was unbearable," Fendley says.

But the members have decided the church has to be rebuilt. Modest plans were drawn up. Pastor Fendley wrote a letter to Spalding County, requesting permission to build on a lot across from the Porter property. Fendley decided that the old half-acre lot where the church stood was too small to rebuild there, too small if the church wanted to grow; there were also "hoops to jump through," she says.

"People in our modern world want to go to a pretty church. Maybe that is something we old folks don't understand, but it's true. Soon Vaughn [United Methodist] will be a new, pretty church, and people will come to be with us." Fendley wrote those lines in the same letter. With insurance from its sanctuary and Sunday school, and contents within the buildings, Vaughn United has $155,000 for the project, but is still $63,000 short.

After the tornado, Billy Briscoe propped a big wooden cross against the front door, even though the entire back of the church was open to the daylight, to ward away the looters.

And there *were* looters. In the rubble, in the aftermath, in the dark, during the next couple days, before FEMA came and GEMA came and support groups donated to the people of Vaughn trash bags full of clothing, there was no protection, even by the police. Everything was there, in its apocalyptic disarray, ripe for the taking. West McIntosh Road had yet to be blocked, so traffic going to Atlanta or Brooks or Peachtree City from Griffin, or vice versa, formed a two-lane, incessant line—gawkers. So the looters were able to see all this *stuff* in front of them, and tried to stake their claim to what they could find. "It's a free country!" someone yelled at Bebe Goolsby, when she asked him what the hell he was doing. It was a stranger, waist deep in one of the decimated houses across the street. Bebe was John and Brenda's daughter, and had been given the nickname "The Bitch"—because she never put up with any shit in Vaughn. She could be loud. She was brusque. She was tall, and stocky. Thirty-three years old. She loved her parents and was often there with her kids and husband, she had ridden bikes up and down the street as a teenager, it had always been a quiet place. Now this? She walked across the street to the would-be thief's car, took a loose brick, and smashed the back windshield. "What are you doing?" he yelled.

"It's a free country," she said.

She stood outside the next few days, like an eagle. "I wanted to help protect the people that raised me," she said.

She saw a man driving a rollback trailer come and park it in Kenneth's yard. She accosted the driver, who said he knew Kenneth, that he was merely there to help; but she worried that he had really just come to steal all Kenneth's old cars. She stayed up nearly seventy-two hours straight with Paul—The Sheriff—and Mike Porter, holding bricks, keeping watch; people were trying to steal scrap metal out of the lots. They tried to steal a Jeep. In a television report from the scene, Paul Porter was asked what the Vaughn residents were doing for protection, and he lifted up his shirt to reveal a holster carrying a Smith & Wesson .44 magnum with hollow-point bullets. He told the newscaster that he was not afraid to use the gun—hence his nickname. The citizens of Vaughn had imposed a martial law: shoot to kill, lest anyone remain alive to sue them after the fact.

Not long after Vaughn was destroyed, a United Methodist Church official drew a map and counted that in the end, the community comprised barely two dozen structures, including two barns. Thirteen of those were totally razed.

In the early twentieth century, Vaughn used to be an actual town, with a post office, a mailing address. A man named James William Vaughn had settled there with his family and started a plantation in the late 1800s. He donated some of his land, and the place adopted his name. A few years later, the Southern railroad was built straight through town, a pair of iron veins pumping commerce through its heart. People rode the train to go work in the textile mills. They came in from other cities, stayed in the Vaughn hotel. The train even brought the first lady, Eleanor Roosevelt, one memorable day, long ago. But then the railroad was pulled up. The cigar factory closed. The soap factory closed. Three old country stores were eventually boarded up and torn down. Weeds grew in the vacant lots, strangling some of those memories. In 1989 James William Vaughn's home, made out of pinewood, was set on fire and burned through the night, to the ground. It had survived more than 100 years. Nearly everything was gone, except for the homes on Bendview and West McIntosh. The modern Vaughn was no longer a town, but it was still a home. Many who lived there had grown up there, had known it their entire lives. Could either barely recall the old days, or had heard tales about them. It was a place where people still said they lived, though now it was technically Griffin.

Vaughn still had a sense of place. Until the tornado took that, too.

The people of Vaughn did get help. And it was very quick in coming. The Red Cross showed up the next day and a nurse looked after a severed fingernail on Mike Porter's right hand. The United Methodist Disaster Relief team arrived and used chain saws to cut up trees. People had to have a way to get in, so that was the first order of business. Pushing piles to the side of the road. Clearing paths. Church volunteers were there for thirty days, beneath large temporary tents, helping clean up the debris. There were fifty-five other church groups who volunteered, and around 1,200 people onsite, depending on the time of day. The residents had food, water, Porta-Potties, a place to take a shower. Prisoners in orange from Spalding County worked in the yards, on the roads, and Brenda English grilled hamburgers for them as a thank-you for their help. FEMA came, with its voluminous paperwork, offering those without insurance a chance at a loan. John English got a grant of $30,000, not nearly enough to help him rebuild. A woman named Brenda Wolf, who lives a couple of miles away, a churchgoer at Vaughn United Methodist, brought coolers, water, snacks, helped set up computers.

After the volunteers went away, an anonymous donor provided Susan and Shalena Barreto a temporary house for a few months, and then all of a sudden they were homeless again. They'd lived in a van before they lived in Vaughn, and spent three years saving money, fixing up that little house, trying to buy the land. It was nothing, just one room, made of cinder block. The tornado had changed them; they could not keep calm at any hint of a storm. Several times, no matter where they were—for instance, eating a pizza by the windows of a restaurant—they'd gotten in their car and driven as far away as they could, trying to outrun the weather. Once they stopped in North Carolina; another time, Maryland. They were hysterical. "The biggest thing it took was our peace of mind," said Susan. "The Doppler, if we see it, and it's red—we take the car and go."

"I've been praying for the people [Susan and Shalena] who lived in that block house," said Mr. Crowder. "They were so nice to me. I used to tell that girl she was my girlfriend, and she'd laugh. They used to bring us clothes, and shoes."

John and Brenda English had lived in their house since 1997 and did not have insurance, because they had just put the house in their names. For years, John had been trying to get the name of the house transferred from her brother's. Now they were living in a little blue house next to John's shed, which they'd owned for a while and had just never rented out.

An anonymous donor asked one of the pastors to hand-deliver checks for undisclosed amounts to the people in town. Bebe and Mike took a collection bucket from the cars passing by and stopping on West McIntosh Road, and raised $1,400 that was split evenly.

The Sheriff decided to rebuild. Paul Porter's mother had lived in that house, and the memories of her, and his life there, overwhelmed him. He couldn't let everything be lost; he couldn't pack up and find someplace else. When asked what the house meant, he couldn't even talk about it. He tried. A weathered man, who was prone to scold his contractor, to call himself a "true redneck," who looked imposing behind the mirrored lenses of his shades—well, when he tried he froze up. Choked back a tear. Looked away. Paul was one of the four people in the community who had insurance. So he didn't get any money from FEMA. When he'd purchased the total-loss coverage from State Farm, he had commented to his agent, "I can't ever imagine a situation in which I'd need this."

An hour after the tornado hit, he was on a cell phone, starting a claim. It would be two months before they finally broke ground. Poured a foundation a month later, for both his house and his new workshop, and also a little two-story home for Amanda. He and Mike had been living in "the dump," which was the Holiday Inn Express down in Griffin. The tornado shook The Sheriff. He had specifically requested a double-reinforced steel safe room in the basement of the new house, big enough to fit his neighbors in Vaughn, should the need arise. High winds made the hairs on the back of his neck stand up. He wanted a damn tornado siren, right there on the edge of his property. It's funny what it did to people. John English woke up during a car trip and screamed at his daughter, "The tornado!" Some of his relatives, including his brothers, were helping him rebuild Brenda's mom's old house. It was a slow process. He was out there every day, white T-shirt pulled over his chest, hat shielding his face. They bought two-by-tens from Home Depot with what they'd received from FEMA. Ms. Willis had chosen to rebuild, too. She was keeping her foster children.

Near the rubble, a yellow school bus pulled up. It was the afternoon of the first day of kindergarten. Amanda Porter's daughter, Krista, ran from the bus stop, where her mother was waiting, and they held hands as they walked up the hill.

"My baby's getting off the bus!" Amanda shouted. She had been sitting under a tent, smoking a cigarette, watching a truck back onto the foundation of her father's new home. This was Vaughn, in the sunlight. It had never been much, and it was even less than it had ever been. The bus pulled away and Amanda took Krista inside to do homework.

The Briscoes could not rebuild. No, they were struggling, after the tornado. They had to move into temporary church housing a few miles away; they had loved living in Vaughn. They had been there for about two years. Their little girl, Gracie Bug, chased lizards and bugs through the woods and brought them into the trailer, where her mother would find them in the bed, on the floor, on the couch, in the rooms. Gracie played with Krista and they both climbed trees. Billy and the kids rode go-karts up in and around the woods, on the trails.

Amanda Briscoe came back and looked at what was left of their trailer one day this past summer. She stood in the grass, where her bedroom used to be; pointed at the lot and described where the pictures fell onto the mattress that was on top of them. The elderly woman who owned the lot was not going to do anything with it, had decided to keep the insurance money, was not going to put a new trailer there. Since Amanda and Billy did not own the trailer, they didn't have a choice; they couldn't afford to come back, and had no opportunity to.

"It used to be beautiful here," she said, looking at the hole, across from the church, where the only thing standing now was that propane tank.

"Now it's just ugly." They'd gotten $5,300 from FEMA. Enough to buy a new little car, to share, after their SUV was destroyed. They put the rest of the money in a safe.

In the days and weeks after the tornado, many people swore they saw a pair of doves in what was left of the trees. Some had never seen doves before, and so the birds had appeared as wonderfully and unexpectedly as something pulled from the hat of a magician. They were spotted in several places, came to be regarded as heavenly, descended to protect the decimated town. Amanda Briscoe said she saw them because they were nesting in that oak tree that fell and crushed their roof, the tree that saved her family; two white doves, just sitting there. Surely, they were a sign. A symbol. They flew inside the rubble of the church and sat on the doorstep outside, before it was condemned and torn down. The town had been through so much, and the people who were staying there, who had stood their ground, who had decided to rebuild, who had refused to leave—even the ones who were coming back to look at what they used to have, one last time—they all needed something like the doves, to lift their spirits. And that's what the doves did. Everybody saw them. Amanda Porter saw them. So did Brenda Wolf and Sandra Fendley. Enough people who saw them believed they weren't just a stroke of luck, just like they didn't believe that the tornado was a terrible stroke of luck, either. The doves were there for a reason.

Paul Porter saw the doves. He saw them in the rubble. He saw them in the trees. He saw them on the days before he returned to his job at the Kmart distribution center. He watched them, as he smoked cigarettes, as he drank Gatorade and bottled water, as his skin got darker as he stood every afternoon in the sun. He saw, too, how everyone else around him reacted to the doves.

So The Sheriff didn't tell the truth.

He didn't have the heart to let anyone know they were just a couple of pigeons.

Justin Heckert on using technology to enhance the details

It is easier to get published in the digital age because there are many more places that take stories. You can get your story published *somewhere*, no matter what it's about—but that's not saying you'll get paid for it. What will set your work apart is the quality of reporting and writing; and both of those, in my opinion, can be improved by taking pictures while on the scene.

I've always found it helpful to take pictures and video while reporting to enhance the detail of things I'm trying to remember. That way I won't completely have to rely on my memory and my notes (I do try to be fastidious about jotting down details). Using my phone to record something that happens during reporting seems natural to me and mostly unobtrusive—depending on the situation.

While reporting the story above, I used my phone a lot, to take dozens of pictures of the aftermath of the Vaughn tornado. Pictures of the houses, of the people, the lay of the land of that tiny town, a type of visual documentation. I even took a video of a tour that "The Mayor" gave me, walking me around through the rubble.

I took pictures of all of the stuff I came across in the town: broken signs, a set of steps leading to nowhere (that used to lead to a house), old maps, pictures of the land back in the early 1900s, residents' personal pictures of how the houses used to look. While I was writing the piece, I could just scroll through my phone pics and not solely rely on my memory when trying to describe the town, the proximity of houses, or what resident lived next to the other. I could write down in my notebook, for instance, the colors of the trees, how the ground was pulled up and spread over everything, but using pictures is a way to be 100 percent sure. I used to take pictures with disposable cameras while I was reporting and then get the pictures developed when I was ready to write. With smart phones, using pictures and video to aid reporting is so much faster, easier, and more immediate.

There is big demand today for embedded video, audio, and compelling photos (as there always has been), but I still believe the *writing* is ultimately what will make a long-form story into art. While taking pictures and video have their place in helping to aid reporting, nothing can stir a reader or prickle the arm hairs like a well-turned phrase. Or a beautiful passage in a story, a description beyond what you, yourself, are seeing in a photo.

I don't believe it's that different from how it used to be, even ten to twenty years ago. Write good stories. That's it. You'll get noticed. Sure, there are different means of spreading the word about stories now, like Longform and Longreads, aggregators of interesting nonfiction content, and you don't have to be published in a huge place to get a lot of eyes on your story, which *is* a lot different from how it used to be. But you do have to write good stories. That's the only way I know how to develop any kind of audience.

PART II

First-Person Journalism

PART II CONTENTS

CAUGHT UP IN HISTORY'S STORMY WAKE WITH ETHEL KENNEDY

Mary McNamara

I go to the Beverly Hilton to interview Ethel Kennedy, the subject of a new HBO documentary, "Ethel," which airs Thursday. The film is by her youngest daughter, Rory.

I walk through the door and there she is, straight up and picture perfect, and for one heart-stopping, utterly unanticipated minute I am 4 years old again, watching my father sob in our living room. He was always a big man, quiet and calm, but now his glasses are on the floor and his face is in his hands and the sound he makes is frightening enough to send me out the front door and onto a neighbor's lawn.

This is the first truly vivid memory of my life. The day Sen. Robert F. Kennedy died. And now, here is his wife, offering me her hand.

She is a small woman but solid, especially beside Rory, who is tall and slim with those Kennedy eyes and the family smile. Ethel looks precisely like what she is—a well-dressed 84-year-old grandmother (and great-grandmother) who put on lipstick, some good jewelry and a smart ensemble to do something she isn't especially keen on doing because her daughter asked her to.

She has bright and watchful eyes and she smiles at me, thanks me for coming. The first mouth-drying minute extends to a second minute and I am convinced that I will not be able to do this, to sit and calmly ask any of the questions I so cavalierly jotted down.

No, I am just going to sit here and stare at Ethel Kennedy while the tattered tapestry of my childhood unhitches itself from storage and unrolls inside my head.

It is impossible to overstate the role the Kennedys played in the lives of families like mine, Irish Catholic Democrats who saw the Kennedys as symbols of social revolution. Not just the final rending of all those No Irish Need Apply signs that haunted my grandparents' memories, but a new breed of young politicians who demanded, from themselves and those around them, a life of service.

The Kennedys spoke of our moral obligation to help the poor, and that responsibility extended to government. The faithful adults of my early memories—public school teachers, liberal priests and Peace Corps volunteers—all believed.

To lose Jack was bad enough; for Bobby to follow so quickly and horribly was overwhelming. In our house, every president lived in the shadow of an alternative reality—what would this country be like if Bobby Kennedy had lived?

All of which came rushing back to me, with inconvenient intensity, within the cream-colored walls of the Beverly Hilton.

Fortunately, if you have done a thing often enough, there is part of the brain that takes over when other systems are failing. So for a few minutes I was able to conduct an interview while pretending I wasn't having an incomprehensible emotional breakdown in front of Ethel Kennedy, and soon enough I wasn't.

Ethel is a woman of few words, both in the documentary and in person. She answers questions directly but simply and is happy to defer to Rory, a successful filmmaker, who talks quickly and smoothly, clearly trying to make this day, in which there would be many interviews and a press panel to follow, as easy on her mother as possible.

Rory says that resurrecting her father and the politics he espoused was not why she committed to the film. Not at all. Sheila Nevins, the president of HBO Documentary Films and with whom she has often worked, had, after years of discussing other Kennedy-related films, suggested it.

Rory had previously shied away from chronicling her family, but very much wanted to share her mother with the world. She did not think, however, that Ethel, who has turned down interview requests and book proposals for decades, would agree.

But she did. Because "Rory asked me to," she says now. "And you can't say no to Rory."

Having seen the film, this is easy to believe. It is a joyful, loving and fascinating back-window view of an iconic family at a time of great social turmoil and political divisions, many of which remain today.

Not surprisingly, the most heart-wrenching moment comes when the family discusses the assassination. Ethel cannot, and her animated face goes still, almost blank. And though the narrative continues, with much focus on her strength, she does not come back until the chronology catches up to Rory's birth. Ethel's eyes light up, "That was the joy of my life."

This is close to where the documentary ends. Although Rory's initial impetus had been to showcase the woman she had only ever known as a single mother, the film focuses almost exclusively on Ethel's life with her husband, moving inexorably toward the day of the 1968 California primary and the Ambassador Hotel.

"When I started looking through the archival footage," Rory says, "I realized that she was always there." She interviewed her mother for five days as well as all but one of her eight living siblings. They are, Rory says, a storytelling family, and it shows in the fond humor and easy cadence of tales oft-told—the menagerie at Hickory Hill, the letters "Daddy" wrote to each of his children at one point or another, the near mythic status of their parents' love and "Mummy's" stoicism.

"Mostly it felt like home movies," Ethel says, which is true to a point.

But of course Rory knew going in that while much of the narrative is happy and hopeful, there were also "sensitive areas." And she didn't know how or if her mother would answer.

"I was a wreck," Ethel says, with a self-mocking grimace. "It's a very busy life. It was like when someone asks you to auction off a weekend in Hyannis and you say, 'Fine,' and then the day actually comes. Now what?"

For Rory it was a unique opportunity: to spend five days asking her mother about her life. Although it becomes clear in the film that the children are comfortable being open about the events of their lives, you get the sense that Ethel has kept the private narrative focused on her husband.

Everyone refers to "Daddy" as if he had died a year ago, or two; almost 45 years later, he remains a vital presence in the family. Ethel says she is not comfortable speaking in public or being photographed or answering questions about herself; in fact, her daughter admits, there was nothing about "this whole process" that her mother enjoyed.

How then to explain the years as a campaigning spouse, the thousands of people invited to her home, the endless appearances and photographs? "I did that for wonderful people," Ethel says. So it's OK if it's for other people? "Wonderful people," she says with a gentle pointedness.

Did it feel, as it felt to many, during those turbulent years, that the country was running mad, falling apart? "Sometimes," she says. "But then there were two and a half years when it seemed like change was possible."

The spirit of the work her husband began is alive, she says, but "no one is talking about the poor [the way the Kennedys did], about helping people's lives get better. We don't have the leaders."

She has never talked about that day when everything changed, she says. "Everyone deals with pain at some point, why dwell on it?"

Others, including recently the likes of Joan Didion and Joyce Carol Oates, have found solace in exploring that pain, but Ethel shakes her head. It may bring resolution for some, "but not for me. Rose Kennedy said that after a storm, the birds still sing. You just get on with it."

"People focus on the dark things," Rory says, pointing out that this interview is trending the same way. "On the tragedy. But there were more happy times than sad."

She is right, of course. For many Americans the deaths of the Kennedy brothers were so personally painful, the loss so profound that the men and their families became, almost instantly, the stuff of myth, symbols of what might have been and was not. That is, after all, the essence of tragedy.

And tragedy does seem to haunt the Kennedys; Ethel lost one son to a drug overdose and another to a skiing accident; a daughter-in-law recently hanged herself. But the living children of Ethel and Robert Kennedy are all vital, successful people, and here is Ethel at the Beverly Hilton doing press at the behest of HBO. Life does go on, has indeed gone on.

Even so, certain moments remain fixed in time and the people of those moments remain fixed as well. The living evoke the dead and the memory of what those deaths meant. That too must be a burden, for Ethel Kennedy and her children, to see in other people the endless permutations of love and grief, and the need for them to see it in them.

I wanted to tell this lovely woman who has seen so much about my father, about how he wept in a way I never saw him weep again the day her husband died. About how he spoke of him often and with infectious admiration. But I did not. At 84, she helped her daughter make this movie and that should be enough.

I closed my notebook, thanked her and Rory, walked out of the hotel and took the elevator to the parking garage roof and got into my car. Then I took off my glasses, put my head in my hands and cried. Because my parents are gone now too—and I couldn't tell them that I had just met Ethel Kennedy. 🎴

Mary McNamara on voice and humor

If you want to be a writer, you cannot be afraid to look like an idiot. Seriously. That is part of the job description. Being a journalist, as opposed to a novelist (which I also am), is great conditioning for this, because you will make mistakes, a million readers will point them out (and many will call you names) and then you will have to write a correction and cc all your editors, some of whom have always suspected you weren't all that. Whenever my kids feel bad about messing up, I tell them that when Mommy messes up, it goes in the newspaper. (And if I really want to impress them, I tell them that people will tweet about it.)

When reporting, it's essential to keep asking questions until you understand a topic well enough to explain it to others. As a reporter, you cannot be shy or pretend you're smarter about something than you are. I remember interviewing a brain expert, and I had to keep backtracking him to get him to explain what, to him, was very simple stuff. It was very embarrassing, but it was my job. (See above: Looking like an idiot.) Because if you don't understand something, there is no way you can credibly explain it to other people.

You cannot be a good writer if you don't pay attention, to both what you're writing about and the words you are choosing to do so. When I was an editor, I had a great writer who was doing a story that required her to interview a great many people. When it came time to write it, she was overwhelmed by her notes—hyperventilating-overwhelmed. So I forbade her to look at her notes. Write the story the way you remember it because you were paying attention and the important points are floating at the top of your brainpan. Obviously, she had to look at her notes to write the story that we published, but the quotes and details that she remembered right away were, not surprisingly, the most powerful tools to tell the story.

The best writing does everything audio, video, and photography can do all at once while offering the reader company on the story's journey. That company doesn't have to be kind or sweet or even sympathetic, but the writer's voice reminds us that we are not alone in experiencing anything—even the sudden emergence of painful truth. And what greater service can we provide than to stand with each other as we discover wonderful, difficult, horrible things?

My voice has many permutations that depend on what I'm writing about, why I'm writing it, and who I'm writing it for. It can be thoughtful and poetic, terse and irritated, sentimental or objective. The biggest characteristic is probably humor, which is a very handy tool for making a point. People usually laugh because something is true, and the next thing they do is take a breath, and in that breath they will inevitably think about why they laughed, and your point slips in with the oxygen. (You can see I am not a science writer.) I am a huge fan of Dorothy Parker and Jean Kerr, both of whom could be biting and enthusiastic, which to me is the essence of being a great writer—that ability to swing between the opposing emotions without losing your balance. And if you do lose your balance, not being afraid to do it again.

My voice is also a personal voice, which is sometimes trickier than it seems. Although the first person is very much in vogue these days, it comes with the very real danger of narcissism. Not everything that happens to me is interesting or relevant to many others. Not every experience can be filtered through my tender, angry, baffled heart.

TO JUST STAY ALIVE

Robert Langellier

"I don't believe people are looking for the meaning of life as much as they are looking for the experience of being alive."
—Joseph Campbell

"Sometimes I imagine, you know, being dead. It might be exciting."
—Minnie

Demon creatures of the nursing home

The hallway of Decair Place is a stale tube. It feels sterile and gives off a polymeric aesthetic of wheezy lifelessness. A sense of discomforting mortality flows through any nursing home, where the sheer volume of death, all packed into one building, outstrips any other venue outside of hospitals and warzones.

I'm a volunteer here. On my first day, in March 2012, I don't see any people. I see creepy little ghost things in wheelchairs, and they're all coming for me. They move as if both the ground and the air itself were made of tar, sluggishly walking or wheeling back and forth, back and forth, slinking up to nurses and visitors like me and chilling them with their wraithlike stares and open mouths.

This is, to be sure, massively insensitive.

But anyone who's made a cursory visit to a nursing home knows the inward mental vortex created to avoid imagining your own long-term future. I am young and I don't belong here. This death doesn't apply to *me*.

I walk down the first hallway, hoping to encounter no one. Near a nurse's station there is a woman in a chair, rocking back and forth. I make eye contact, despite my effort to avoid her. I smile and say hello. I'm awkward. She keeps looking at me, rocks back and forth slowly, like a rubber ball riding an ocean wave. Saying nothing, going nowhere. It doesn't even matter that I'm there. She doesn't see me.

Next I encounter Ralphie. He's almost completely bald, and his jaw hangs loose like it's come unhinged. He speaks a loud, excited gibberish, and when he does, that swinging jaw moves up and down like he's chewing. The reason I know his name is because it's taped onto the back of his wheelchair. He won't stop talking to me, something about slipping out of his chair and having 911 called. But he seems fine, so I nod and say "uh-huh" and move on.

Forget it, I'm out of here.

There's a man in a motorized wheelchair by the front door who looks about 40, wearing only a gray t-shirt, gray briefs, a calf brace and shoes. His thousand-yard stare betrays his lack of cognizance, and his bare legs indicate his lack of recent sanitization. Mechanically, without impetus, he tilts his wheelchair, arching it upward and backward. He looks like a Transformer, everything in slow, terrifying movements. Finally he hangs there in a weird, precipitous angle, suspended in the middle of the walkway. I smile and walk by without saying a word.

These are alien people. I'm afraid of them. I sure as hell don't want to talk to them. I'm 20, and not supposed to be surrounded by so much death.

Elsewhere, though, I'm surrounded by my own uninteresting peers. I don't particularly care about the elderly, but I saw this as a way to find interesting people. My new job as a volunteer at Decair Place is to distract residents from the stale emptiness of their environment. I'm to befriend people who have lived lifetimes of freedom only to be institutionalized in their final years, and to try to reconcile them with that fact as well as I can with a board game. I'll start next time.

Enter Minnie

There aren't many sprightly 90 year olds; Queen Minnie is an exception. Queen Minnie is a queen, she proudly declares, because she lives in a room by herself. A curtain whose guiderail bisects the ceiling is pulled tightly against the wall, rendering the salmon-colored draperies nearly nonexistent. The whole room is Minnie's, and it is huge. About 15x10 feet, it has two beds (both hers) and two tall stoic wardrobes (both hers) and three chairs (all hers). It has a bathroom with a toilet and a sink. Against the wall is a flat screen television tuned to Disney. That's hers. There is the curtain. And a window. Really it is no different than all of the other rooms at Decair Place, but it's all hers.

Minnie's room gives her great comfort, because it's one of the few things that she has left that is all hers. Or almost hers, anyway. It's technically Decair Place's, and it will be someone else's just as soon as she is done living. But today it is hers, and the plain, light green bed covering is hers, and the blurry watercolor of a bikini-clad, beach-bathing woman on the wall is also hers.

Minnie doesn't look a day older than 75. When I meet her, she's standing outside her doorway with an element of youthful cockiness in her posture, chatting with passing residents. Her nails are freshly painted, dusty rose, and so we bow to each other in lieu of damaging the drying polish; her hand is so skeletal I might have broken it anyway. Her lips are drowned in intimidatingly red lipstick, a blazing hue that strikes an assertive counterstance against her very not-red skin. Her hair is slightly longer than the standard short clip of an elderly woman's hair, but it is wild and curled and dyed perfectly black. The rest of her is all movement. Her fingers dance around, and she is quick to step, with fast strikes and a look of brightness. "I can't do much else, but I can certainly walk faster than the rest of them," she says. Despite her garish adornments, Minnie has a certain gentleness, a nimbleness.

She is lucid. One can tell from the way her eyes look at you when she talks, or how they catch movement, that she's still a functioning human being. She notices you. She is vivacious, infectiously effervescent for her age, and bored as hell. She wakes up, eats breakfast, sits around, takes part in a designed daily activity, eats again, and waits to become tired.

A bent tack, Minnie is still sharp but worn past her use. Like all of her Decair Place neighbors, she's past the age or state of making decisions for herself. It just wasn't dementia that landed her here, as far as she can tell. It was dehydration.

While Minnie was living by herself in St. Louis, her children—the lawyer-politician, the tax collector, the psychologist, and the librarian—discovered she wasn't eating right. Minnie interpreted this as not eating right; her children interpreted it as an oblique sign of dementia. They convinced her to move to Decair Place, in a Missouri town where her son the lawyer-politician lives. They gave away her house and many of her material possessions, and so far have visited four times, she claims, in the 15 months she's been there—about one visit per year per child. Then again, two of her children live in California. "People have lives to live," Minnie says.

For the most part, she's lived hers. While most of us have working life goals, Minnie lives for meals and for "getting the hell out" of there. The latter is a pipe dream; after all, she has no home to return to even if she could choose to leave. Her current life falls into a category similar to high-risk inpatients of psychiatric hospitals and large dogs in apartments. "The next step from here is prison," she says. "I think I've got a life sentence." There are no more Vegas singing auditions, no more gambling-addicted husbands, no more real estate offices, no more children, and no fresh air at Decair Place.

Tomorrow Minnie is going shopping with Annie. She gleefully informs every passer-by of this plan. She seems to know every resident. ("Oh, I'm very popular here. Very, very popular. I don't know why.") It will be the fifth time since arriving at Decair Place that she will leave its keypad-encoded doors. A four-digit password is enough to keep most of the residents locked into regulation, although there are the occasional cases of dementia patients found wandering from their nursing homes. Minnie still has eyes and fingers that work, but she never talks of escape. She pines for "getting out" but never speaks of simply walking out the front door. But tomorrow she is going shopping. "Anything to get the hell out of here."

How to die in America

Minnie feels dumped. And maybe she is. She doesn't seem to belong in the stagnant environment of Decair Place. She might better fit into an assisted living facility, but Medicare doesn't cover the rent there, and Decair Place makes Minnie's family more comfortable with the threat of dementia. She doesn't have a house to move back to. She doesn't handle her own fast-disappearing money—her daughter has power of attorney and manages her dwindling finances. When she's down to $999, Medicaid will kick in. She has a stash of $14 in a tin—one can only get what one pays for. At Decair Place, she can't even walk out the front doors. She can't have a snack when she's hungry. At about 4:30 every evening, she and other residents are shepherded to the dining hall by the nurses, whose care is often more on-the-clock than from-the-heart. Otherwise Marcella may forget to eat.

"When I first moved here, I cried for three weeks," she says. It's a harsh transition, one that is unprecedented in the frequency with which it occurs today. On the scale of human history, taking care of 80-year-old humans is a new deal starting in the 20th century. U.S. life expectancies have increased by 30 years since 1900, according to the Centers for Disease Control and Prevention. Science and medicine are beckoning with bony fingers to longer and longer life spans. The MacArthur Research Network on an Aging Society predicts that by 2050, when my own parents will be 90, women will live to be on average 92 years old and men 84. That's up from 78.7 years today. Those extra years mean trillions of dollars being funneled into long-term care for aging elders not ready—or unable—to die. With an aging American society, a fifth of Americans will be over 65 by 2030. This means more people in nursing homes.

The first reaction is to avoid the issue. To say, "I'll never let myself live in a nursing home. I'll never let my parents live in a nursing home." Easy to say. But women and men are both breadwinners in the 21st century. Often neither can be caregivers for their parents. Although the Centers for Medicare & Medicaid Services (CMS) says that 70 percent of elderly people will have family and friends as their sole caregivers, a U.S. Department of Health and Senior Services study indicates that if you live to 65, you'll have a 40 percent chance of landing in a nursing home at some point. And as of the most recent National Nursing Home Survey in 2004, an average nursing home stay is almost two and a half years. You can't stay young forever, and unless you're lucky, you can't die when you want to.

For every queen, a king

King Raymond looks regal enough: a Navy cap that never leaves his head, with white wisps of hair escaping from underneath, perfectly carved wrinkles that give off just the right air of sagacity, and a wooden cane, itself wrinkled with spiraling ridges.

The King has a disarming smile as persistent as the Navy cap. In it you can see his perfect set of upper teeth. It's only when he talks that you can see how all his bottom teeth are missing save for the middle ones. Raymond is a good-natured man of the people—one of the regulars in the hallway. Most times of the day you can see him roaming or sitting in his throne on the visitors' chairs, surveying his kingdom. Bestowing his full-faced grins on geriatric subjects.

Raymond is the twinkling-eyes kind of elderly person. He's the one that lacks bitterness, that sits patiently with those whom he can't understand and who can't understand him. He is a good king. The people like him.

And the king must have his queen.

Raymond is not a shy man, but he is a relaxed one. He doesn't seek out company as much as he allows it to come to him, preferring to toss greetings and warm chuckles from his throne. But there is Minnie. For her he will get up and make his way to his next-door neighbor's room. Raymond is old, but he is not dead. He knows what he wants.

Since Minnie moved into the home a year ago, she and Raymond have spent a lot of time together. Raymond would come grinning into her room and watch TV on the flat screen 20x30" Element with her, and sometimes the nurses would shut the lights off early, leaving the two together in the dark—the closest thing in a nursing home to going to the movies. Minnie would leave her door open to dissuade any suspicion, but still the nicknames "Queen" Minnie and "King" Raymond were born.

The royal family is not without its troubles. Minnie likes Raymond, but she's not exactly ready for commitment. People don't get married as young as they used to, she says. "Hell, I'm 90 and I *still* don't want that. I mean, I like spending my time with Raymond, but it's like 'whoa let's not get too serious here.'" Not that that stops Raymond's advances—he tells her he wants her to move in with him.

Minnie can talk for an hour nonstop about Raymond, relationships and sex—and she will. Every 10 minutes or so she takes care to make it clear she's not into him, before continuing. But of course, he sometimes gets lost in the three hallways of Decair Place, and she feels it's the neighborly thing to guide him home and visit with him when she finds him. And of course sometimes she simply gets bored and stops by his place to chat.

What she doesn't mention is the excitement of the bare thought of forbidden romance. It's reminiscent of high school trysts steaming in parking lots, groping in theaters, and coming through backdoors into bedrooms after midnight. But at Decair Place, the parents are up all night. There are no secret meetings.

Minnie turns to me, says, "It never stops, honey." It's what she gets for being one of the prettiest girls in the home. "You're never too old for it," she adds, laughing. There is no magic screen hidden in the nursing home's front doors that makes you forget about sex.

The troubles with ambulating

The problem with being in care service is that your product is people. And via the identity property, your people are products—the thing you're being paid to take care of. Minnie is the metaphorical equivalent of a fragile parcel to a UPS deliveryman, an investment account to a portfolio manager, or a sheep to a shepherd.

So, liabilities. Falling residents are risks of lawsuit or loss of business. At the very least, it can lead to bad reports. Every 9–15 months, CMS surveys Medicare/Medicaid-funded homes and reports their deficiencies, and in Missouri the Missouri Department of Health and Senior Services inspects twice a year. Search the Internet and you can easily find a nursing home's 2567, a federal form that lists and describes all violations of a nursing home, including level of severity and potential for harm (almost one in five Missouri homes were cited for "serious deficiencies"). Infractions can be anything from lack of proper fire escape routes to physical abuse of residents. If cited homes don't fix infractions quickly, they can be hit with civil money penalties, have Medicare/Medicaid funds withdrawn or in more serious cases be completely terminated. In one sense this system pressures nursing homes to keep up their standards of care requirements and minimize harm. In another sense it means Minnie has to use her walker, whether she needs it or not.

Stubbornness never rests for Minnie. Her kids might have taken her house away, but she won't let anyone take her legs. Again and again the same scene plays out: Minnie pushes her walker aside in her room, chin up, and beelines down 2 Wing, moving as briskly as any 45-year-old half her age, stale air blowing through her permed hair. Again and again: "Minnie, where's your walker?" "You need to use your walker!" "You can't be walking around without your walker!" In slow, loud tones, the nurses treat Minnie like a foreigner who will somehow understand "WHERE, IS, THE, BUS, STOP?" but not normal speech. F. Scott Fitzgerald famously said that exclamation points are like laughing at your own jokes. The butts of the jokes in Decair Place are the residents, cognitively buried below the institutional motives of the nursing staff. Comically expressive volume is employed as an infantilizing compliance tool. It sounds a bit conspiratorial, but stretched smiles and overenthusiasm are not always employed to make friends with residents, but to coerce them back into their rooms and to stop complaining incoherently in the hallway of 3 Wing.

Minnie grumbles and returns to her room to grab her walker. It's adorned by craft supplies from the Activities Room: feathers, a large banner with her name on it, colored streamers. A decoration project with Annie, the activities director. It looks like a wrapped present as much as it does a walker. "I just want to feel young, even if I can't be," Minnie says, leaning over it as she heads back out her door, slowed by the pushing of the walker.

Nursing homes are a delicate balancing act. One side of the beam is safety, the other side freedom. Too much freedom equals too many injuries (and CMS citations). Too much safety equals institutionalization, dependence and depression, and eventually sweeping systematic critiques. Minnie wants to walk, but Minnie's daughter wants her to be breathing. Minnie's daughter handles the money. Looks like we have a winner.

The walls get tighter

Minnie's shrunken world is getting smaller by about 50 square feet. She's been lucky so far, but in May—a week from now—she's getting a roommate, and she's pissed about it. Her stuff is sprawled across both wardrobes and tables. The new clothes she bought with Annie aren't going to fit anywhere now. Over the course of the week she nervously waits, like a college freshman finding out with whom she's sharing a dorm room.

When she finally arrives, Minnie's attitude shifts abruptly. Ruth Greer is a gruff, round woman with a cynical eye. Like Minnie, she's more lifelike than most of the other residents, at least mentally. In April, before she moved to Decair Place, she fell trying to go to the bathroom when she wasn't supposed to be moving on her own. "I remember the walker flying up, and me not being able to catch it." Now she's bedridden and bitter with a leg-sized cast on. The process of fixing it has been arduous, and it will take months more. Ruth claims it took a long time to get x-rays, which then failed to get to the doctors. "Someone could probably sue them if they kept track of everything, but who wants to go through all that red tape?" "Liability" starts to become a term I understand more and more.

Ruth is as fluent as Minnie in vitriol for the nursing home system. Over this the two bond and instantly become friends, gnawing at the world from their beds. They're coping with more than boredom; they're coping with social uselessness. From a productivity standpoint, they are now the saps on a capitalist culture that raised them to detest idleness. These women are Depression survivors. They've spent their whole lives working jobs and building families, and now wait every day to fall asleep. It makes the boredom all the more scarring. They're not just failing to engage their stimuli; they're failing to engage in the world.

Raymond goes to the hospital the first time

Minnie's ex-husband died two decades ago, age 69. He was a Navy man in World War II for nearly four years. Just like Raymond. Minnie speaks of her former marriage with the nostalgia one affords to the tap water of the town one grew up in. That is to say, with a somewhat pleasant, mostly indifferent half-smile. She and her ex-husband divorced years before his death, and she doesn't have any outward signs of sadness on looking back. Or rather, glancing back. She's alive now, even if she's living on the institution's schedule. And it's the people who are alive now and pay attention to her who interest her.

Raymond has been gone for a while at the hospital. It's not the first time and it won't be the last. Often, Minnie has no idea why, or when or if he'll be back. This time, he returns, but only to move out. Not to a different home, but to the opposite end of 2 Wing, where he'll be closer to the nurse's station. In a nursing home community it's like moving to a different neighborhood. For example, Minnie doesn't socialize much with people in 3 Wing; it's too far away. So the one or two minute walk down the hallway holds weight for her. She can no longer peek around her doorframe into Raymond's room. His failing health is taking him physically away from her.

After dinner one day in April, residents slowly file back to their rooms. Having moved, Raymond has even more difficulty finding his room than before. This Minnie puts on herself, escorting him down the long green hallway to room 202, the last one on the left. Minnie lays him down on his bed and props a pillow, sets up his cane and turns on his 13-inch. He looks content, spacey, like an old, dilapidated angel. The ever-present smile is slightly more pronounced whenever Minnie is around. He glows in her company. For the next five minutes, Minnie stands by his bedside, right at his head, passing the time. She yells everything, as his hearing is severely dulled. In the dull environment around him, perhaps it's better that his senses are so. Minnie wonders if maybe that is why he is able to smile at everything still.

They look like a couple, although Minnie's role is blurred between that of a romantic partner and a mother. It's not entirely certain which one is propelling her down the hall to 202. Certainly, she says, it's the mothering, as she denies any romantic aspect of their relationship. As the two wrap up their conversation, she leans over, and the two kiss the air and laugh. Minnie departs, grabbing her walker in the hallway and carrying on past the nurse's desk just outside.

Minnie and Raymond are an odd pairing to the casual observer. Minnie is racked with worries, and Raymond is calm and carefree. Minnie is active and still clear-headed, and Raymond has a mild dementia that may or may not account in large part for his carefree attitude. And sure, maybe they aren't sneaking into maintenance closets or the Physical Therapy room to hook up, and maybe they aren't true loves or even real loves at all and maybe they are two elderly people stalling out a few more years in a nursing home with no notable life change to look forward to beyond when the next haircut day is and what's for dinner and maybe the opportunity to connect-by-flirting with someone they know it's way too late to start with. They make a good fake couple, anyway.

Smoking angel

Cute young girl is a badass angel who smokes. Angela is a bullet train in the hallways, with long businesslike strides, yet with the brakes of a

2009 Corvette, stopping on a dime to talk to residents. She's considerably younger than the other nurses, in her mid-20s, and has dirty blonde hair pulled into a ponytail and a smooth, made-up face, all complimented by flowery pink scrubs. Soft features, but there are no princesses in Decair Place. She commands just as much respect from the residents as the other nurses. She just gets their friendship, too. And she's made a lot of friends. She's like a classic all-star mom, speaking to each resident succinctly and sincerely as she power walks from 3 Wing to help a woman go to the bathroom down in 2 Wing.

One of the perks of being a CNA is on-the-clock smoke breaks. Just outside the courtyard doors to the left is a small, screened-in outdoor room that looks out on the picturesque white gazebo. This is Angela's home base, where she takes residents out to have a smoke when they (or she) need it. Right now, Edith wants a smoke, so Angela rounds up her two regulars, Edith and Raymond, and takes them outside to the smoke room.

Raymond takes a dignified seat and puts his cane up, takes a menthol from Angela and has it lit. He's fine on his own, puffing in silence from under his Navy cap in the corner of the room. Angela focuses her attention on Edith, whose motor functions cannot be trusted to handle cigarette ashes without her wearing a heavy lead apron for protection. While the woman speaks in what seems to be unintelligible murmurs, Angela responds fluidly and in full. She can speak her language. To me, Edith might as well be speaking Xhosa. In scrubs, I could just as well give Edith a cigarette and sit beside her, but Angela takes care to hold whatever conversation she can with her. All the while she repeatedly taps Edith's cigarette butt into an ashtray and works her own, and Raymond puffs and grins.

Angela looks around the near-empty room. "We used to have so many smokers," she says, a bit of wistfulness in her voice. "Now there's just a few left." Angela's friends don't stick around too long.

She's been doing this for a few years, and this isn't her first home. Edith sits motionless in her wheelchair; Angela leans back and takes a drag, relaxing fully for the first time since I've seen her. She's of the age (and the looks) for screaming nightclubs and partying, but these are her people. "They're all pretty much the same no matter where you go," she says.

Eventually the fire hits the filter, and it's out of the quiet of the smoke room and back into the quiet of the home.

Angela wheels Edith down the hall of 1 Wing at the blistering rate of 3 Gs—she has business to attend to. Raymond is left alone, nothing to do for the rest of the day but oversee his kingdom. He sits down in his throne, the aging sea-green velvet armchair.

"It's almost like a prison," he says to me. "Only it isn't." And the bastard smiles. A big, honest, no-glib-no-sarcasm-no-kidding *smile*.

He's right, though, in more ways than he knows. Not only does Decair Place keep him within its institutionalized walls, but it *needs* him. Of all U.S. nursing homes, 70 percent are for-profit. Prolonging life is profitable. The longer you keep people alive, regardless of their quality of life, the more checks get cashed. And the sound of money wakes the market up. Homes have gotten more competitive, and as the number of 65-year-olds shoots up more than 50 percent in the next couple decades, it'll get even more competitive. More homes, more beds. Gotta fill 'em. When private contractors build new prisons, the cells have to be filled. It's no different here.

To just go outside

The Activities Room is a mess of children's activities: board games (mostly puzzles), racks of greeting cards, craft supplies, paint handprints on the wall, plastic tennis rackets and Velcro gloves that surely no resident has ever used, a Wii with the game Jeopardy, old movies and cassettes, and a community pet turtle named HC.

I poke my head outside to Minnie across the hall. "Do you like jigsaw puzzles?"

"I did, when I was 12," she calls. No dice in the activities room. Instead we do what everyone else does when they're bored: take another walk.

A glass pair of double doors enters out into the only pocket of fresh air that many residents ever get, a small, enclosed courtyard with a garden and the gazebo that no one really uses. Around the edges of the walkway are flowers that add Decair Place's only flair of color and non-urine-related scent. There's even a trio of redbud trees triangulating the circular path, two of which are still alive. A beautiful garden surrounded by a ring of living purgatory.

We sit down on a bench, and Minnie reminisces about her ex-husband. In another time there were singing auditions and gambling in Vegas. There was youth in St. Louis. "He was good to me, introduced me to different things, took me to nice places." But that was a long time ago. The sum force of all that memory brings but a cynical smile to her face. "He gambled too much," she says. "I was married to him I think about 100 years."

Eventually we go back inside, where we find Raymond seated upon his throne.

"Would you like to take a walk?" His eyes gleam in a way that they don't when he talks to me. Minnie gets up close to him, so that he can hear.

"I can't right now. I have company."

"What?"

"I CAN'T. I HAVE COMPANY. Maybe later!"

"Well, I just thought you'd want to take a walk with me."

"Well I'll just think about it."

There's a 10 second silence. Finally Raymond turns to me. "Who are you here for?"

"Minnie," I say.

Raymond's eyes get big and switch to Minnie. "Oh! I've never heard you called that before!"

She turns to me. I can't tell if she's hurt. "He doesn't know my name."

"I used to know," he says, grinning.

"No," she says. "No you didn't." To me: "He recognizes me when he sees me, but he doesn't know my name."

"My memory is bad," Raymond laughs.

There's another awkward silence, when Raymond looks at me with those crystal, empty eyes and happy smile. I don't know what he makes of these exchanges. I don't know if he even knows they happened. But he has that smile, and Minnie can't keep herself from coming back to him. I remember months ago when she told me about residents mistaking lovers for their own deceased spouses, on account of their dementia. "Or maybe that's just what they want you to think," she had told me then, winking. Raymond's Navy cap sits snugly on his head. It's hard to say who, if either of them, is playing forgetting games.

Meanwhile, Mr. Conrad, shaky old fellow in a wheelchair, only just capable of moving, wheels up to the door to the courtyard. I hold it open for him. Nothing, sits still. I'm faced with a long, awkward showdown where Mr. Conrad refuses to budge. I am determined to help, but not determined enough to find out if he's capable of conversation. A nurse comes up, asks if he wants to go out. "Okay, I'll take him away," she says. But then his feet catch the edge of the carpet, which bunches up and sticks him there while the nurse tries pushing harder.

Mr. Conrad meets her eyes and he looks like he's about to speak. His lips tremble and his fingers quiver in gathering the air and the jaw muscles required for speaking. I get the sense that he feels himself speaking but knows that nothing is coming out. The strain on Mr. Conrad's face is agonizing to watch, and it soon becomes evident that no words will be escaping.

Raymond is watching and smiling at me through all of this. I realize that there's a hidden hierarchy in the home. Each patient, regardless of their lucidity, has someone to look down on, to silently ridicule behind their back and say, "Gee, I'm glad I'm not a nutcase like them." Senility here is a game of relativity. Mr. Conrad's feet are still caught on the rug. "They drag him backwards," Raymond says, to help the nurse. "They drag him backwards 'cause he can't get his feet up." "Oh, I see," she says. She tries again to push him normally. This time his feet pick up and she lets go. He begins to walk his wheelchair ever so slightly, in painful inches. It's an aching process. He slowly veers to the right and goes straight to the side wall, against which is a long table loaded with a panoply of plastic flowers. When he hits the table he reaches out with a loose fist and seems to swipe at the arrangement, and again and again. We all just stand, watching him. He might be cudgeling his dumb frustration into the flowers, or he might simply be reaching out to touch them, to test if they're real or fake or just to get a feel of the texture. There's no real way to tell. And that's the problem. But he doesn't have Raymond's infectious smile on his face.

Speaking of which, Raymond is still grinning at me. Finally, finally, finally the nurse takes over and guides him away into the hallway. He disappears. And within a minute Mr. Conrad has wheeled himself back to us, the nurse having freed herself of him. He again moves toward us and slams quietly into the door. He puts a hand on the door handle and pulls, doing nothing to open the door but plenty to run himself into it once again—the feeblest escape attempt in the history of incarceration. I stare at him, knowing if I open the courtyard door for him again, the same scene will play out. I wonder how often this happens, the numbing and pointless repetition of it. "Let's go back," Minnie says in an effort to leave.

We go out and turn down the hallway together, and behind me I hear Raymond: "Are you trying to get outside? You got yourself too close to the door to get it open."

The door closes

It's May 4, and Minnie won't talk much. She seems distracted, looking hyperopically beyond me.

Recently she found out her children sold her truck. A reasonable decision—a private room at Decair Place costs $4,730 a month, and what is Minnie ever going to do with a truck anyway? Drive to the dining hall? Anyway, her license was taken away long ago.

But it's not what her truck means to her. She could care less for having a truck. What she cares about is not losing one.

Throughout the day, she has difficulty focusing on everything, and every conversation manages to make its way back to the truck. In the last year and a half, Minnie has had her city, her house, her credit cards, her furniture, Raymond's health and half of her room taken from her control. Without her truck, she is really, truly stuck in Decair Place. She knows she's not ever going to leave. But now she can't even pretend.

"The truck was the only thing left that was mine," she says, tearing up. "It's just one more thing."

The walls start to feel a little tighter.

Later on in the evening we are sitting and talking with Ruth in their room, room 221. Ruth's daughter was here for a visit, but she is gone now, and the chatter falls away. The television is on, distracting us by faint degrees until it consumes the new silence. It's a PBS airing of *The Lawrence Welk Show*, the musical variety show that ran from the '50s through the '70s. This episode is from the early '60s—it's still in black and white. Minnie and Ruth begin to drift off as Welk introduces the young Lennon Sisters. They're singing "Mockingbird Hill," the sound crackling out of the screen and into the room. ("When the sun in the morning peeps over the hill / And kisses the roses 'round my windowsill / Then my heart fills with gladness when I hear the trill / Of those birds in the treetops on Mockingbird Hill.") Ruth, still awake, listens with her eyes closed, hands folded over the TV remote, as if in prayer.

Raymond goes to the hospital the second time

As always, Raymond is seated at the front of the home on his throne. Today he's having eye trouble. "I've been waiting for my appointment all day," he says. "They haven't come."

"What for?" I ask. Nothing. "WHAT FOR?"

"Oh, I don't know. Same appointment as yesterday, and the day before and the day before." He laughs. "I don't even know which doctor it's with. Maybe if I did I would call them." Laugh. "I have an appointment just across the street."

"Which street?"

"Today. I have an appointment today."

"WHICH STREET?"

"Right across the street there. I don't know which street."

This is the last time I see Raymond for a couple months. Shortly afterward, he's gone. According to Minnie, he's back in the hospital, and then to another nursing home. "He lost his location," she says. That's the only explanation. She says he was healthy one day, and the next she received a note that he was healthy but had been transferred. Without him, she seems a little less vivid. Some of her life seems to have been taken out with him. She stops paying as much attention to things. At the dinner table she can't remember whether she's eaten or not.

In a nursing home, people disappear. They come in, they go out. Everyone seems to want to get out of the nursing homes, and the problem is that sometimes they do. Minnie has the vague notion that Raymond is in a different home, but she doesn't *really* know. She can ask the nurses, but she might soon forget again. She can only fill herself with abstract worry.

"Maybe I could visit him," she says. Minnie thinks a visit from her might be a step forward for him. She's convinced she keeps Raymond healthy. Once, she says, Raymond went three days without eating. The nurses, not knowing what to do, asked Queen Minnie to try to convince him. "I got him to eat for me," she says.

This is the only area of her life where she still feels useful. But she refuses to visit him—as if she could leave Decair Place—until she gets her teeth fixed. Minnie has been talking about "new teeth" for two months. Her son, the politician, has convinced her to get dentures, but it's a long process. "He's embarrassed to be seen with me," she says. "He came in and said,

'Minnie, you look like hell.'" Minnie remembers when she was the parent, sitting in her real estate office, her young son coming in with a beard, long hair and no shoes. When she was the embarrassed one.

"Maybe he won't recognize me," she says of Raymond, her face furrowed.

"Maybe he will," I say. She has no idea where he is, no means of transportation and no permission to leave. All she can really do is hope he comes back.

One last dance

Bedtime at Decair Place is around 9:00. There's no exact time that everyone has to go to sleep, but by 8:30 the halls are empty and peaceful, and the nurses make more casual rounds. In room 221 Minnie and Ruth are enjoying the Decair Place twilight, chatting like they're elementary school best friends on a sleepover.

"What would we do without each other?" Minnie asks from across the room.

"Go crazy," Ruth says, smirking.

Minnie gets up from her bed and takes up her walker, moves to grab the remote from the bureau. A couple of nurses stroll by outside.

"Hey Minnie!" one of them calls in good-naturedly. "You best be using that walker, now!"

"Walk?" Minnie calls back. "I don't need to walk. I can dance!"

With the two nurses watching, Minnie moves her feather-adorned walker to the side and starts a slow, graceful step to inaudible music. She's playing around, but there's a surprising enchantment in the fluidity of her aging body. She stays right in time with the soundlessness, a couple steps forward, backward, her arms outstretched in front of her, holding her phantom partner. The lights of the room have their artificial brightness, but it's late and the whole institution is otherwise quiet and dark, allowing her to spin in the silence.

Minnie begins to hum. Some tuneless melody that withers and dies outside her lips, but in here it's an orchestra. She keeps stepping, turning, slowly, as smoothly and quickly as her body can handle. For a moment, she doesn't even seem to be in a nursing home. She doesn't seem to be old. She is completely, entirely, as much as she can ever be, out of Decair Place.

The two nurses, henchwomen in scrubs, come into the room after her. "Minnie!" one of them calls. "You are hilarious!" They laugh and watch her, commenting and joking with her as she dances. Ruth smiles, lying on her bed. Tonight, Minnie is allowed to break the rules. The walker will still be there tomorrow. But right now, she is on stage, auditioning her last part in Vegas. No liability regulations will tell her otherwise. The *la-dee-dum* humming fills the room, and swells to symphonic proportions.

A new smile

Finally, in September, the appointment comes and Minnie is fitted and given a new pair of dentures. They don't fit. She shows me the upper teeth in her room as a nurse comes in. "Yeah, they looked like they didn't match when I saw 'em yesterday," the nurse says as she gives Minnie her medication. Minnie is irate over the bad teeth, and she complains enthusiastically about them.

Yet outside the room I meet Tom, an old white balding head in a wheelchair with a tube running under his nose. He's alert and highly articulate compared with the rest of the residents. He looks at Minnie, and then me, and then grins up at Minnie. "I told you you'd have guys chasing you around once you got your new teeth," he says. Minnie smiles with her new teeth, flattered. They might fit awkwardly, but they look pretty good. She still has to go back to the dentist to get them fixed, and until then she can't wear them much. But they're new and they're hers and they're the first new thing that's been hers in a very long time.

Sleeping hallways

In mid-September Raymond makes a triumphant return to Decair Place to a rousing crowd of congratulating nurses. His skin is pale and sickly now, and for the first time since I came to Decair Place I see him without his Navy cap. The first time I've ever seen him look different. Without the hat he looks older, frailer. "He's holding on," Minnie says. He doesn't talk so much anymore as much as stare vacantly at walls.

For the rest of the time I know them, the relationship between him and Minnie starts to cool. With Raymond's hearing shot and his faculties as withered as some of Decair Place's least capable residents, he becomes difficult to communicate with. Minnie stops going to visit him much. The last time I see him, in December, King Raymond's new seat is in a wheelchair, dethroned from his regular armchair near the front door, and he sits in it in the corner of the hallway, passing hours blankly, almost gone but feebly holding on.

Back to September. Minnie is asleep fully dressed when I arrive tonight. The fluorescent lights on the wall are still on. She's wearing her cheetah print sweatpants, and at the foot of the bed is her cheetah print coat—some of her last assertions of agility. At her bedside is a big pink bottle of hair product—one of her last assertions of vitality. Bouquets of fake red, pink and white flowers decorate the room, mixing like a plastic watercolor with the artificial pink and green comforters on the two beds. There's a clock that constantly blinks 12:00. There's an atomic clock on the windowsill. The second hand is the only thing that moves in the room, along with the blinking bedside clock. Time passes and nothing else happens.

I pace the hallways waiting for Minnie to awake. It's late now, and quiet. Most of the residents have gone to bed, and other than a blind woman in 3 Wing whistling and mumbling, "I'm too tired too tired mamamama too tired too tired mamamama," the hallway roamers are nowhere to be seen. The emptiness carries a strange sense of calm, one that feels like it doesn't belong here. The usual quietness of a nursing home as I've experienced it is always underlain with the anxiety of restriction. There's a certain vague, inaudible volume that hums over the discomfort and malcontent. Minnie hears it, and I hear it, and to the best of my perception every other resident I know can hear it. It's right now, in the empty hallways, that there is no discomfort. It's all hidden away now, behind doors, under bed sheets, with the lights off, away from my view. I don't have to deal with these people. For once, it's really quiet. I see one nurse walk by, give me a strange look. I see the spiral design on the green and white walls, a strand of gold paint curling and winding along at hip height, wrapping itself around every doorway, tying them all together. I wend my way around to 3 Wing, all the way down to the big lounge, where residents don't even go in the daytime. It's dark now. The TV is off. I return down the hallway the way I came, realizing it's likely that Minnie won't wake up until the morning. Why would she, when all she can do is walk tiredly through lifeless lounges?

When I reach the corner of 1 and 2 Wings, a shrill electronic screech suddenly annihilates the silence and fills the entire hallway. A residents' body alarm has gone off. It keeps ringing in high-decibel succession until a nurse comes in and shuts it off. A body alarm is a thing that some at-risk residents have strapped to them, and whenever they venture to move too much it fires off a sonic explosion that brings the nurses running. It's to prevent people from falling out of their beds or their chairs and hurting themselves. Liability protection. It's a thing that is fortunately starting to be phased out of nursing homes around the U.S.

Finally, after 30 seconds of earsplitting sirens, the situation is under control, and if anyone's still asleep on this end of the wing they're probably dead or deaf. Even in the restored quiet, the spell of silence is broken. I don't feel the hypnotism from before. I'm fully re-attuned to this place and the people behind its doors. No one knows peace until it's broken, after all. I go to the opposite end of the hall and peek into Minnie's room. Still asleep.

Grand theft walker

It's hard to perceive deterioration in a place where everyone's expected to be deteriorated already. But in Minnie, her vitality begins to slip out in noticeable increments. By late September, there's a stark change in her appearance. She no longer dresses up as if she's going somewhere. Her clothes are more comfortable, her hair less composed. It no longer has the lusty black sheen it once had. Now it's a dull, faded gray-black, unkempt and left to fall at early morning angles. Ruth moved out a month ago to another home. Minnie used to be afraid of getting a roommate; now she's afraid of not having one.

She complains with less frequency about using her walker. It has become an instinctive part of her body, a quad-legged appendage that shoots from her hands. She does still abandon it from time to time, but it is no longer an act of rebellion so much as an act of forgetfulness. At dinner, she asserts that her tablemate Francina's walker is her own. Grabs it, walks it back to her room, where a nurse eventually has to confront her. Minnie resists, claiming ownership of the walker that looks nothing like hers.

"Minnie, doesn't yours have the little feathers on it!" the nurse says, loudly and exaggeratedly. "The colored feathers!"

"Feathers? Oh, I don't know."

The nurse is forced to go on a walker hunt around the home, until she finally finds it sitting unattended, right next to Minnie's dinner chair. Brings it back, returns Francina's walker.

Almost all the colorful décor from her walker has eroded by now. All that remains are a few tattered feathers that stick taped to the crossbar, a pathetic remnant of its former flash. I'm tempted to rip the damn things off, restore it some dignity, but I don't. I let her hold onto them.

The new Minnie

By mid-November, a new roommate, Carolyn Fanning, has moved in. Carolyn is more cognizant than Minnie (in fact she reminds me of Minnie when I first met her in March). She is a perfectly good ambulator without a walker, and she talks about her roommate as one talks about caring for one's little sister.

Minnie keeps asking me the same questions, over and over. Every ten minutes or so: "You still have all your jobs?" "Do you still have all of your jobs?" And each time she asks I'm thrown off guard. I don't know this Minnie—I remember the arrogant, lithe 90-year-old standing outside her doorway, rolling her eyes at the incoherent residents and the caricatured nurses.

She doesn't remember anymore what time of day it is. She doesn't know if she's just had breakfast or dinner. When her children sold her truck, it was the last physical property of Minnie's to be taken from her. But at least she had the memory.

Memory doesn't disappear overnight; it sneaks away over months, leaving behind traces that disappear themselves later. A quiet killer. Memory, more than owning a truck, makes Minnie human. It gives Minnie her past, and by extension, her future. Without it, a whole bunch of her fizzles out.

Soon we go on a walk, looking for Raymond. Minnie doesn't talk about him much anymore. There's not much to say. We don't find him, and Minnie gets turned around in 1 Wing, so I direct her back to 221. Later, I recall some of the symptoms of dementia onset: *Neglecting appearance. Getting lost at home. Loss of articulation. Repeating questions or stories.*

Not all of Minnie's fiery resistance has been quelled. It's just retreated to further indignities, clinging to what it can still resist. A wheelchair now sits at her bedside, undecorated, untouched. "I don't want to use that thing," she says dismissively. "I don't want to get boxed in in that." The same hostile sentiment directed to the walker months ago. She still ambulates okay on her own, though a little wobbly. The nurses still remind her to use her walker, even when it's in her hands.

In the same way that memory slips away, comfortableness slips in. At some point, I stopped finding her out of place. It seems to me now that she belongs here, that her yearnings to get out are more like escape fantasies than righteous injustices. After a while, I don't think one could handle the cognitive dissonance—that she should not be here, but with no reasonable way for her to live on her own—so one's brain simply justifies and settles.

A year and a half is enough to break Minnie in to her environment and to make her accept it. With so much less vigor than before, she seems truly, for once, to be a Decair Place resident.

What is most sad is that it isn't entirely the nursing home's fault. Decair Place did not invent aging, even if it helps it along. Whether it's September of this year or the next, there will come a day when Minnie can't remember if she just had breakfast or dinner. There is little but the universe to be blamed. After all, this is not a hospital, an institution for renewal, for revitalization, for birth or rebirth or reanimation. It's not a temporary stop for temporary patients with temporary illnesses. It's not a place of healing. It's Decair Place.

To just slip away

Between 60–80 percent of nursing home residents have some form of dementia. Many are incontinent, blind and/or deaf, and some cannot even form sentences. These are medical nightmares.

But one can't simply die anymore. One deteriorates under the miracle of modern medicine until she's reached a near vegetative state, where still she's kept alive, wandering the pale halls of an Alzheimer's ward. It's only after years of this that she might reach an actual vegetative state, teetering on the brink of death itself, when she's yanked back up by her feeble brain activity with the godsend of life support, suspended there in half life for another week or two before the faint blip of the heart monitor finally fizzles out. Our magnanimity thrusts this decay on ourselves and our parents, because they don't want to die and we don't want them to die.

There they are, half alive and half dead, wheeling back and forth in chairs in front of me. That's how you die in America.

Robert Langellier on being a young writer

Young writers don't know what to write about. Sit down and write a list of all the themes of your coming generation. What will be the major stories of your age? In my story here, I began by thinking broadly of aging in the modern world. Look further ahead than terrorism and gay rights. Then get more specific: the sucking straw at the bottom of Lake Mead later this century, and the exodus from the West. The rebirth and eventual boom of Detroit. Those are great themes. Those are the stories that will define a time. Take your list and shove it in your friends' faces and scream at them until they scream their ideas back at you and you have something comprehensive and passionate. That's step one.

Young writers feel they need to be or look pure. Accept that good morals spring from bad morals. I want money when I'm old, so social security concerns me, so thus do nursing homes, and thus I am Minnie and Minnie is me and you. It's okay for it all to be about you, because that's what social justice is born from. Vanity fuels more writing than we let on: start from yourself and move outward.

Now you have the arrogance to swim and something to write about—next, how to write about it. I used to very consciously avoid stylistic influences. I thought that each major influence narrowed your perspective on the world and thereby limited your potential as a human being. I thought that an empty canvas was a perfect canvas. I still believe that an empty canvas should be on your mind just as much as a finished one.

But from Ernest Hemingway to Junot Diaz we are told to be livers before writers, and living inevitably hurls paint on your perfect canvas. That's okay. Go to the places of your dreams. No one will stop you. Talk to the migrants, the CEOs, the baseball players, the roughnecks, the poets, the sex addicts, the children, the mud, the trees, the sun. They'll talk back.

While you're talking with them, read poetry, read the *New York Times*, read *Le Monde*, read Jack Kerouac and John McPhee, watch documentaries, listen to punk rock. Writers need to be inspired by more than just facts. If all you read is the *Guardian*, you'll be dry, and no one will want to read you. When I write poetry, my prose becomes more beautiful and composed. When I report, my poetry becomes more charged.

One of the last things a writer does is write. Don't tear your eyes out. Of course, you don't know what you're doing. Great kings and conquerors didn't know what their borders would look like until they died. You watch the borders develop.

You'll get a thousand rejections before you get it right. It took me two years to sell "To Just Stay Alive." I still haven't made a penny off it. Some investments are for the long term, and some things you do just because you're dumb. You've decided to be a writer, so you've already accepted a life of romantic, professional, and financial rejection. Maybe we'll all regret it later. For now, not a minute.

VIDEO GAMES WITH A REFUGEE

Sean McLachlan

"Are you American?"

The little boy with the big brown eyes was sitting on the couch next to mine in the lobby of my hotel in Najaf, Iraq. He was dressed in jeans, a button-down shirt and sneakers. He peered at me over the edge of his iPad. I looked up from my email.

"No, I'm Canadian. You Iraqi?"

"I'm Lebanese but I live in Syria. We move back to Lebanon now."

"Your English is good."

"I go to the international school." He held up his iPad. "I'm looking for games."

"You find any good ones?" I asked, smiling.

"Yeah, you want to play?"

There was something about this kid that reminded me of my own son. Maybe it was the obsession with video games. Maybe it was because he was bilingual. Maybe it was because I was missing my son so much.

"Sure," I said.

He came over to my couch and plopped down beside me. I logged off my email and put away my laptop. He shook my hand—an oddly adult gesture—and told me his name was Mohammad and that he was 9 years old.

"I've been to Syria," I told him. "I liked it a lot. Where are you from in Syria?"

"Sayyida Zainab. Want to see it? It's on Youtube."

"Sure."

Then he showed me this video—bodies wrapped in bloodstained sheets being buried in a mass grave.

"They're dead," he said in a low voice.

I couldn't think of what to say. This kid was 9 and this was his reality. I've spent the past seven years protecting my son from the ugliness of the world. Mohammad's dad probably did the same thing until his country fell apart. After a moment I turned the video off.

"Don't watch that, it's sad," I told him.

"OK. Want to play some games?"

The speed with which his mood changed shocked me. I was still numb from what I had seen.

"Sure, Mohammad. Let's play some games."

Yes, Mohammad, be a kid.

He'd downloaded a bunch of free apps. We played one where Obama and Romney shoot ping pong balls at each other. I played Obama and won. It was close, though. Mohammad was obviously experienced at video games.

One of the hotel employees passed by.

"See that man?" Mohammad said. "I hate him. He do this to me to tease me."

He crossed his eyes. Suddenly I felt protective. Some guy was teasing Mohammad? For a moment it felt like someone had teased my own son.

"Can you do that?" he asked.

I crossed my eyes and wiggled my nostrils at him. He smiled.

"My brother can move his ears."

"I can't do that. Can you do this?" I rolled my tongue. He did the same.

We searched for more apps as the massacre at Sayyida Zainab replayed in my mind. One app took my photo and Mohammad used a razor to shave me bald. Then we played a game where a cat and dog throw bones at each other over a fence. I tried to let him win while he tried to let me win. I eventually won at letting him win. To assuage his sense of Arab hospitality he fetched me tea. Then we played a parking game.

"My father had a car but somebody take," Mohammad said, his voice going low again.

I flashed back to the video. What else did his family lose as they fled Syria?

He wasn't so good at parking. He kept hitting other cars. Eventually he gave up and got onto the app store to look for more games. One ad showed a woman in a bikini. He put his hand over it.

"Don't look, it's bad," he told me.

"OK."

Mohammad's two teenaged sisters, jeans showing under their abayas, sat at another couch nearby and occasionally added to the conversation from a distance. They told me they're on pilgrimage here. Najaf and the nearby city of Karbala are sacred to Shia Muslims. I was here seeing the same shrines.

"How long you stay in Najaf?" Mohammad asked me.

"I leave tomorrow."

His face fell.

"Oh. Let's play another game," he said.

"OK, Mohammad."

My group was already gathering to visit the local shrine of Imam Ali, which Mohammad's family had already visited. They were soon headed off to Karbala.

"You'll love Karbala," I told him. "The shrine is very beautiful." Like Syria used to be, I wanted to add.

"You not going to Karbala again?" he asked.

"No. Sorry, Mohammad."

Everyone was boarding the bus now. Reluctantly I got up and said goodbye. Mohammad looked sad.

"Keep practicing those games, kid," I said, forcing a smile.

Then I got on the bus and never saw him again.

Sometimes you meet people on your travels that stick with you long after you say goodbye. The 9-year-old boy who likes video games and survived a massacre is going to stick with me for a long time—that and the fact that a couple of those bodies were smaller than he is. ▨

Sean McLachlan on standing up for yourself and your stories

The best advice I can give to beginning writers is to be yourself and not worry about your audience. The public is invisible, fickle, and for the most part unknowable, so don't worry about establishing a readership. If you write well and consistently about topics that interest you, your readership will develop naturally. Many beginning writers worry far too much about the impression they're making. Do the highest quality work you can, and hope for the best. If a reader reaches out to you, by all means reply in a friendly and professional manner. I love hearing from readers. But don't worry too much about being on this year's social media bandwagon. Get into the best markets you can and deliver a quality product.

There's been a sea change in the style of writing that's in demand. Mobile devices and computers encourage a quicker reading style. My online editors are constantly pushing for image-driven short pieces. Short, buzzy pieces are fine for some subjects, but others deserve more depth. Push back against the trend toward trivialization. You can't write about Syria in a listicle. You can't do a Top Ten slideshow on illegal immigration. Well, you can, but you'll look like a chump. Some topics are complex, and the only way to cover them properly is with a longer, more detailed piece.

This doesn't mean you have to always write in-depth analysis. You can sometimes find a subject that evokes the topic in a creative way, like this story about the Syrian kid wanting to play video games with me. Mohammad needed to hold on to some of his childhood, while the harsh reality of his life kept breaking through. My editor, Grant Martin, immediately saw the potential of the piece. I hardly ever had to push back with him. Someone higher up in AOL Media, however, wanted us to publish a photo of Mohammad playing video games. The reason why this would be a bad idea should be blatantly obvious to anyone. Instead, we illustrated the online story with a link to the YouTube video Mohammad had shown me. That illustrated his story far better and kept him safe.

It can be difficult for beginning writers to stand up to editors. Remember that you have one advantage over your editors—you know the subject better than they do. Explain to them why something needs to be done in a certain way. If your reasons are good enough and presented clearly enough, you'll win out more often than not.

Push to broaden your range too. Like many professional writers, I do a range of writing, including reportage, essays, travelogues, reviews, history books, short stories, and novels. On a single day last week I reported on an art opening, worked on an archaeology booklet, and wrote a chapter of my next post-apocalyptic novel. Most writers have eclectic interests, so why limit yourself? One of the great rewards of this career is exploring all the things in the world you're curious about.

REAMING THE CUBE

Jason Effmann

8:05 a.m., Grand Entrance

The fluorescent light above my head is flickering between almost and completely off as it continues its prolonged and erratic demise. Over the wall to my right, a short, thirtysomething pair of muttonchops slurps coffee through the Pez-sized hole of a Starbucks cup. He's sporting a nylon tracksuit jacket, cargo shorts, flip-flops and a wool stocking cap. It's a look that says July. And January. With our only window at the far end of the hall it's hard to tell, and this is all Steve's worn since moving in eight months ago.

Steve's business cards say *Designer,* but he has taken on the additional role of sentry, routinely warning us in advance of our marketing manager's arrival. Ted's appearance in the hallway launches Steve into a soft whistle that slides down in pitch, as though something is falling from the sky. The closer Ted gets, the lower the whistle drops—and woeful are the mornings when Ted gets stopped in conversation, freezing Steve on the same note for several minutes. When at last Ted rounds the corner and enters the cube to the left of mine, the disproportionately loud crash of his backpack against the thinly carpeted concrete floor provides the impact and the punch line Steve is looking for. But before anyone lets out so much as a snicker, Ted is drowning out the team with a push of the speakerphone button on his coal-gray, office-issue phone, signaling that quiet hours are over and the work day is to begin in earnest.

The monotonously friendly female robo-voice trumpets Ted's progress through his voicemail to the entire office via the square-inch speaker: "WELCOME TO THE PHONE MAIL SYSTEM. PLEASE ENTER YOUR PASSWORD."

Four beeps, all of the same pitch—probably zeroes. "YOU HAVE (pause) SEVEN (pause) NEW MESSAGES. TO LISTEN TO YOUR MESSAGES, PLEASE PRESS THREE." Another beep. "FIRST MESSAGE, SENT. . ."

And that seems like as good a cue as any to bury the Apple-issue white ear buds deep into my ears, crank the instrumental mix I've created especially for this occasion, and pray for deliverance.

The cubicle's first lie is woven into its name. For it is neither a cube—as one might logically assume—nor in any way suitable for use as a bedroom, which is the word's origin. (*Latin,* cubiculum, *from* cubare, *"to lie down."*) Rather, the one I occupy measures eight feet across by 12 feet deep, with 5-and-a-half-foot walls—just tall enough so that most men and only about half of the women can peer over it. I know of nothing good in this world founded upon deceit, and the cube's vices don't stop with its name. Designed in the 1960s—either by staff at Intel or Herman Miller Furniture (neither claims credit)—its intent was to cure inefficiencies and inequities in the workplace. Instead, its flimsy, fist-thick panels are a brick wall to productivity, collaboration and creativity, and can turn work—not necessarily a Platonic Academy to begin with—into a surprisingly lonely endeavor.

For the first four years of my adult life, I'd managed to avoid them altogether. Upon graduation, I joined a gaggle of fellow greenhorns in an experimental newsroom in Chicago's western suburbs, slinging lead sentences over a low-lying partition—a Maginot Line that did little but keep pens from rolling out of sight. Out in the open like the Canada geese grazing across the street, we behaved as any flock would: maintaining constant communication, keeping watch over each other, asking directions on transitions, and pointing out any blind spots or weaknesses. We stuck together, sitting in the same positions at tables in bars as we did in the office. The younger writers learned from the veterans, who kept them out of harm's way until they were strong enough to fend for themselves.

By the time I'd acquired all the necessary survival skills, I was leaving that nest for a magazine gig downtown that included an office of my own. Granted, I shared it with the water heater and custodial closet. But there was also a door to close and a window to stare longingly out of whenever deadlines approached. Both were invaluable in a role I was never really cut out to take and all too eager to leave. Two years in, the job and the city had worn on me. I was ready for regular hours and better pay in a location that suited me. So like a lemming following a cliché over the cliff, I moved west, lured by greener pastures, a milder climate and a role as copywriter at a large corporation. The job sounded creative. The campus looked like a major university. The employees weren't forced to share a single toilet. As I leapt, any concerns about working in a cubicle were lodged in the very back of my mind, alongside 80s-era basketball players and my middle school locker combination.

One rule in life I have subsequently learned to stick by is to always look before you leap. While the role was everything I'd hoped, the only space available upon my arrival stranded me far away from the five other writers in the company, making learning how to do my job remarkably difficult. For the first year my main concern wasn't how to succeed, but how to move closer to either the team or the window—if I wasn't going to have the protection and camaraderie of the group, the least I could get was a little sunshine. When it became apparent that I wasn't going anywhere, and when some of the other writers began to fall prey to the sharp teeth of corporate reality, my survival instinct kicked in and I began to look around for a way to hold on to both my job and my sanity until I figured the place out. And one of the earliest and easiest conclusions to reach was that the cubicles we all inhabited were like zoo enclosures—offering the thin illusion of solitude, while allowing anyone to peer over the wall and see what you've got that they might be interested in. If you wanted to keep your ideas or your gum to yourself, it wouldn't be a bad idea to lock them in your cabinet when you step away from your desk.

9:27 a.m., Sneezing Fit

Our cubes are arranged into tidy lines of five, sharing a middle partition with another five. In effect, everyone faces someone else, though the wall typically prevents that unless both parties are standing (hey, it happens). The teams are all bundled together: producers, designers, marketers, product managers, and me. I am the sole writer for a team of 20, third in a cube of five, essentially in the middle of the row. It is the only time in my life I have felt crowded and lonely at the same time.

Directly across from me is Julie, a producer whose sneeze could knock jets out of the sky. It's one of those "ha-CHA" sneezes that sounds like a black belt trying to break a cinder block with her elbow, and it's always loud enough to jolt me out of my seat, even when I'm wearing my headphones. Julie has a severe pollen allergy and two germ-infested elementary schoolers, so sneezing has become her calling card. And on this particular day, she's putting together a notably voluminous string of scream-backed nasal evacuations. I lose my train of thought, and another product name slips out of my head and into the ether.

Colds here are passed around more frequently than PowerPoint presentations. If a kid brings a bug home from school and gives it to a parent, it'll infest our office for the next month. That's because most people feel an obligation to show up to work regardless of their condition, and without regard for those who suddenly find themselves within range of patient zero. These mucus troopers not only deliver their work on time, but add their virus as an attachment. I've never been as sick, as often, as I have since working here. No wonder the convenience store on campus stocks three types of cold medication.

Basic ecology reinforces the prevailing employee suspicion that nesting in cubicles may not necessarily be good for one's mental and physical health. No other animal operates in this manner. They either congregate in open space, believing there's strength in numbers, or go it alone, tucked quietly away with their solitude and self-reliance. Not a single animal in its right mind would limit itself to only one escape route, in an area rife with its own species. There'd be too much competition for resources, too much chance of predation or the spread of disease. My Environmental Biology professor would argue that if my coworkers were birds, most of them would be dead by now.

On the plus side, at least the birds that remained would get offices.

10:58 a.m. Chatter

"Hey Doug, you there?"
(Mouth full of something) "Ted, that you?"
"Did you get my proposal?"
(Slightly more comprehensible) "Uhhhhhh. . . No, did you e-mail it?"
"Yesterday."
"Oh, yeah, here it is. Thanks."
Since the arrival of the cubicle, words have replaced smoke as the greatest source of pollution in office buildings. With the false sense of privacy

that a 66-inch-high wall brings, there is none of the polite consideration that one gets, say, on public transportation. People consider themselves free to inject themselves into any conversation, and to make their point at any volume possible. For those whose jobs predominantly involve roaming from one meeting to another, that doesn't present much of a problem. But for anyone who is required to sit, think, and generate a coherent thought, the environmental effects of a cube are akin to trying to write poetry from the bleachers of a livestock auction, where the call and response between the first cow and the herd escalates in volume like a giant game of bovine Marco Polo.

Those cries for attention and direction are understandable. In a large company such as this, with thousands of employees and only so many corner offices, the vast majority spends their time passing through a maze of identical cubicles to get to the one with their nameplate perched atop it. Over the past seven years, I've unpacked boxes, painted ceilings and rearranged the furniture in four different homes, only to depart five times a week to come and push pins into the dolphin-gray walls of the same cubicle I've had since 2005. It has outlasted five pets, two cars and one marriage. Yet, on occasions more frequent than I'm comfortable admitting—if, say, the elevator stops a floor earlier than expected while I have my face buried in my phone—I walk into the wrong one by mistake, startling both myself and the rightful occupant.

Which at least partly explains the marking.

There is a ritualistic marking of territory that goes on in most cubicles. Steve refuses to participate in this, explaining, "I don't want to give anyone the idea that I'm happy here." To everyone else, however, that's exactly the idea they're trying to convey—or if not happy, at least firmly entrenched. With no door, front gate, moat or drawbridge, it's natural to feel under threat of invasion, to want to define and defend your 528 cubic feet of turf—no matter how undesirable it would be under any other circumstance. No one truly buys into the idea of job security, no one holds their fate in their own hands, so we take the one physical thing we can affect—a space designed to be impersonal and temporary, fitting anyone by suiting no one—and try to give it a sense of personal permanence. We try to make it a home away from home, when in reality it's just a room at the Best Western with the door kicked in.

That doesn't stop people from trying. The athletic employees affix race bibs and basketball jerseys to the walls with clear pushpins, while proud mothers weigh down desks with framed photos of their kids and dogs. Producers add bookcases. Designers wallpaper over the backdrops with gigantic posters that look incomprehensibly cool. But on any corner of the poster there is always the pushpin, beyond every poster edge the gray wall. No matter how different our jobs, we all inhabit the same basic space, and no desk can be raised high enough to see the forest for the reams of recycled printer paper.

12:33 p.m. Lunch

The fruit flies are at it again. I went to grab the banana I brought in yesterday, and three of them leapt up from behind it like they were going to rob me. Custodial has put traps on the tops of our cube walls to fight this ongoing occupation, but the fruit flies have no interest. Personally, I don't blame them. There's enough real food to go around in my cube alone.

I have a habit of eating at my desk. I like to cook, so most of the time the smell of leftovers spills over my cubicle wall and into the adjoining open space. Ted is constantly asking me what I have on the menu for the day. Sometimes it's homemade macaroni and cheese, others times slow-cooked pesto lasagna or stir-fried peanut noodles. My response draws audible oohs. The food itself draws fruit flies. And the act of eating it seems to attract fly-bys. Whatever and whenever I have lunch, it's almost always interrupted by someone stepping into the doorway and cornering me about a project. There I sit, a deer in headlights with pesto on his muzzle, while someone rambles through intricate details from a meeting I should have attended but wasn't invited to. Two things always run through my head at this moment. The first is that this conversation could've have waited until I finished. The second is that I shouldn't be eating in my cubicle in the first place. This is my one opportunity a day to break bread and my antisocial behavior, and I'm spending it with my back turned on the world, as usual.

The cube certainly has something to do with this. But so do our own hang-ups. I get to decide how I'm going to react to the two people who are talking, literally behind my back, about the project I'm working silently on barely four feet away. Just like I get to decide whether to eat the lonely cupcake on the counter behind me, the one left over from Julie's birthday. The cubicle's own noncommittal nature—neither open nor closed, private nor public, quiet nor loud—forces us to make the choices. And while its construction may slightly favor isolation, it does ultimately leave the decision in our hands as to whether we embrace a pack mentality or retreat into our wood-veneered shells.

The problem: it only takes a few fighting over who gets to be the alpha dog to send everyone else scrambling for cover.

4:47 p.m. Exit

As I lean all the way back in my chair and stare up at the two pinkening fluorescent bulbs—the world's most depressing sunset—I am thinking about leaving. Not for the evening. For good. And not immediately. But I have begun to wonder, mostly out of curiosity, how long I can cut it in this cubicle. It's natural to want to move on, up, or even just across, particularly when you've loitered for so long in a space that feels so temporary. It's like waiting for a bus that's five years late. As I close my eyes to give them a reprieve from the light that's bombarded them for the past nine hours, I come to the conclusion that's the point of cubicles—to make you itchy for change and challenge, to not get too comfortable and complacent. At least that's how I'm justifying the daydream that Julie's latest sneeze knocks me out of. It's another screamer, the sort that causes grocery store employees to chime in "Bless You" over the intercom. I tighten my jawline and shorten my timeline.

According to recent history, there appear to be two distinct methods of cubicle flight available to individuals: The Door or The Ladder.

The Door is easiest to visualize. At the end of a particularly frustrating day at work, you place your hands on top of your desk, push up, stand up, turn around, and walk out, never to return again. You leave the always cozy, occasionally infuriating confines of a cube farm and escape back into the wild. It is also the hardest to execute, because saying you're going to throw away a satisfying career at a stable company that pays you well and actually doing it are two entirely different matters. I am aware, even thankful, of the fact that this place has made me soft, that leaving at this point and in this manner would be the human equivalent of a Yorkshire terrier joining a wolf pack. That's the type of leap that requires confidence and a ferocious will, and separates the copywriters from the writers and the graphic designers from the artists. And I might not be fond of my cube, but I have yet to muster up the courage to call myself a writer.

So Ladder it is. Only it, too, presents some significant and inextricably linked problems. First, a ladder of this size with this many people on it can take an eternity to climb; there are 20-year veterans still holding meetings with their employees in cafeteria booths. And if you resolve to bypass those somewhat lengthy timelines, trying to expedite your rise to one of the higher rungs may mean questionable decisions or somewhat regrettable actions. I've watched incredibly talented, completely lovely people forgo the strongest aspects of their work and their personalities in order to one day be able to shut a door and eat their lunch in peace.

There is a third option beginning to crop up now, one that requires none of these sacrifices on the part of the employee. It is to follow the instructions Reagan gave Gorbachev and *tear down that wall.* Convert the zoo into a safari. Replace cubicles with open spaces. Get rid of the cages and turn people loose, trusting in their abilities and in the better aspects of their nature. Make the office a place for ideas instead of jealousies. The rows where the facilities folks have removed all trace of cubicle parts seem larger, livelier, almost unrecognizable from their counterparts just a row over. The same could be said of the people working there. They bounce around. They are raucous when the mood calls for it, respectfully quiet when a few among them need silence to work. It fills me with envy. And hope.

Last Wednesday I called facilities to ask if they could take my cube walls down. It's not my call to make. But it seems only natural to let an animal stretch its legs now and again, before its instinct tells it to bolt. 🔲

Jason Effmann on streamlining writing
and getting out of the way

I knew from the age of eight that I wanted to be a writer. I volunteered to write the family Christmas letter before we even had a family Christmas letter. I relished every writing assignment we ever had in school—not because it was an easy A, but because it always felt like play to me. Telling a story is creative play. As a writer, you are a magician conjuring reality out of thin air, and people will always want you to show them something they cannot see for themselves.

In college, my professors typically described my writing as "wordy," "heavy," or "purple"—a bruised and bloated literary corpse. In the four-year period right out of college, I made foolish mistakes at a thousand miles an hour while trying to copy the writers I most admired. When I moved from newspaper and magazine writing to more commercially based opportunities, my word count went from five thousand per month to about six. This is only a mild exaggeration. The streamlining process had an impact on all of my writing—that quicker, sparer style just sounds better. It has more velocity, and now I'm taking that style and stretching it out to longer forms.

One day I'll get to stop going to work, but I'll always be a writer. For as long as I'm able I will always be playing around on a keyboard, trying to make the words ring as clear and true on the page as they do in my head.

When a story's done well, it looks like a tango, an elegant series of steps executed in graceful sequence and perfect rhythm. But for me it always starts out looking like the Electric Slide—a lot of repetition, a lot of bumping into others, a lot of missed beats and awkward, drunken movements. It takes me a long time to get the choreography right. I'll put the first few paragraphs down, write the fourth, then dive back into the first three to carve out a better path from one to four.

A lot of my focus during revision is on getting out of the way of the story. Anton Chekhov's rule that if you hang a rifle on the wall in the first chapter it has to go off by the third is one of the best pieces of advice a writer can carry. Often, in the reporting of a story, we get delicious quotes or details that we feel intense desire and pressure to share. But if they're tangential, they don't belong. Great stories make you feel like you're strapped onto a racehorse. You're not taking in the entire view—just the landmarks and actions that are essential to getting to the finish line intact and in front.

Find what makes your voice and the story you're telling unique and compelling. Twist the medium to your message—it's only a medium, after all. None of this is sacred.

A SAD THOUGHT DANCED

Suan Pineda

His rancid odor, of midnight smoke soaked in days-old liquor, broods around me. Somehow, intense smells at either end of the spectrum incite the same reaction. Heavy cologne. Sewer water. It's the same. The man dangles a bottle in his trembling, muddy hands, and tumbles toward me. And his beard—his beard bears the signs of many wandering nights, like this one. I prepare to sidestep him as he approaches me, but the zigzagging couples shish-shinging their feet on an improvised dance floor detour his path.

"El tango te llama," he growls as the swarm of tightly embracing dancers swallows him. "The tango calls you." This tango, in Plaza Dorrego in San Telmo, Buenos Aires, nestled under the sweet daze of dim lights, is carried on the bandoneón's cry through the whistling tree leaves, transpiring in the streets where Argentina recovers five years after its gravest economic crisis.

Maybe it's the fetor. Maybe it's a drunkard's aphorism. Maybe it's the distorted lament pouring out of an old record player or the newness of my *milonga* journey's first stop, but here under the muted Buenos Aires sky, I feel close to the heart of tango, which perhaps beats more intensely after a testing ordeal. This tango is mortal, with flesh and sweat and stench—too human for my glamorized fantasy.

"Tango is a one-way journey," Romina Lenci cautioned me before my trip. "You don't come back." Romina has surrendered to that fate; she has danced tango for more than a decade, and she sees no return. But that just emboldened me. I guess I'm just as intoxicated with the possibilities of tango—with the romanticism of surrendering to a stranger, with the relief of not knowing where I'm going and not caring—as any other rookie, as any other outsider. But I have another morbid yearning: I want to confirm that doomed Argentine cycle, epitomized in the back-and-forth, twisting steps of tango. Tango, after all, is the well where Argentine thinkers and corner drunkards look for *la argentinidad.*

I throw a furtive look at Guillermo Segura, who, in utter contrast with the drunkard, stands stoically beside me, his tall, clean-cut silhouette squeezing through the mountains of shadows that stand shoulder to shoulder on the dusty wooden dance floor. Languid feet fly like birds over the peaks and valleys. Guillermo, eyes half-closed, remains silent, but occasionally blurts out little snippets about tango, about his life.

He started dancing tango after he separated from his partner.

He despises the old-fashioned tango rituals.

He's just waiting for Argentina's next crisis—economic or political.

"Every ten years there's a crisis"

Tonight, nothing seems to surprise Guillermo. Not this decaying lushness, not all the hype about his country's miraculous recovery. In early 2002, the value of the peso dropped 75 percent. Five presidents took office in ten days. Half the country fell below the poverty line. Five years later the new president, Cristina Fernández de Kirchner, seems to continue Argentina's new chapter, which was started with her husband, Néstor Kirchner. But even this new chapter is tainted by doubt (reports about misleading inflation numbers emerge) and pessimism (economic gains still haven't solved pivotal social issues).

And to that, Guillermo seems to stand unfazed; he submerges himself in tango and waits for the next low. "Every ten years there's a crisis," he says. It's a learned line that almost every Argentine disguises as a self-sabotaging joke. "It's mathematical," he grins as he counts in his head—just a couple more years. I wonder if he could smell the storm coming.

To survive their tribulation, many Argentines are pinning their hopes on tourism to bring the country's economy back to health. Tourism, an industry that boomed after the recession, is Argentina's third source of revenue, bringing in more than $4 billion in 2007. And in times of crisis, improvisation—as always—came in handy; the tango scene was reinvigorated with an increasing number of lessons and clubs. From three-figure tango packages at the Buenos Aires Hilton, to shows in La Ventana and Madero Tango, to low-key, low-budget classes in hostels such as Sandanzas, tango is the well Argentina is drawing from for its selling essence.

Its people, however, can't help but cloud those hopeful signs with skepticism.

Here, in the half-lit Plaza Dorrego, in a culture of muffled extremes and controlled debauchery, nothing appears to have changed, yet everything has happened. Signs of the nation's revival are clear though fragile, as they lie alongside the scars: graffiti decrying corruption and calling for presidents to step down scratch historic buildings; a beautiful boy huddling in a street corner, clothes torn, eyes shut, lost.

Avenida Corrientes: a twilight zone

Having seen enough, Guillermo tries to figure out our way out of the labyrinthine cobblestone streets of the tango barrio.

"San Telmo disconcerts me," he mutters as we dodge the cracks on the impossibly narrow sidewalks. We move swiftly, breathe in spring's silvery air, leave block after block behind us, cross over spilled garbage, pass the tumultuous Plaza de Mayo, where pigeons flock during the afternoon. Their flight, a mirage of lazy days, deflates the brewing intensity of innumerable protests. Then, the ever-expanding Avenida Corrientes, that decadent boulevard that harbors the city's sensibility and broods tango, unfolds before us.

It is around 10 p.m.; the streets are waking up for the famous Buenos Aires nightlife. There is no better stage than Corrientes to showcase its contradictions: the glitzy theater plays and hectic nocturnal revelry amid the constant rummaging of *cartoneros* (collectors of cartons) among the garbage.

It's like a twilight zone, *la argentinidad* and the blinding lights in an unusually deserted Corrientes. The street widens, and on its concrete horizon rests the translucent Obelisco, defiantly piercing the blue night. Guillermo is warming up to me now and is more talkative. So I ask this question, which I figure these days is as normal as asking how someone is: "How did you survive the crisis?

With a nonchalant tone, he said he was OK.

A physicist at an oil company. OK.

Did he want to leave the country, like the 300,000 who fled the recession? "I like having a place to belong to."

Buenos Aires is his home. And that's that.

Tango: resignation and rebellion

We leave Corrientes and descend into the dim grotto of the *subte*, the metro. Our next *milonga* is several stations away. Encased in this metallic worm, blank stares and lifeless expressions seem to fade in the fluorescent daze as time creeps by with each lulling revolution of the train. A slender girl sits across from us, her black-tight legs crossed, her hair entangled in a bun, and in her lap, a tango-shoes bag. I can't wait to get out.

As the train makes a stumping stop, Guillermo points out that just a few blocks away are the slums, called *villas miseria*, which ironically are what the most luxurious buildings look out over. After the crisis, many moved into shantytowns and have not come out.

He falls silent, again.

I wonder if Guillermo's deadpan expression and sporadic blasts of laughter are a disguise for that ingrained melancholy so well known in tango, an amalgam of resignation and rebellion to a condemned cycle: 1966—rise of the military dictatorship; 1976—dirty war; 1989—economy melts down; 2002—half the population falls below the poverty line after years of illusory bonanza. The trajectory of Argentina's roller-coaster history seems to eerily mirror tango's serpentine yet cyclical path. "Every ten years there's a crisis," I remind myself; I've heard it so many times.

La Glorieta: scene of contradictions

Ten blocks and a *subte* ride later, we arrive at La Glorieta, a pavilion in Barrancas de Belgrano, one of the well-off parts of town. La Glorieta is a *milonga* hot spot during summer and spring. On this late October night, it's packed. A nerdy-looking guy twirls his partner, the girl from the metro, counterclockwise. She does the *caminado* (walking) with her eyes closed and the side of her head glued to her partner's.

I look around. It's fair ground: all ages, nationalities, and skill levels. Amateurs, who stay in the middle, to veteran *tangueros*, who loop the outskirts of the round pavilion.

"The *milonga* is a place that gathers very special people, lonely people, whose heads are a mess," says Romina, whose ancestors have danced tango for as far as she can remember. "Some people go to therapy, others go to *milongas*."

In the months after the latest crisis, Romina noticed differences in the *milonga* scene: some perfunctory, some profound. To dance, people didn't fix up as nicely as before. But they would go to the *milonga* after a *cacerolazo*, where, banging pots and pans, they would protest against the government.

La Glorieta is getting crowded. I huddle in a corner, still insecure of my tango skills and still rusty with the do-you-want-to-dance rituals. Guillermo has already done a few rounds. From one end, he spots me, and with an energy I haven't seen before, he walks toward me grinning and introduces me to Regina Alleman. Poised as a delicate tulip, Regina talks with that Argentine cadence and glides her slim frame in the arms of a *milonguero*. I think Regina is a Buenos Aires native until she says she moved here from Switzerland two years ago following the call of tango.

It was the paradox that attracted her. "The city, like tango, has this contradiction: joy and sadness, people that are open and people who are mistrustful [living in the same place and time]." Though she arrived three years after the economic meltdown, Regina can still perceive the fear in people. "However, [the crisis] did yield something positive," she says: "People live in the moment."

In this moment, beads of sweat glide down foreheads, heels and sneakers mingle in a poetry of movement. It's been almost an hour since I arrived at La Glorieta, and the crowd is overflowing. The music—a mix of old and new tango—fills the plaza: Los Reyes del Tango, Juan D'Arienzo, Orquesta Fernández Fierro, Osvaldo Pugliese and an occasional batch of salsa, rock or swing between rounds of tango.

The last note dies away, but lingers in memory. The crowd spreads to all directions, and I reunite with Guillermo at the foot of the stairs where a line of girls are taking off their heels and changing into tennis shoes. Sandra, a petite brunette with a quick smile, packs up her tango shoes and pulls out a map from her bag. We join her and agree to go to Porteño y Bailarín, in Riobamba.

The night is young.

A sad thought danced

On the meandering route 29 bus, our newly formed trio navigates the clogged veins of a proud, bruised Buenos Aires, the city of Jorge Luis Borges, of "the uncertain yesterday and different today," the home of 11 million souls. A bump, a turn, a stop. I begin to feel Buenos Aires' beat. Through the fingerprint-stained window, I see patches of light and darkness; European-style buildings and unassuming houses; shadows swallowed by the light of a night lived as day.

Porteño y Bailarín bears a more formal demeanor than La Glorieta. Guillermo is not fond of this smoky place: He doesn't like the old rituals, like the *cabeceo* (when a man asks a woman to dance with a head movement), that are still practiced in traditional *milongas*, and the two dance floors—one for veterans (all dressed in dark attires, sitting stoically at minimalist tables) and another for the younger, rookie crowd, squeezed in the back.

Sweet cologne, aired wine, used air. We make our way through the hall. A few heads turn, murmurs tickle our ears as we scurry among tables. I'm walking walked paths, of immigrants, of prostitutes, of taxi drivers, of pathologists, of seized memories. In the back, we find a spot. Is this *la argentinidad*? Squeezed between social lines, among the cracks of a tired valley, walked over time and again? Reinventing, reducing, resuming the journey to a known end?

Extremes, in the end, meet at the same place.

"Do you tango?" a man asks me from his corner, skipping the *cabeceo* ritual, breaking conventions.

"No," I say from my end. I'm tired. I'm afraid. I'm not ready to plunge into the endless walk of tango. Not tonight; tonight I can only watch.

But Guillermo, despite his reservations about the place, lunges into a tango with Sandra. It's better to dance than to stand still.

"Tango is a sad thought you dance," Enrique Santos Discépolo once said. The venerated tango lyricist's simple definition is in each step Guillermo propels and Sandra anchors—two shadows merged in their solitude, furling, breaking the monotony of the green walls that shelter their ephemeral escape from reality.

I watch them as I silently count the number of years to the next crisis. Five or four. That omen invariably hangs over every Argentine's head. But this night is old and tango is alive in Buenos Aires.

Guillermo walks me to a corner and helps me grab a cab back to my hostel. We promise to see each other the next day; we don't fulfill it. I get into the taxi. The city shines through the cab's window. The humid streets emanate a heavy, fishy mist, and once in a while I see dead pigeons on the sidewalks. 🔲

Suan Pineda on the beauty of language

Spanish is my first language. Mandarin is the language I speak at home. And English, for a long time, was a stranger. My encounter with English—in drips and drops during my adolescence, then in a flood during my early adulthood—was abrupt and somehow hostile. As a foreigner to the language, I felt edged out of a realm that loomed forever distant.

Elusive and tempered, English came from me in apprehensive and indifferent bursts. Learning a new language—and I mean, really learning it, to the point in which the voice that comes out of your mouth, the words that you write in that language sound not only at least partially true but also have a tinge of some familiarity—can be a violent endeavor, of taming, of domination, of resistance. The speaker and the spoken—at odds, first and forever, and then, with hope and some relinquishing, a hint of harmony.

Feeling exiled, I didn't understand its aesthetic and failed to grasp its beauty.

After years of learning it in school, of getting immersed in it during my first years in an American college, and particularly after several torturous writing classes, I started to regard English differently. I learned to love and employ its compactness, its crispness, its simplicity. The world unfolded anew before me—it was as if English had given me a periscope with which I could peer into my surroundings.

Verbs—oh, the richness of English verbs!—adjectives and phrases started to shape and even, perhaps, grant new sense to my experiences—however mundane they were. Piano music pouring out of a flower-rimmed balcony in a numbingly hot Madrid dusk turned into a poetic image that has been edged in my memory in words, twirling around me like a refreshing breeze.

English, learning to write and to find my voice as a writer in it, has changed me profoundly. Exactly how I cannot say, but I can attest that it has become, after years of heartache and joys, a space where I no longer feel estranged, where I'm at the same time bewildered and comforted. This is not to say, however, that my mind-set and worldview prior to my incursion into English have been subdued or silenced. Discovering the beauty of English not only enriched the possibilities of my writing in Spanish but also opened new avenues of perception and expression in the languages of my childhood.

The richness of seeing my surroundings in these three different registers—each one informing or silencing the other depending on the circumstances, my surroundings, my temperament—is how my voice has come to be. Each language occupies a unique space and conjures a distinctive feeling.

Mandarin is home. Spanish is heart. English is mind.

These are rather simplistic and absolute categories, so I should say that these are extremely porous and most times seem to work in parallel when I write in any of these languages. It is in the merging, the clashes, and the temporary reconciliation of these linguistic currents where I not only find my voice but also shape the way I look at the world when researching and writing a story.

However, the polyvalence of languages and the baggage and cultural context that they carry is a double-edged sword: it can be both utterly stifling and a great fountain of unexplored metaphors.

Now, more than a decade of living in the United States and of inhabiting English, so to speak, my voice—at times trembling and at others strangely reassured—is one in which these three languages, these three worlds, with all their richness and conflict, somehow reconcile.

THESE MOUNTAINS EAT MEN

Sara Shahriari

It was a Friday morning, and I was sitting in a mineshaft in Bolivia with 20 miners and a bag of entrails at my feet.

Four white llamas were slaughtered earlier in the day. Throats cut, they bled to death quickly. The miners masterfully butchered them, setting aside the meat for a dinner celebration, and the blood and entrails for Tío Supay, god of the mines. Ruy Lopez, one of the mine's directors, told me that preparing the offering correctly is crucial, so that Tío Supay will accept it and be appeased. Three miners died while at work in these mines last year, so honoring El Tío is a matter of life and death. If he's happy he can lead a man to wealth—if not, he may feast on his bones.

Working underground is a dangerous business here in Oruro, one in a string of mining towns that stretch along the mineral-rich Andes, where equipment consists of rubber boots, a headlamp, and a helmet. Dynamite explosions, collapsing tunnels, and poisonous gasses kill fast. Lung disease kills slowly. Either way, extracting tin and silver and from the rock is a brutal life, and although they are Catholics, everyone here recognizes other powers and pays tribute to Tío Supay.

Part of that tribute is drinking a lot and chewing wads of coca leaves, a stimulant that gives the miners energy. Dust particles and cigarette smoke swirled through the air like fog in headlamp beams. The beer, poured into a single communal plastic cup, made the rounds again and again. Every once in a while a milky white container filled with grain alcohol made a pass.

245

The miners shared stories as we floated on a cloud of booze and smoke. Ruy came to work in the mines after his father died young, leaving his sons to support the family—an experience many of the men share.

Soon it was time to make the offering to Tío Supay. Men took the bags of bones and entrails to an abandoned part of the mine, where they carefully distributed them, finally splashing blood on the walls. Then we all picked up and moved so that El Tío could feast in peace, in the dark, undisturbed.

Emerging from the mine into the afternoon sunlight, it was hard to believe that the world outside still existed. The darkness, the mood of the miners, the booze and stimulants made everything outside seem like a blazingly bright dream. But the party wasn't over yet. Llama was served in the miners' hall and the beer flowed even faster. The next day I woke up with a thumping hangover.

Two nights later I was on a crowded bus rocketing toward the city of Potosí as a lightning storm traced brilliant flashes over the dark plains. I wanted to understand more about the world of miners, the how and why of their work in these brutal and dangerous places.

Potosí was home to one of the richest silver mines the world has ever known and a great source of colonial Spain's wealth. People say you could build a bridge from here to Europe with silver that came out of the Cerro Rico, or Rich Hill, the mountain that dwarfs the city—or build two bridges from the bones of the African and Indian slaves who died mining and minting it. The city has a beautiful colonial center, testament to wealth that has since faded.

To the south the Cerro looms, a broad, rust-colored cone. Though it has been mined day and night for nearly five hundred years, a recent increase in mineral prices after a long slump is drawing more people to work the many small mines here in one of Bolivia's poorest regions. Some prosper, and stories of mattresses stuffed with cash are believable when a Hummer rolls through Potosí's narrow streets. But that remarkable prosperity reaches very few.

Patricia lives in the Calvario miners' encampment, at the very top of a series of steep stairs that lead up a hillside. The climb left me gasping for air. Patricia is a Quechua Indian wearing a knee-length velvet skirt, flat sandals, a cardigan, and two long black braids draping down her back. She is 28 and can barely read or write. The encampment was originally built by the state, back in the days when the government controlled more of Bolivia's mines, but today it forms a poor neighborhood where Patricia's family of seven squats in a one-room cement house with a tin roof, a rough concrete floor, two twin beds, and old dressers stuffed with clothes and blankets. The kids' clothes are dirty. There are a few dried pieces of meat stored in the rafters for meals.

Standing in front of the house all you see is the mountain. It dominates everything. Patricia's husband is a miner, but he left to visit a neighboring town two weeks before I met her. She says she's sure he'll be back, but she's not sure when. While he's gone she spins llama wool, sews, and washes clothes to get by, earning just a couple dollars a day—much less than the $150 a month her husband can make.

That's part of the world that surrounds the mines, but I also wanted to see conditions inside and speak with more workers. Enter Reynaldo Ramírez, a miner with an interesting second job that doesn't involve pickaxes and hauling heavy metal trolleys loaded with rock. Instead he guides a steady flow of visitors, drawn to the notorious and fascinating mountain, through its dark tunnels.

Reynaldo led me into one of the many mine mouths that dot the mountain, through a colonial stonework arch, legacy of the centuries the Cerro has been tunneled, dynamited, and dug into a maze that no one fully understands. Those who work near the entrance to the mine are lucky. It's flat. There are tracks and carts to move the rock in and out, fresh air filters in, and in most places you can stand upright. Going to the second level is not so easy.

Several hundred feet into the mountain, we reached a sort of crossroads, where dark tunnels stretched off in all directions toward the deeper levels. Here, as if on a throne, sits Tío Supay. Found in many mines, he is a man with long horns, a beard, and an erect penis, festooned with paper streamers and scattered with coca leaves—an amalgamation of the colonizing Catholic's image of a devil and the old beliefs in the sacred nature of mountains that existed before any Spaniard set foot here in search of silver. Beyond him, we began to descend via a steep three-foot-high tunnel. Crouched on our heels, we slid 30 feet into air that was suddenly hot and laced with suffocating dust.

The heat, the knowledge that hundreds of feet of rock rose over me, the splintering wooden posts supporting the tunnel, the thin air at 14,000 feet.

I still can't understand how tourists make it to the fourth level of the mine, or how Agustin, a 14-year-old miner I met, works on the sixth level for nine hours a day, six days a week, under hundreds of feet of rock in the burning heat at the heart of the mountain. To enter the mines is to feel the presence of Tío Supay everywhere and to understand that no matter how much blood and sacrifice you offer the Cerro in exchange for the mineral it gives up, it is easy to be eaten by the rock underground in the dark.

An hour later I stumbled out into daylight, squinting and struggling for air, and followed Reynaldo to meet Agustin's mother at her home. A 49-year-old woman who speaks only Quechua, she was sick with stomach pains and lay huddled in her bedroom, which is also the kitchen.

Agustin's father recently died of silicosis, the lung disease that kills many lifelong miners in their 40s and 50s. There is very little safety technology in the tiny mines in the Cerro Rico, and even the small things people could do to preserve their health, like buying masks to guard against the deadly dust, often go undone amidst the fatalism and daily relationship with danger that define their lives.

Now Augustin works because he has to support his mother and younger siblings. He plans to return to school next year, though I can't quite believe he'll get the chance. With no family to help and very little education, his life is now a circle of necessity, and the mine is the only form of survival that he knows. Even for those with education and the chance at other jobs, the tunnels are seductive, because in every miner's heart there's the hope that the next explosion, the next level down, the next tap of the hammer will mean money, security, even riches.

Augustin sitting outside his house, the gray rock dust still caked around the edges of his face and his fingernails, already looked like a ghost to me, and my heart broke for him. I had seen and heard what I came to learn: the necessity, hope, fatalism, and danger born in a world where the mine is life and death. Despite the white llamas and the blood sacrifices, even as the mountain gives miners the means to eat, to put a roof over their heads and send their children to school, it claims them. That's just the way things are. ▨

Sara Shahriari on being a successful freelancer

As a full-time freelancer based outside the United States I pitch a lot—at least four times a month, and often much more. There are several key ideas to keep hold of while pitching, the most important being understanding the publication you are pitching to. By reading several issues or scouring a website you can get an idea of the kinds of stories editors are looking for and use that information to model your pitch. If the wording and focus of a pitch are already in line with the publication, then I believe a writer stands a better chance.

Second, editors are extraordinarily busy people who generally don't have time to slog through a draft that needs drastic changes. In my experience, they like to hire writers who have already written the kind of story the editor is searching for. So if you want to work for a specific magazine or other outlet, concentrate on writing stories that will show the editors at that publication that you are capable of doing just the kind of work they need.

Most editors will get your pitch via email, so think a lot about how the pitch will appear on a screen. If an editor opens an email and sees a thousand-word block of text, he or she might put off or even delete such a major undertaking. I usually send fairly short pitches: just three paragraphs. The first one teases the story, showing why it is interesting and readable, the second uses a few facts and figures to establish the story's relevance and importance, and the final one gives an account of whom I will interview and how I will structure the story. That final paragraph, my plan of action, is important because it shows the editor I understand the topic enough to know how to report it. Then I attach links to two of my strong, recent stories.

Finally, having some sort of contact with the editor, whether it is through a colleague who can put you in touch or because you formerly worked or interned for the outlet, greatly increases your chances of getting a response to your pitch. Once you are in touch, build relationships with editors through consistent communication, sending quality stories and in general treating your editor as a respected coworker or manager. Being a writer editors can count on for good stories and strong collaboration will bring you more work.

I'm not saying that surviving as a freelance journalist is ever easy. In fact, not having health insurance through an employer or a steady paycheck and having to manage all your taxes and business administration yourself are issues I encourage all journalists to seriously consider before entering the freelance field. At the same time, freelance has offered me the opportunity to write almost exclusively about topics that are of great interest to me.

It's also important to be able to work across different types of media so that you can be competitive. For a long time the idea of the "backpack journalist" made me roll my eyes. How could anyone be an outstanding photographer, video producer, writer, and radio reporter all at the same time? Just managing all the equipment necessary to produce high-quality reporting for every possible form of media at the same time seemed absurd.

After several years of working internationally in the field, I've come to realize that the ability to work across platforms doesn't mean I have to do work in them all, all the time. It's good to have one or two specialty areas but also gain a basic understanding of as many additional skills as you can.

PART III

Personal Stories and Memoirs

PART III CONTENTS

Without Completely Falling Apart
Jessi Hamilton
A phone call from her father informs Hamilton that her aunt has
been raped. Reeling from the pain of loving someone who's been
deeply hurt, she discovers that rape harms a family as well as the
victim.   285

When Nationalism Trumps Race
Melanie Coffee
A young African American reporter covers an anti-Muslim protest in Chicago after 9/11. As rioters scream "Down with brown!"
she is fearful for her safety until she realizes that, for once, their
racism is not directed at her.   289

Soul Train on Mute
Michaella A. Thornton
In rural North Carolina, Thornton is stranded for two years in
the Teach for America program. Through her eccentric and racist landlords, she realizes that her own biases can further the distance to meaningful social change.   297

1202 Park Avenue, 1999
Sona Pai
Three soon-to-be college graduates live in their first real home. As
they revel in the freedom of sitting with their shoes on the couch
and smoking inside, they learn to grow up.   311

FAYE'S ASHES

Shane Epping

When my wife Mary and I prepared for a two-week summer trip to Spain, we packed lightly. My friend Ramón lived in Galicia, located in the northwest corner of the country, and I hadn't seen him in 17 years. We were good friends in college and he took care of me more than once when I needed support. Ramón and I lost touch for a few years but once we re-connected I made an effort to not lose him again. After an almost unspeakable sadness engulfed my wife and me that spring, we accepted Ramón's invitation to visit him and his family, trusting our friendship hadn't faded at a time when Mary and I needed to get away. Our baggage included two carry-on suitcases, a backpack, and my camera gear. Everything we needed for the trip was within reach on the plane. Nothing was out of our hands. And even though we weren't taking much with us, we would be leaving something behind. Our daughter, Faye. She died in the spring and a spoonful of her ashes would eventually enter the Bay of Biscay on the northern coast of Spain. A part of us would forever rest in a foreign land, where neither Mary nor I had ever been or may never return. It would be the first time we ever let her go.

The first leg of our journey began in St. Louis where we boarded a plane and flew to Toronto. We ate in the Canadian airport where overpriced, really bad hamburgers would later take their toll on my insides. Once we were in the air, the pain in my stomach was sharp. And then the plane began to shake. Turbulence. "Monsieur? Monsieur?," the flight attendant repeatedly asked as she tapped lightly on the folding door. I said nothing. I held my head in my hands and closed my eyes. "Monsieur? Monsieur?," she said again. A few minutes later, I returned to my seat. Mary was taking pills to combat her recent fear of flying so the less said about feeling out of control the better. For both of us, it was an uncomfortable journey.

Much of the flight was overnight so when I saw the light emerging above the clouds, I noticed it immediately. I grabbed my camera from beneath the seat and began to make photos. The early morning colors silhouetted the wing of the plane. From top to bottom, the spectrum included black, blue, yellow, orange, red, and black again. The contrast was strong and I couldn't believe more people weren't awake. I may have seen more beautiful sunrises in my life, but I don't know when. I thought about lead singer Jeff Mangum of Neutral Milk Hotel and his lyrics:

> And one day we will die, and our ashes will fly
> from the aeroplane over the sea,
> but for now we are young, let us lay in the sun,
> and count every beautiful thing we can see.

Mary was listening to her iPod and she shared an ear bud with me. The Avett Brothers played "The Ballad of Love and Hate":

> Love arrives safely with suitcase in tow,
> carrying with her the good things we know,
> a reason to live and a reason to grow, to trust, to hold, to care. . .
> Hate stumbles forward and leans in the door.
> Weary head hung down, eyes to the floor.
> He says, "Love, I'm sorry," and she says,
> "What for? I'm yours and that's it, whatever.
> I should not have been gone for so long.
> I'm yours and that's it, forever.
> You're mine and that's it, forever."

The combination of a beautiful sunrise, lyrics to one of my favorite songs, and the fact that we were carrying Faye's ashes, made me cry. This was my introduction to Spain.

As the sun set on August 27, 2011—the year before Mary and I traveled to Spain—we celebrated our fourth wedding anniversary in Rocheport,

Missouri, the same place we were married. Our table was next to a window and included a view of the sun sinking beneath the Missouri River. We had two big reasons to celebrate. Mary was pregnant and we planned to call our parents after dinner to deliver the news. Mary had had a miscarriage the previous year, so we were happy to have another chance at parenthood. We first called her parents in Omaha and then my mom in Moberly, Missouri, where both she and I were born. My mom, a caregiver for her father who passed away after fighting Alzheimer's and her mother who had recently endured brain surgery, was in need of good news. She wanted something to look forward to that wouldn't end sadly. A baby represents the antithesis of death. Birth is life. An only child, I was offering Mom a chance to be a grandmother for the first time. None of us knew it at the time, but that offer would be unfulfilled. All of us would outlive a child yet to be born.

After the miscarriage, Mary's visits to the doctor were an emotional roller coaster. We heard a heartbeat and saw a small embryo after the first sonogram. There was an option to determine the baby's gender but we chose to keep it a surprise. When my friend Yanni visited that fall, he asked if I hoped for a boy. I said that I didn't care. I had seen a documentary about a child born with Trisomy 18, a genetic disorder in which an infant has a third copy of material from chromosome 18 instead of the usual two copies, a fatal abnormality, and it hit me hard. The baby's name was Thomas and he only lived a few days. Watching a couple lose a child after a full-term pregnancy is almost impossible to witness. Many other friends couldn't finish the video. It was too hard. So responding to Yanni's question, I said, "I used to say that I expected to have a son, but I honestly don't care anymore. Boy or girl, I just hope it's healthy." A few weeks later, Mary and I would find out that we would be living in Thomas's parents' shoes. What was impossible for others to watch was going to be our lives. And there was nothing we could do about it.

At 20 weeks of pregnancy, the doctor suspected a problem and sent us to a specialist the same day. When we entered his waiting room, the mood was noticeably different from the one we'd just left. People in this room weren't happy to be here. Like us, they were here because of a serious problem. The décor was immaculate, calming, spacious, quiet, yet full of gloom. After conducting an amniocentesis, where a needle was inserted through

Mary's abdominal wall, then through the wall of her uterus, and finally into the amniotic sac, the specialist withdrew amniotic fluid for a genetic diagnosis. He overnighted the fluid out of state for examination and told us he would contact us in a day or two. His deadline came and went, forcing us to wait longer than we expected. He finally called Mary and told her that our baby had Trisomy 18. He or she might not make it to birth, and if so, life expectancy wouldn't be long. We decided to find out Faye's gender and give her a name. The journey was going to be a short one. We wanted to bond with her immediately. Mary was halfway through her pregnancy. The next four months she carried a baby, not knowing whether the unborn child's heart would keep beating. Mary was attentive to Faye's movements and questioned the baby's health when there was prolonged inactivity. Sometimes Mary wondered if she could carry on. Her only hope was that she could eventually hold her daughter, alive, for at least a few minutes after birth. We turned down all offers for baby showers and we decided not to decorate a nursery. Prior to the Trisomy 18 diagnosis, Mary bought a personalized onesie with a camera on it because I'm a photographer and she knew I'd love it. I wondered if the outfit would ever be worn.

For Thanksgiving, Mary and I hosted a turkey dinner for our immediate family members. There were four generations at the table: my grandmother, my mom, myself, and Faye. Before we ate, I read a poem by the Dalai Lama XIV, about never giving up, that a friend had sent me. Even though Faye's fate was in jeopardy, I hoped for the best. I hoped she would live. When my grandmother had brain surgery the previous summer, the doctors said that her quality of life would never return. My mom and my uncle chose to remove her feeding tube and to take her off of the oxygen machine. I stayed with her in the hospital while Mom drove to Moberly to get more clothes. I sat next to her bed and watched the St. Louis Cardinals play baseball. They were her favorite team. The nurse told me that Ba probably wouldn't live through the night. Everybody gave up on her. Six months later, I helped Ba walk up the stairs of my house before she sat at the dining room table and ate the turkey I cooked. Ba never gave up. We hung the Dalai Lama's quote on the inside of our front door for several months until Mary tired of it and took it down.

When we arrived in Barcelona, Mary and I were exhausted. It was morning in Spain, but we hadn't slept. Our hotel room wasn't ready yet so we had to wait a few hours before checking in. We left our luggage in the lobby and roamed the streets. We started with champagne and quiche on Las Ramblas, the famous walkway where tourists are known to pack the sidewalks between Plaza de Cataluña and the Balearic Sea. The architecture was big and bold, ornate and beautiful. People of many ethnicities surrounded us. English was not the dominant language. Alone together, we were strangers in a strange land, far away yet where we wanted to be. After some sangria at a nearby public square and another cocktail at the hotel bar on the roof, we lumbered back to our room and lay down for a nap. We woke up near midnight. Well-rested but jetlagged, we hit the streets. Unlike Columbia, Missouri, and most other places we've lived, the streets of Barcelona were occupied in the middle of the night. We navigated the narrow Old Town alleys for several hours, willing to go wherever they'd take us next.

When we awoke the next morning, I felt overwhelmed. I had purchased two guidebooks about Spain while in Missouri, and the sections on Barcelona were extensive. I didn't know how to proceed. We only had a few days in the big city, I doubted I'd return anytime soon, and I felt obliged to see everything notable in the city. I also wondered where we should leave Faye's ashes. We were close to a beach—should we go to the water immediately? Deciding between sightseeing and relaxing was a challenge. Mary suggested we take in only one site a day. Sagrada Família church, designed by Antoni Gaudí, was our first stop. Under construction since its inception in 1882, the church is one of the most impressive structures I've seen. With columns designed to look like trees in a forest, the architectural details are dazzling. It was here that I prayed for the first time about Faye. Mary and I sat on a pew in the front of the church before resting on our knees and communicating to God. I'm not real sure why I prayed, except to say that I was inspired by my surroundings. Gaudí devoted much of his life to this legacy, and it wasn't lost on me. I made sure to photograph his tomb in the Sagrada Família Crypt before I left. Our remaining time included Park Güell, the National Art Museum of Catalonia, La Boqueria, Montjuïc Castle, cafés, a 40-euro sea bass at the Port of Barcelona, and late-night dancing at a *discoteca*. We never made it to the beach. Faye was still with us.

After leaving Barcelona, we took a train to San Sebastian and slowed our pace on the northeastern coast. We stayed in a hotel on the beach and went for a swim soon after our arrival. I've always been attracted to the ocean and water. I enjoy the sense of peace as well as the risk of not being able to touch bottom, and the ability to keep going. Perhaps this is why I wanted part of Faye to forever stay in the ocean. It's an area of the world where mysterious, beautiful things happen beyond my sight. Yet I couldn't leave Faye's ashes here. The beach was full of people. I hoped to find a place that was more secluded and off the beaten path.

Near Faye's due date of April 3 we had met with the doctor. It appeared that Faye was doing well but not going to arrive on her own. The doctor scheduled induced labor for April 12, which meant we would arrive at the hospital the day before. On April 11, I wrote a letter to my daughter:

> *Dear Faye,*
>
> *This is your dad. Tomorrow, you and I will meet for the first time. You've probably heard my voice during the past 41 weeks while you've been inside your mother. I hope you recognize me. I've kept you off of Facebook and out of public view for most of the time you've been preparing to enter the world. It wasn't until recently that I decided to show you off. This was my decision and I hope you agree with it.*
>
> *For most of my life I've been afraid of being a dad. I'm 39 years old and past the arc of when most men enter fatherhood. I have a few reasons why I hesitated from having a child. My perspective about responsibility is probably the biggest hurdle. Being a good father is one of the most important things a man can do with his life. And this might be why I've avoided it. I would hate to fail you—it would be my biggest regret.*
>
> *I want you to know that I'm ready for you to be my daughter. I will show you what's important in life. You'll discover music, photography, the ocean, movies, running, poetry, books, and most importantly, love. Nobody will hurt you. Life will be beautiful. The doctors say that you won't make it because you have a disease called Trisomy 18. This is no fault of your own. I'm worried that your introduction to the world will be a struggle. I worry that you'll struggle to breath and that your heart will have trouble keeping you alive. I think this is why your mom hasn't come anywhere*

close to going into labor. I think you know that you're safe on the inside.

Unlike most people, birth could be the antithesis of life for you. I don't really know what to tell you. And I don't know how to help you. You'll be surrounded by your mom and me. We'll be there every second. We will never leave you alone. I want you to do what you have to do to find peace. I think you might be the only one who knows what that is. Before you're even born, you'll have to carry a wisdom that's beyond me or anyone else in the room. I wish it were easier. I'm a strong person and I'll help you, but I want you to help yourself, too. If you need to let go, that's ok. You will not be forgotten. You will not be forgotten. You will not be forgotten.

I'll see you tomorrow. I love you.

Dad

When we arrived at the hospital later that day, the doctor listened for Faye's heartbeat. She couldn't find one. Since we had seen our doctor two days earlier, Faye had died. Mary burst into tears and screamed, "Noooooooo!" She had made it 41 weeks with Faye, and all she wanted was at least a couple of hours to be with her. I was shocked. I said nothing.

The next phase of the trip was renting a car in San Sebastian for a westbound drive to Santiago de Compostela, where Ramón lived. We planned to drive for two days, spending a night along the way in a small town called Gijón. Halfway to our destination, we stopped at Bilboa, the birthplace of the friend who'd sent the hopeful Dalai Lama quotation that I had read aloud at Thanksgiving. If he hadn't been born, my life experience would have been lessened. Being born is the best gift we can offer the world. I made a few pictures of the Guggenheim Museum, and we continued our trip.

Finding our hotel in Gijón was hard. Directions led us close to our destination but failed us at the end. Few people spoke English, and we didn't know where to go. Excitement rose when we found an Internet café but dissipated quickly, after we continued to miss streets, make wrong turns, and overlook landmarks. Finally we found our hotel, La Colina, a small structure on top of a cliff, with only eight rooms. The view from our room was the most scenic I've seen. Two large windows revealed views of the ocean to the east and cliffs to the south. In the distance, I could see a small, secluded beach. To find it, a person would have to be intentional. I knew this is where I wanted to leave Faye. Mary agreed.

The next morning I woke up early to photograph the sunrise from our room. But it was cloudy and not as picturesque as I hoped. I went back to bed and later awoke to rain. After we ate breakfast at the hotel's cafeteria, it was 30 minutes until checkout time. I asked Mary if she wanted to go with me to place the ashes in the Bay of Biscay, part of the Atlantic Ocean. She said yes and left the room before me as I packed my camera gear to protect it from the rain. We didn't have much time so I ran after her. We were both completely wet within minutes. The trail to the ocean was slippery, and we had to measure each step to keep from falling down. When we finally reached the shoreline, a boulder blocked us from the beach. Undeterred, Mary rolled up her pants and entered the water. I took off my shoes and socks, raised my camera bag above my head, and followed her. The waves crashed our legs at knee height. Mary unpacked Faye's ashes and went into the water by herself. She spoke to Faye and told her what was happening. I stayed on shore and made pictures of them with my camera. After she finished, I placed my camera on a rock and made a photo of both of us. We could see our hotel on top of the cliff and realized how far we had come in such a short time.

We left Playa de Serin without Faye and continued west to Ramón's home in Santiago. Located in northwestern Spain, this is the final destination for those who make the historical pilgrimage known as the Way of St. James that begins in southern France and ends in Finisterre. Although Mary and I didn't walk all those miles, we unintentionally made the same trip as others have been doing since the ninth century. We sat at the place the Romans called the end of the earth, and we saw a never-ending horizon of ocean. I hiked down a steep cliff to dip my bandanna in the water before using it to cool my face. I felt refreshed, if only temporarily.

Despite years of separation, Ramón and I bonded immediately. Mary told him about our trip with Faye, and he cried. At the University of Chicago, Ramón had been a biochemistry major who graduated with honors. After the death of his grandmother, who lived in Spain, Ramón reassessed his priorities and took her final advice to be happy. He is now a tattoo artist. I suspected that he might want to tattoo me.

The idea was a swallow, a bird that always returns home, and the words, "LET GO." He asked for the last few grains of Faye's ashes to mix with the ink for a tattoo on my inner left arm. After he finished, he asked me to tattoo him. He knew that I had never inked anybody. I asked what he wanted me to write, and he said, "LET GO."

Shane Epping on artistic influences and the storyteller's toolbox

For reasons unknown to me, I was strongly attracted to existentialist writers when I was young. I remember reading Dostoyevsky's *Crime and Punishment* as a junior in high school and being attracted to the idea that none of us can escape the self-destructive thoughts in our heads, no matter how smart we think we are. Other favorites included Shakespeare's *King Lear*, Tom Stoppard's *Rosencrantz and Guildenstern Are Dead,* Thomas Hardy's *Tess of the d'Urbervilles,* and Kurt Vonnegut's *Slaughterhouse-Five.* They all commented on humans' ridiculous state of being in an unjust world. I don't think I really understood the dark humor in some of them until years later. While in college, I read a lot of stuff outside of the classroom that would stay with me: Tom Wolfe's *The Electric Kool-Aid Acid Test,* Ken Kesey's *One Flew over the Cuckoo's Nest,* J. D. Salinger's *The Catcher in the Rye,* Anthony Burgess's *A Clockwork Orange,* and a few more books by Vonnegut, who would become one of my favorites. After graduating from college, I read Ayn Rand's *Atlas Shrugged* because it was the longest book with the smallest font that I could find, and I needed something to distract me from my job at a law firm. I also developed a strong interest in cyberpunk, with a particular affinity for Neal Stephenson's *Snow Crash.* Charles Bukowski's *Ham on Rye* blew my mind. In later adulthood, I have fond memories of Adam Berlin's *Headlock,* Andre Dubus's *Townie,* Cormac McCarthy's *The Road,* Stephen Chbosky's *The Perks of Being a Wallflower,* Irvine Welsh's *Trainspotting,* and Jonathan Franzen's *Freedom.* All of these books contributed to my complicated views of the world, or perhaps they shined a light on something that was already there.

When I was younger, I wanted to read the darkest shit I could find. Nowadays I don't really have a strong interest in doing so. I think the world is hard enough. Sometimes I want to read about how beautiful the world is. In terms of artists, Ansel Adams has always been my favorite photographer. He could have been a professional pianist but he chose photography. He appreciated beauty in all art forms and didn't pigeonhole into one form. He is quoted as saying, "You don't make a photograph just with a camera. You bring to the act of photography all the pictures you have seen, the books you have read, the music you have heard, the people you have loved." I love that.

Contrary to the song, video didn't kill the radio star. Likewise, the Internet will not kill the writer. It's quite possible it will do exactly the opposite. Writers can now reach a worldwide audience in an instant. Editors are probably more important now than ever before. So is having the right box of tools.

In graduate school at the Missouri School of Journalism, I split my curriculum between writing and photography. Whether using words or photos, similar themes contribute to strong storytelling: details, scene setters, transitions, and tension, for example.

As a professional photographer, I attended MediaStorm, a weeklong workshop in Brooklyn. This is where I learned to polish my skills and to give people in my photos a voice. I now write stories, make photos, and collect videos. A photo can be great on its own, but it's not unusual for it to be stronger with a well-written caption or accompanying audio to provide context. This is where video can prove the best instrument in a storyteller's box of tools.

Communities of like-minded storytellers are equally important assets. It helps me remember why I want to be a photographer and why I don't really want to do anything besides tell stories. There are countless reasons to quit, and many of my friends have left the profession. The job market is brutally competitive and low-paying. People love photos, but they don't love paying for them. The only reason I do what I do is because I want to.

AFGHANISTAN: A LONG ROAD HOME

Lois Raimondo

Late at night I sit in my apartment in Washington, D.C., watching U.S. leaders talk on television about the war on terrorism. Afghanistan moves in and out of these conversations, as it does with the headlines. One day there's a lethal flare-up on a mountain stronghold. Later the situation is "controlled," and newsroom pundits move on to other hot spots like Iran, Kashmir, or Somalia. Then my phone rings. The call is from Afghanistan.

It's my former translator, Ahmad Zia Masud, now a negotiator for Afghanistan's hastily formed Ministry of Defense. He calls me often by satellite phone from mountaintops, villages, and caves where he is meeting with resisters to reform—Taliban fighters, independent warlords—who, after decades of war, are reluctant or unwilling to lay down their guns. Sometimes Masud and other negotiators are threatened and forced to retreat. Soldiers then move in, and the hills resound once more with war.

"This is a very dangerous time for my country," Masud tells me. "Every day I see disaster. The young boys, they know only war, nothing else. What will happen to them? I believe food will come, factories will come, but now the people are suffering. Even if peace comes, so much has died."

From last October into December, Masud and I worked together day and night on the parched hills and plains of northern Afghanistan, where I was on assignment as a photojournalist for the *Washington Post*. Masud was in his eighth year of forced exile from his home in Taliban-controlled Kabul, working mostly for the Northern Alliance leadership. When hundreds of foreign journalists began descending into Khodja Bahauddin, site of the Northern Alliance's government headquarters, the foreign ministry assembled an army of translators. Masud, with halting English, but well connected, wound up with me. He is a devout Muslim and father of three; I an unveiled, unmarried, Western woman. Neither of us imagined how our minds and lives would mingle and be forever changed.

From the start we covered frontline stories, which required a steady diet of Russian military maps, bareback rides on mountain-bred horses across frigid rivers, a phone book filled with satellite numbers for field commanders, and a stomach for black tea. Some days mortar fire thundered constantly. Other days were still. The United States had announced that it would launch air strikes on Taliban positions, but the Northern Alliance frontline commanders we were meeting with weren't being told when. So they held their men in check, awaiting the U.S. campaign that would allow them to take the offensive against the weakened Taliban territory. The pause created space to report beyond the front lines and provide social and historical background for the conflict. Camera in hand, I set out to document the "collateral" consequences of the war. From dawn to dark, Masud and I bounced around in a Russian jeep—human marbles in a thin tin can—to find people and their stories.

We wandered, like archeologists, through physical and emotional fields of destruction. We met young students, hungry for knowledge, whose well-tended schools had been commandeered by Taliban troops and turned into garbage-strewn, graffiti-marked military barracks. We located families, three generations deep, displaced now to bare-boned refugee camps. Everywhere we went, we found fragmented communities; human lives ripped apart to hospitals, prisons and cemeteries. Along the way, sharing hundreds of miles, our own stories unfolded.

Educated at Kabul University, Masud was still a consummate student at age 32. He carried a small, lined notebook in his chest pocket, which he filled each working day with new English words (once when we were under fire, he yelled, "Make yourself small!" Laughing, I shouted back, "You mean scrunch down?" "Scrunch" made its way into his book.). He has immense curiosity. Yet Masud had chosen to avoid all contact with Western cultures abroad and instead became a religious-political activist, nurturing strict devotion to Islam among his people. My own curiosity had led me to spend more than a decade living in remote, mostly impoverished, corners of China, India and Tibet—none so ravaged as Afghanistan.

The prison at Khodja Bahauddin was made of clay. Small dank cells had one tiny hole cut high in the wall. While I was waiting to interview some Taliban inmates, guards and low-risk prisoners circled me, muttering ominously. I looked to Masud, my vigilant protector. He spoke sharply, and everyone backed off. The prison director opened a cell, offering me any Talib. I peered in and discerned, barely, six hunched figures. We entered the cell. As I began to sit, Masud warned me of "small friends," our code for lice, fleas, and other creatures that had gotten into our sleeping bags in a bunker near the front lines. I squatted to talk with the prisoners, who ranged in age from 17 to 43. Every one of them claimed they had been drafted, under threat of death, to fight for the Taliban. They talked of their crops and families, wives and children left behind. Later the prison director said, "Maybe they are farmers. But they killed our soldiers. They should die." Shortly afterward one prisoner did die, of illness, right before our eyes. "Have you seen people die?" I asked Masud. He exploded in anger: "This is new for you. War, death and dying is our way of life."

Such suffering failed to dim Masud's sense of hope. That hope was rooted in a deep devotion to God, which I learned through his long, joyful renditions of Koranic stories. Our trips by jeep or horseback were punctuated each day by sunset prayer, even when shells were flying. Despite the constant threat of danger and death, Masud and other Afghans I met strove for normalcy in their lives. Imposing the rhythms of religion, they transformed one more day of war into one more day of peace. We broke Ramadan fast at sunset with still-warm bread made with prayerful hands in an outdoor oven—soldiers, civilians, and one foreigner seated on the ground, a complex human circle bound by simple bread. The teachings of Islam seemed to temper potential violence in a poor and desperate people. Yet taken to fundamental extremes, the same faith was also motivating Taliban fighters just over the next hill, who wanted to kill, certainly me, but also their Muslim brothers. Masud was more of a brother than most. He, like most Taliban, is ethnically Pashtun, one of the few working with the Northern Alliance.

Once, when we were deep in the desert, Masud announced that if he were governor of an Afghan state, he would rule by Koranic law, ordering immediate execution for adulterous men and women (this he offered as proof that Islam held women in high esteem). Muslims who converted to

Christianity would also die. I had seen this man comfort despairing widows, disarm deranged soldiers, play with childlike abandon, and respond with patience to foreigners who knew nothing of his culture. Such compassion, playfulness, and respect seemed at odds with his fundamentalist fervor. I wondered where he housed such rigid rules and didn't yet realize that my landing in his world was causing those walls to tremble.

One day we visited Lalaguzar, a sprawling refugee camp near Khodja. Weeks earlier I had watched a boy there toss a tiny ball made of plastic wrapped with twine. The sand-colored ball was constantly disappearing or unwinding. Later, in a far-off town, I bought a soccer ball. Masud and I returned to Lalaguzar and wandered through miles of indistinguishable tents, looking for the boy. Giggling children, all hungry for play, crowded around. As I offered a kicking lesson, some women peeked at us from behind a tent. Masud kicked the ball, and one of the women kicked it back. "Oh, no," said Masud, only half-joking. "Maybe her husband will kill me. I played soccer with his wife."

That afternoon we returned to Khojda and sat with tea on the concrete stoop outside my room. Masud poured the tea, then abruptly confessed that he felt conflicted in my presence. "It is a sin to be with you, talking friendly in this way," he said. "I must pray very hard every night after leaving you."

I wasn't ready for this. We had been working together, almost every day, for weeks. "You are saying I am a sin?"

"Yes. A man must not speak friendly with a woman who is not his wife. I love my wife very much. We have rules. You are not Muslim. But this is not the main thing. It is dangerous. You should be covered." I instinctively tightened my scarf around my head. "The people of Afghanistan do not want you here."

"I see." I stayed calm but inwardly stunned because, until then, I had thought we understood each other and communicated in ways that were, at times, extraordinary. Now I was a sin.

He went on. "Nobody wants foreigners here. I hate America. In too many ways, I hate America."

His words sank into silence. We had already discussed what we both viewed as the rampant materialism of the U.S. culture. Masud believed that American peacetime society, rife with crime, was the inevitable consequence of spiritual bankruptcy. He feared that Americans in Afghanistan—soldiers, journalists, businessmen, even peacemakers—would carry with them these same cultural values. I could see, I agree with, some of what he said. Now my Afghan translator, who was becoming my friend, seemed to equate me with an enemy. I was a sin from a nation he loathed.

Tears welling up, I surrendered. "Okay, I understand." Then I looked up and saw tears coursing down his face. "Masud, why are you crying?" "I cry because I have hurt you," he said. "Speaking with you is a small sin; this is a big sin. The heart is a holy place, and we must take care to never hurt one another. I am sorry. Now I must leave." He rose to his feet, planning to resign as my translator. We were both off balance, but I wanted him to stay. "Wait. Please. You will be part of Afghanistan's new government. Contact with the West is now inevitable. You will have to deal with foreigners, if for no other reason than to protect what you feel is precious about Islam and Afghan culture. You can be both bridge and gatekeeper for your people."

The optimist and the fundamentalist were tangled in a web. In the end, Masud chose to stay. He was beginning to trust me, and that troubled him. Because I was not Muslim, he had assumed I would never understand his world. Yet my work had taken us together into the raw lives of strangers, giving us common ground where we could challenge each other's thinking. He entered new words in his notebook that night: "flexibility" and "cultural relativity," ideas we discussed at length. We then retired to our separate quarters for exhausted sleep.

Life in war-torn Afghanistan is reduced and elevated to elemental action. Yet, despite the brutality that such living must breed, I was a constant witness to great generosity.

When the war heated up, Masud made it his business each day to get us to the front line for battle and back to safe haven by night. He had friends in both places who helped when they could. One position we returned to often was the post at Kapahasan Hill, a series of underground bunkers built in the hills facing Taliban strongholds in nearby Taloqan. Masud and I went first to commander Zuhoor's bunker. Welcomed by him and protected by Masud, I felt safe. This evening in a small underground chamber Abdul Rozaq, chief radio operator, worked the ancient wireless, a crackling lifeline powered by a car battery, checking on men posted along the mountain's 28-mile Northern Alliance front.

Commander Zuhoo, age 30, a strong, soft-spoken man who read himself to sleep each night, was issuing orders to his men. As his charges, very young and awfully old, departed for the dark unknown, he urged each one to be careful. The U.S. bombing campaigned had finally began. Taloqan was next, and the Taliban were desperate. Someone would certainly die before this night was over.

The young commander, who started soldiering at 15, turned to us and asked if we wanted any sugar in our tea. He apologized for not having any food and then said he must leave. But if we needed anything at all, Rozaq could find him by radio. Next, a soldier strapped the commander with supplies so he could lead an advance minesweeping team down into the valley, into the heart of Taliban territory. Rozaq, who never left his post, spoke as his leader headed out. "That man, my brother, my father, he is worth a thousand ordinary soldiers."

We all fell silent, feeling the long reach of the gentle commander, imagining his footsteps moving in darkness, knowing that battle was near. Masud and I went out for air. The mountains were magnified in moonlight and unearthly still. There was no electricity, no air pollution, to disrupt the night sky. It was alive with stars, bright bits of dust floating in a giant cup of jet-black tea. You breathed deep on top of Afghan mountains and inhaled the universe.

Later that night the silence was shattered by the restless, suffocating thud of Taliban rockets. Inside the bunker, I asked Masud to explain how both the Northern Alliance and Taliban soldiers could use the broad Islamic concept of jihad, or "struggle," to sanction killing fellow Muslims. "It is complicated," he said, suddenly smiling. "You like, I use my new word 'complicated'?" he paused. "We believe there is only one God, Allah, and our life on earth is to serve him only. Unfortunately, the human is weak, and unwise mullahs, with wrong thinking, disobey the law of the Koran and lead the people in a dangerous direction. This war is about power, not God."

"But how does a good and gracious God, as you describe yours, justify killing in his name?"

"Oh, Lois. I am a weak teacher for you," he said. "Our God does not want the people to be killing. Long ago the Muslim world was under attack by Christians who wanted to make all of Islam disappear from Earth.

Jihad was about survival. For us jihad with weapons is a last resort. It is a very desperate thing. The greatest jihad, our God teaches us, is jihad of the heart."

The next morning I was blasted awake before dawn by thunderous explosions. U.S. B-52s had found their mark at Taloqan. Oddly, I felt secure lying against the bunker's earthen wall. I had become so deeply immersed in the assignment that my attitude matched my translators, the surrounding soldiers, operating Muslim belief that one cannot save oneself from death. When your time comes, you will go. This calmed me as I worked.

I thought of the Northern Alliance soldiers, who, outnumbered and outgunned, had been fighting a war far from home for more than six years. With every bomb that fell from the sky, each man was closer to going home. But home to what? Loved ones dead. Towns and cities destroyed. Farmlands riddled with land mines. I would soon return to the United States, whose planes were flying overhead. Masud would spend the rest of his life cleaning up the mess from this war and others before it.

Still in my sleeping bag, I turned toward the bunker's blanketed doorway. In the dim light of dawn I saw a silhouette. With eyes closed, palms up, lips moving in silent prayer, and cheeks wet with tears, Masud was talking with his God. I closed my eyes, allowing him privacy, and turned back to the wall, knowing I could offer nothing that would help him. My own tears fell silently, separate from his, but into the same earth. I was learning in this paradoxical world of rigid rules and barely controlled chaos, that there is a certain beauty in boundaries. The discovery did not come without pain.

This bunker had been a place of great intimacy, where hardened warriors huddled around dim kerosene lanterns late at night, listening to their commander read aloud from tattered pages of Persian poetry, delicate stories about brave young men riding off on horseback to fight the good war, leaving behind trails of flower petals that their loves could never follow. Now they were on the move, a restless river of men flowing along the dusty dirt road leading to the enemy-occupied regional capital Taloqan.

Five thousand advancing Northern Alliance troops halted at sundown in a narrow valley stretched between foothills of the Hindu Kush. Their general, Dawood Khan, with advisers and bodyguards, climbed an adjoining hill overlooking the city. They laid their scarves on the rocky ground and, kneeling close together, prepared to pray.

The surrounding hills abruptly exploded with fire. A murderous cacophony of mortars, rockets, and machine guns hammered the soldiers,
a ragtag lot of men merged from farms, villages, and military forces over
weeks growing. They scattered in all directions, frantically diving for cover
in a narrow valley locked between rock walls. The commanders continued
to pray. I moved in what seemed like slow motion, making pictures. The
bloody bodies of land mine victims were being rushed back through the
ranks. Soldiers began to run in panicked retreat. Suddenly, a voice stopped
me in my tracks. "Allah Akbar! (God is great!) Forward! Allah Akbar!"
Looking over my shoulder, bending to the commanding voice, I saw Masud standing firm in the midst of a massive retreat. Blocked by the passion
of his war cry, the fighters slowed, stopped, turned and continued to battle.
I settled back in making pictures. Masud's voice continued to echo through
the valley.

In that moment he was a stranger to me. But in his voice I heard his
history: The young boy of seven who watched wide-eyed as Russian tanks
rolled into his hometown of Kabul; the idealistic university student who
saw two of his closest friends die at his side defending their city from the
Taliban; the dedicated husband and father willing to die that day to make a
better future for his people.

When the sun came up the next morning, Masud and I walked the streets
of newly liberated Taloqan. Friends whom he had not seen for years rushed
at him from a celebratory crowd. They toppled over, laughing and hugging.
I watched his joy expand with every acquaintance found alive. Meanwhile
his wireless radio crackled with urgency—critical work that must be done
in this transitional moment. It fell to Masud to set up new vanguard headquarters in Taloqan and to negotiate with remaining Taliban holdouts.
He managed the radio, relaying orders and issuing commands, struggling
throughout to keep an eye on me, worried about the surging crowd of men
pushing in close to get a glimpse of the foreign woman. I shouted above the
noise that I was okay, that he should move ahead. We both knew that with
the liberation of Taloqan, our separation was imminent.

Masud called to me: "I do not want to leave you." Then suddenly, ap-
pearing before us, was a young man, Nasir Sabawoon, a neatly-dressed
schoolteacher recently returned from training in Pakistan, speaking nearly
perfect English. "Can I help you with something?" he asked.

Masud was suspicious. This was too coincidental. The Pakistani connection worried him. The perfect English. Masud interrogated him roughly
while Nasir, seemingly used to such exchange, casually provided answers.
Questions went about his family, where he stayed and studied in Pakistan,
which mullah did he follow. Satisfied for the moment by the answers, Masud approved him to stay with me for the next few hours (with another Masud-appointed soldier accompanying) while he took care of critical
business and also conducted a more thorough background check on my
potential new translator.

A few hours later I moved into Nasir's mother's house, in the "ladies
quarters," one room that housed his mother, six sisters, several nieces,
three granddaughters, and now me. Fresh bread was baking in the family's
clay oven. A tree with giant lemons grew in the courtyard. Children chased
each other in circles while two beautiful women, diaphanous scarves
draped around their heads, laughed while sweeping a colorful intricately
knotted Persian carpet, gesturing for me to join them. I had come out from
the desert and landed in a fairy tale. Which, we all know, must always end.

A month later, time had come for me to leave. It was snowing. Masud
had come to say goodbye. "How do I say goodbye to you," I said. He struggled to reply. "You have been my closest friend. You have taught me 'flexible' and 'complicated.' I am a different man because of you." He paused. "I
can no longer hate America because you are there." He gave me gifts for my
nephews, three small vests of leather and fur. Then he put his hand over his
heart, and we parted.

Masud worked his way south over snowy mountains to Kabul where he
reunited with his family, briefly, before being called upon to help secure remote hostile regions of the country. When he phones me now, he tells me
of the "total devastation of physical structures, land, and people's minds."
He worries that aid from the U.S. and other foreign powers will degrade
his culture. He cringes when new Afghan leaders who have lived most of
their lives abroad talk of a "new Afghanistan" and "globalization." I've never heard him sound so tired or so sad.

"These people do not know my country. What must we call this? 'Cultural relativity?' Remember our time with that word?" He laughs quietly.
"We are a very religious people. Our ideas are very different. I am afraid
for Afghanistan. These are the things you must write about. Otherwise, our

words will have no soul." I ask if I can tell our story. "If it can help the world know the beauty and peace in Islam, then you must tell it," he said.

Before I left Afghanistan, an American friend gave me a gift, six simple words of encouragement. As Masud and I moved with the war across northern Afghanistan, we shared these same six words between us. When I was face-to-face with the wrathful fury of an American-hating Talib, Masud spoke them softly to steady me. When he went undercover deep in the mountains on mission to turn Pashtun Talibs into Northern Alliance allies, I did the same for him. I, now, comfortable in the United States, he, wrestling with an increasingly splintered "coalition" in Afghanistan, end our long distance phone conversation with six simple words: "Be smart. Be brave. Be afraid."

Lois Raimondo on understanding media and manipulation

Since I've worked both sides of this equation, almost equally, as both narrative journalism writer and documentary photographer, I have practical and visceral experience of what one accomplishes that the other does not, or, more dramatically, cannot. The degree of difference is most recognizable in the best work from both sides. Those practitioners—of word or image—have nuanced understanding of how their media operate and so push the boundaries of possibility.

There is no escaping the fact that story itself changes as it gets taken up, translated, into differing forms of physical transmission. The mistake too often made—in my experience most often made by web editors with less experience of deeper narrative forms—is to assume that every situation or story (speaking journalistically here) can be equally represented in any one of the specific multimedia modes.

All forms of storytelling involve manipulation. The most informed consumer of story understands both the devices and limitations of each form. Industry-wide, awareness of how each mode gets made, and then how readers and viewers absorb that particular product, allows for better decision-making on the front end. I do believe that each mode—word, image, video, audio—can tell a story, but it is important to recognize the inherent partiality of each tale. Individual modes offer specific viewings, but they are not interchangeable in either content or capability. To assume so is to ignore the realities of technical and sociocultural conditioning that surround the creation and absorption of all today.

One of the most critical components of content and message difference between various modes of telling is time, as both a concept and physical fact. Good writing relies on imagery and metaphor to create shared space with the reader. There is a process of slow but steady knowing that occurs when the picture gets word-painted in the imagination of someone taking in that story. The time investment the reader makes to travel in that world resonates both forward and backward. The experience of interacting with the information weaves a tapestry of trust (if the story is good enough to hold attention and interest).

Photographs, even as they freeze one single moment in time, share some of this same "woven trust" sensibility. The stillness of the image allows the reader-viewer to explore the space with her or his own intelligence, absorbing, going back to rethink or clarify content. The "reality" of the picture, in and of itself, projects a credible truth. In this sense, for me, still photography and the written word share a piece of common ground on the side of intake.

But the examination must go further than that. Because while both the written word and the still picture can lie, people assume pictures don't have a point of view. And so pictures are "evidence" when words are "hearsay." What every photographer knows to be true is that every frozen moment of "truth" represents the image-maker editing out a hundred other, sometimes contradictory, options of framed report.

My concerns come when there are gross or radical manipulations of reality being made, particularly in video reporting where both technology and audience expectations make it easy, and that video is being assigned, supported, and pasted alongside word and image report as equal and accurate. Journalistically, they are not equal or interchangeable.

Video reporting (the practice of which is most often referred to as multimedia) is rarely, if ever, subject to the same scrutiny applied to journalistic copy. Rather, the expectation is that in order to hold the viewer's interest the edited piece should be kept at under four minutes, transitions should be smooth, not choppy, and that audio should be clear, sound bites poignant, minus all the still and quiet weaving ways by which a word story works. Multimedia is authoritative and directive, sweeping the viewer along in an expertly designed moving story. An old, pre-multimedia equivalent would be a five-year-old child traveling in a small wooden boat through a dark cave of singing international dolls in the "It's a Small World" exhibit at the 1965 New York World's Fair. Child's eyes wide with wonderment, while the boat is being pushed and guided every second by an unseen, underwater, motorized track. There is no place or space for the viewer to fall off the track or separate from song.

Knowing how it all gets put together is much less romantic than the "Small World" ride. It makes one a much more critical and sometimes cynical viewer of content. I think it can also make for a much better reporter—and storyteller.

ENGAGING SOCIAL RESPONSIBILITY

Besa Luci

At the time it was just my story, not *the* story. Hundreds of people had started crossing the border from Kosovo into Macedonia. The line of cars kept coming to a halt as the border police maneuvered the day's flow. Those passing by on foot would immediately hop into taxis with final destinations still unknown. And a fifteen-year-old girl, hands tucked in a jean jacket gazing down at the pavement, waiting on her own.

The journalistic instinct is to get that story—to capture the human element of an event that seemed political—the long-anticipated day that NATO would begin its air-strike campaign against former Yugoslavia to stop the ethnic cleansing in Kosovo.

But fourteen years ago, when I was that fifteen-year-old, I balked at the foreign journalists crowded around me. The last thing I wanted was to be asked questions, because standing there scared and alone, I thought I had no answers.

That was my first real contact with the media, and at different times in my life it has been the object of my confusion, hatred, and passion.

Growing up in Kosovo during the '90s, the truism that the personal is the political was a lived and embodied experience for me. I never missed the opportunity to hang out in coffeehouses where people met after protests to discuss politics. However, I am not the generation of socialist pioneers who fervently supported Yugoslav Olympic teams. I also didn't grow up among the protesters who threw rocks at the police.

These are the stories that my parents, sisters, and their friends would tell me and more often recall to one another. My stories are those of how I understood the immediate world around me.

I remember the late-night gatherings at our apartment. My parents and their friends sat chain-smoking over bottomless glasses with Konjac. Though the cast of friends and family would change, the scene was always the same.

They would intently watch the edition of the Serbian news but not for information. They'd watch it to learn what new propaganda was being promoted by Milosevic's nationalistic policies.

Angry shouts at the TV set were a constant fixture in that routine. After the news ended, my parents and their friends would engage in heated debates and disagreements.

I found it fascinating that an anchor could so heat and fuel their debates. I hated how they argued, and I developed a deep-seated disdain for the news, believing that newscasts were designed to make people angry and argumentative. I didn't understand why my parents and their friends would continue to crave it.

What I failed to understand was how Serbian coverage of the wars in the region indicated what would eventually happen to Kosovo. How Serbia saw the wars around the country was evidence of how it would conduct its own war against the Kosovar Albanians.

It wasn't the news that showed me most clearly what was happening to Kosovo; it was my mother's dinner parties.

My mother, a pathologist and professor at University of Pristina Medical School, was particularly vocal about the effects of Milosevic's policies on health care in Kosovo. She was among the many doctors who lost their jobs to their Belgrade colleagues being brought to Pristina to replace them. Western academics and activists who visited Kosovo came to dinner at our house to speak with her and listen to her ideas.

She would tell them about the Kosovo Albanian parallel society, and how with the majority of schools taught in Albanian closed down, Albanians were opening their houses to teach school in our language.

My mother's persistence was what amazed me the most. Despite the lack of progress it was possible to make, she went on teaching, researching, and publishing. But she was particularly proud when my sisters and I spoke with her guests and told them our adolescent political views. They ate and drank in our home and left in amazement as to how well we all spoke English.

This is one story many international journalists and NGO workers visiting Kosovo especially liked. They also visited our schools and at times even left confused as to whether we had always been full of hate or if it was the result of power-hungry politicians. At times we gave them the stories they wanted to hear, and soon we began to believe them ourselves. But most of the time we were satisfied with the mere fact that someone was interested in our stories, that somehow we also mattered.

But despite the astonished look on our visitors' faces, our stories of social and political injustice, of parallel self-organization, never reached international audiences, which always made me wonder why. And by the time Kosovo became "newsworthy" for international coverage in 1999, I was introduced to a journalism led by selectively constructed images.

For me they were images that reinforced dominant stereotypes of the Balkans as a place where pain characterized much of everyday life. Images circulating in the Western media were full of vodka-drinking peasants and horse-drawn carriages. There was no coverage of the real social injustices that surrounded me every day. The stories that needed to be told were simply absent from the news, and the problem was so widespread that I didn't know whom to blame.

So as the fifteen-year old girl at the border, I thought I had no answers for the foreign journalists. That is because they kept asking me the wrong questions. They insisted on knowing *why* my parents had decided to stay in Kosovo. I wanted to speak to *how* my childhood and growing up had been subject to a constant experience of inequality.

For the following fourth months, I became a refugee and went to stay with my sister in Bulgaria. She was a senior at the American University in Bulgaria (AUBG), a school I would later attend. One of my strongest memories of the time remains a student's commencement speech.

She stated that AUBG students had lost their "at home." They had somehow lost their pasts because they were no longer the ones who were writing it. Whether they had actually ever participated in its writing was not questioned. But there was a general feeling of loss. Their "at home" had changed.

They would no longer be accepted in their home countries because somehow their identities had been compromised. In the West, they would never fit in, remaining too different. Their accents would be valuable commodities. They would be the native scholars from that liminal space that showed where Europe ended or perhaps began. Or at least they would hope so.

It was refreshing to adopt the idea of a fragmented self and identity. Being marginal, fitting nowhere and everywhere at the same time, was somehow empowering but also alienating.

I continued my professional and academic journey in trying to make sense of these pasts and memories and our role in them for the future. Quickly I discovered that as a child, my version of democracy had been somehow idealized, at times even naïve.

That is because over the past fourteen years, I've continued to be placed as part of region viewed merely as a source of conflict—fitting within constructions of the "transitions to democracy" and postwar societies. Our collective narrative in Kosovo didn't necessarily translate into an earlier belief that with independence all problems would be solved. In fact, this transition has often translated to a new form of denial to move freely and to exist as a Kosovar. And when one doesn't participate as an equal, it only adds to a general feeling of loss.

But for me it has also produced a social responsibility to engage the political, as within such competing readings rise important issues of relations of powers, and awareness of the importance of paying attention to individual stories. I try to reclaim a sense of authorship over the narratives coming out of Kosovo by participating in their making and writing. I remain convinced that individual stories and voices should not be lost.

I no longer see myself belonging to a place that needs to capitalize on the image shaped and transmitted by international media and politics. Today there is a new belief and assertion in agency, a belief that history is something we all can possess and that marginalized narratives and memories can be recorded. And that is how I see my place, because there's nothing wrong with showing your weaknesses, and there's something special when you notice and speak to them on your own. 🎴

Besa Luci on journalism that takes time

Regardless of platform, young writers today face the challenge of deciding what kind of writers they want to establish themselves as, and this largely depends on the type of media they engage and the type of stories they come to write about. My advice is to remember that we need journalism and storytelling that takes time—time to examine, comment, and even challenge the ways and shape of our society.

Taking time to listen to the people around you is vital. Most stories begin by researching and reading around the specific topic, theme, cause, or individual that we are interested in writing a story on. But in my experience, some of my best writing has come when I have listened to discussions of family members, friends, or colleagues on the particular topic and tried to understand where their reasoning and points of view came from. In this regard, it is important to always particularly listen to those ideas and opinions that do not align with yours, and to challenge your information pool and your knowledge.

I continue to have a complicated relationship with writing. It often takes a very long time. I'll write a 500-word page just to arrive at the opening sentence that will influences the rest of the story and what I want to say. A significant amount of time is also spent on having my stories bring new discussion and debate—examine what about the story will resonate in a profound and new way. When my writing and stories manage to trigger public discussion online, it reminds me of why I chose to become a journalist in the first place—seeking to find and expose untold stories.

WITHOUT COMPLETELY FALLING APART

Jessi Hamilton

You will never forget that morning. The way you chose to overlook how badly the floors needed to be swept. The flavor of the coffee you'd just begun to sip as you stood there in the kitchen, looking out the window soaking in the early light. The jarring of your phone ringing—seeming too loud and unwelcome at 8 a.m. on a Sunday. The way your dad sounded when you heard him on the other line.

You will never forget the way he said, "Honey, are you at home? I have some really bad news." You were home. And suddenly you felt uneasy. Waiting. Heart on the floor. Standing there, barefoot on your dirty hardwoods holding turning-cold coffee, stuck in the moment between knowing nothing and knowing too much.

And then he tells you.

The night before, just miles from your house, your aunt was raped and robbed by a man who forced his way into her house as she let her dogs out. After he was finished with her, she made two phone calls. One to the police and one to your dad. He'd been over there since 2 a.m.

By 8 a.m., you were his second phone call.

When he called to tell your sister, he forgot to ask her if she was at home, and so he broke the news while she stood in the middle of the grocery store—cart full of food and babies.

You need to be home to process such information.

And it's there, at home, in the middle of your kitchen, where two things happen. You lose your breath. And you get angry. Then you decide you have to do something. But there is no manual for what to do when someone so close to you is hurt so badly. So your sister comes over, still reeling from leaving her grocery cart full in the bread aisle, sits at your breakfast table, and together you decide that maybe the best thing to do is to go over to the house to show your support. And to bring a pizza. When you get there, the police will still be outside, and she will, somehow, still be standing and strong. You'll hug her in the middle of her kitchen and cry because you'll picture what happened there and also because you're glad she's still alive. Although bruised and limping, she's alive.

As much as her womanhood was exploited just hours before, she is still very much a woman. She looks the same as she did the day before. It's just that everything inside has changed.

But here's the challenge. As women, we block a lot of things out. Memories of things that hurt us. Abusive language that was spewed our way. We compartmentalize events so that they don't seem as bad as they really are—sticking them in sacheted and linen-lined drawers. But when your world is rocked by rape, shit gets unblocked.

Now I'm talking about me. The observer. Dare I call myself the victim's bleeding-heart-sponge. The indirect recipient of this world disrupted. Suddenly things like letting the dog out became a feat of bravery. Sleeping through the night in a creaky old house meant my bedtime got pushed and pushed until eventually I wasn't sleeping at all. I spent hours trying to catch the fucker who dared to tread on my family's turf. I helped organize a reward-raising benefit. I planned, I worked, I contributed. Because contributing was easier than doing nothing. Doing nothing might have killed me.

And although I kept (and keep) moving forward, it's different now. My drawers are opened, their contents splayed out like wounded soldiers, bleeding and dirty.

A few weeks after the phone call, I was listening to a song as I made dinner. The lyrics talked about hardly being able to see what's in front of you—ending with a haunting echo of "oh, God—where have you been." A question I'd been afraid to ask. Until then.

A question that brought me to my knees in the space between my sink and my stove. A question that ended with this answer: No matter where we think he's been, it is no disrespect to allow ourselves to feel pain. And loss. And lost. Because when we don't let our souls mourn, we can't fully heal.

What was left of my innocence was shattered, beyond shattered, the morning my dad called me. But the moment I walked into the door of the house where it happened, the moment I saw her as not just a victim but as a survivor, I learned that being a woman isn't about things that society would like me to believe. It's not a scorecard with tallies for the number of successful marriages, each perfect child you have, or even how respected you feel. No.

It's about courage—courage makes you a woman. And strength. And being able to move over and through. Not getting stuck. Fighting back. Being light.

Radiant, light.

It's not about how much is taken away. It's about how much you hold on to. It's what you reclaim as yours. And even more than that, I think it's about honesty. It's telling our stories. Like the one about my family. It's going back to the place where things broke. It's taking back your kitchen. Standing over a bubbling pot, making something to last all week. It's sautéing garlic and onions in olive oil without being afraid that the phone might ring with bad news on the other line.

Being a woman is about being proud. It's about looking at yourself in the mirror—all naked and vulnerable—and accepting the scar on your knee, the cellulite on your thighs, and the shape of your nose. It's loving yourself enough from the inside that the outside starts to shine brighter.

It's opening your drawers and washing what's inside with forgiveness.

So that when your dad calls to tell you that a member of your family has been hurt, you can go to her without completely falling apart. 🔳

Jessi Hamilton on setting the bar high for all forms of writing

When it comes to writing, I tend to practice one thing: ass to chair. (Yes, I read that somewhere.) I believe firmly that every writer can become a better writer and that nothing needs to be said the same way twice. That's the beauty of words: pushing and pulling them to find the perfect way to say something—the way no one else has ever thought to say it before.

I get paid to write copy for advertising. I got into this via a degree in magazine journalism and a desire to change the world with my unique perspective and storytelling. Instead I ended up writing for the local paper, editing a trade magazine, and deeply missing 9-to-5 creativity.

Then an advertising agency took a chance on me. They saw something in me, and I've spent the past eight years writing the words the whole world skims.

But that's okay. Because every day I work with a group of talented people to come up with big ideas and execute them. I don't just get paid to write. I get paid to create, to think, to market, to make people fall in love. Yes, with brands, but still—we're talking about love, people.

Do I ever feel like I sold out? Absolutely. But that's why I keep writing poetry and personal essays. That's why I have half of a memoir in my desk drawer at work. That's why I still care about the craft—constantly reading and absorbing other writing. Writing I can aspire to write. And to beat.

Today anyone anywhere can publish anything they want digitally, from 140 characters at a time on Twitter to pages upon pages of blog updates. It's becoming harder and harder for consumers of words to wade through the overabundance—and bad writing—that's out there.

That's why it's up to us, up to you. It's up to future journalists and current ones to keep writing well. It's easy to write a sentence and hit publish to send it out to a social media network of millions, but what does that say about the craft? About rewriting and editing, about care and patience, about rejection letters?

Not much.

So, please, I urge you: don't get lazy. Don't become complacent. Keep the craft of writing what it is—a craft. Yes, everyone can write, but not many can write well. Set the bar high. Then set it higher.

WHEN NATIONALISM TRUMPS RACE

Melanie Coffee

My hand clenched the steering wheel, and my stomach was in knots. *Dear God, just keep me safe. Do not let them hurt me. . . . What the hell am I doing?*

Everyone remembers where they were that day. People were at work, getting ready for work, getting the kids ready for school. All in our usual morning routines on that particular September 11.

At the time I was a journalist for the Associated Press, and hours after the twin towers fell I was one of the four people who were put on the team whose sole aim was to document all who had died. We were told we were going to work 12-hour shifts, day in and day out, until every last person was documented. Every. Last. One.

Being younger, I pulled the night shift and was about halfway through my shift, sifting through lists of confirmed dead, unconfirmed dead, and unknown, when the news desk heard there was an anti-Muslim protest bubbling up in Bridgeview. We had no reporters available to go, so they plucked me from the Death Beat.

Apparently someone tried to throw a Molotov cocktail at a mosque. We were waiting for the anti-Muslim or anti-Arab backlash to happen in the wake of 9/11, and the first notable incident had just manifested.

My editor walked over to my desk and cautiously asked me to get my notebook. "Be very careful," she said, looking worried, concerned about sending an African-American reporter to cover a racially volatile situation. She gave me a smile and went back to her desk. Then Mikey, one of our photographers, charged toward my desk, cameras slung over his shoulder and a fat lens in one hand. Mikey was like your uncle who drank too much. He had that potbelly supported by impossibly thin stick legs, but he was a tough teddy bear, and you were glad he was there.

Before leaving, he furrowed his brow and pointed at me. "If you get there before me, do NOT get out of your car. You wait. For. Me."

Mikey looked scared. Here was a guy who worked in the war zones of Afghanistan and elsewhere. Seeing him scared frightened me.

Mikey's warning kept echoing through my head while I hustled to my car. Once inside my Honda Civic, I began to wonder. Now what was it that I heard about Bridgeview... I'd only lived in Chicago for about five months, so the suburbs and neighborhoods were still a patchwork of gibberish to me.

Bridgeview, Bridgeview, Bridgeview... Was that where those white kids beat up that black kid on a bike so badly he was in a coma? Or was that Bridgeport? Or some other neighborhood with a bridge in its name?

That general area about twenty minutes southwest of downtown had a reputation for intolerance. I thought about all the horrible things that could happen to a young African-American woman covering what could turn into a race riot. The crowd could take one look at my brown skin, surge toward me, and—I shook my head; my panic was getting the best of me. I had to get it together.

Once down there, I found that Bridgeview looked like your run-of-the-mill suburb. The pristine, four-lane road was lined with strip malls separated by an occasional gas station or Taco Bell. Everything was well-lit by identical, towering lamp posts. A fire red Ford F150 zoomed past with "a U.S. flag larger than the truck's bed. On the other side of the truck was a smaller Confederate flag.

I knew the Confederate flag was touted as a symbol of southern pride, but my guard went up when I saw it. I'd had too many instances when, after seeing that flag, a racial epithet had been thrown or a milder yet insensitive comment had been made about "those people," my people.

Finally I quieted my mind and focused on getting to the mosque. A couple blocks later, Bridgeview looked like a Friday night in small-town America, where everyone cruised the main strip. Music blared from shiny cars that honked at each other, as if to say hi. Kids in hot rods revved up their engines and later slammed on the brakes. Wheels squealed, blackening the road. People hung halfway out of car windows, chanting "U-S-A! U-S-A! U-S-A!" About a block away, there was a pulsating, chanting crowd. I pulled over and called Mikey on his cell. He didn't answer.

His words rung through my head: "Do NOT get out of your car. You wait. For. Me."

Sigh.

I called him again. No answer.

Screw it, I thought. My story was outside, not in the car. I had to go out there.

Heart pounding, I opened the door. The chant changed. "Down with brown! Down with brown! Down with brown!" I looked at my brown skin. "Dammit." I froze. *Dear God*— I couldn't even think of anything to complete the prayer.

Clutching my notebook as if it were a shield, I marched up to the flag-waving crowd and started wading through. "Down with brown! Down with brown!" As I passed some of the shouters, they quieted down. I pressed further into the group to its ugly center: a tallish young white man, shouted above all the rest. "Down with brown!" The hate in his cold eyes gave me pause, but my feet took over and walked me right up to stand face-to-chest with him. I had to raise my voice.

"Excuse me, sir, my name is Melanie Coffee, and I'm a reporter with the Associated Press!"

He stopped shouting and gently leaned over to hear me better.

"Um, I was wondering, what are you doing out here tonight?" I know, I know, lame question. Edward R. Murrow was turning in his grave.

"They attacked our country and killed our people! I want to spill Muslim blood!" he yelled. The crowd behind me cheered.

"And so you're out here because—"

"Because I'm proud to be American, and I hate Arabs and I always have."

I got a few more hate-filled quotes and then slowly slipped out of the pulsating crowd, which had changed its chant back to "U-S-A! U-S-A! U-S-A!"

Afterword I sat in my car, shaking. Then a thought struck me: when nineteen-year-old Colin Zaremba stopped shouting "Down with brown!"

and looked at me, there was no animosity toward me. His hate was scary, but for me it was different that time. For once, a racist had not seen my color. I was viewed as an American first and a person of African descent second, if at all. It rattled my soul to hear "Down with brown," and it shocked me to discover that for the protesters, my kind of brown didn't matter that day. Patriotism had somehow blurred that line between blacks and whites.

For me that line had always been firm, distinct. When I was a child, my neighbor asked me why God made me chocolate instead of vanilla. In college, numerous late-night conversations showed white friends how racism wasn't just a myth. And years later I got into an argument with a white acquaintance who called a black football player a "coon" during the Super Bowl.

But this September evening, I was one of "them." The same "them" that had often hated me, the ones who many times had called out for my ancestors' blood. And it was all because "foreigners" had attacked U.S. soil.

The hatred in Bridgeview that night created an odd form of acceptance—and put me on a different side of the racial divide. ▨

Melanie Coffee on using digital technology
to be a better journalist

With the digital age (it feels so antiquated to even say that), there are fewer gatekeepers to publishing. Anyone with access to a computer can click "publish" and one's writing is out there for the world to see. However, that also means that there is a plethora of bad writing masquerading as journalism.

Readers are aware of that, so to rise above the drivel, ensure that your writing is crisp, clear, and compelling. It's best to have an online presence, where potential employers can see your talents, your engagement, and hire you or at least pay you to publish your work.

The pieces I've written that have gone viral are timely and touch on sensitive topics: Trayvon Martin shortly after the seventeen-year-old was killed. A mother of five who was bullied for having her wrinkly stomach on display at a beach.

It sounds clichéd, but they were real stories about real people. As a writer, I have to make the people in my story more than an "X-year-old, Insert Name Here" person delivering the perfect quote. I have to bring my readers along with me and show them the human beings: moms, dads, uncles, brothers, and friends. When your people recognize that, they connect with it, share your story with others, who in turn share it with more people. It can snowball from there.

Having an established audience can help, and you have to be your own advocate to develop one. When you are working on a story, talk about it through your social media channels to create your own buzz. Share pictures and insights in real time to bring your readers along with you for the ride. Once it's in print, go back and share the final product on all your social media channels, tagging the sources in your story as well as people in related fields who might be interested in reading your piece. Stay consistent with this behavior, produce quality results, and soon your audience will grow. This is also where beat-building comes in, as these people can often turn into sources for future stories.

Beat-building, or developing a beat, is one of the most important parts of being a journalist. It's where you uncover untold stories or stories told in a new light. The first step in this process is to identify educated sources, people whose daily lives are enmeshed in the issue, whether they are advocates, critics, university researchers, heads of think tanks, or everyday people who are relevant to the topic. Next, reach out to those people. Social media make it easier to cast a wider net for cultivating sources. Use the various platforms to start a discussion surrounding your beat.

For example, let's say your beat is higher education, and you are writing a piece about a new policy on how a university handles sexual assault. For the story you will interview proponents and critics of the policy, university officials, a national expert or two, a student-led organization on sexual violence, and regular students. Once the story is done, reach out to a couple of experts in the field that you didn't use for your story and begin a conversation. For instance, ask the Rape, Abuse and Incest National Network if the policy goes far enough or what they think will be the long-term implications of such a policy.

Two things have been accomplished with this question: You have pointed out your story to a knowledgeable source, and you have also created the beginnings of a possible relationship between reporter and source. Both of these are essential for building a solid beat.

The last step in the process includes being aware that the source's thoughts can easily spark a follow-up piece or address the wider issue of sexual assaults in a different light. Write that story and begin the beat-building process again.

Another way to use social media to develop your beat entails using scraps of information that were trimmed from the story: they make great fodder for social media platforms. Retrieve something from the cutting-room floor to compose a tweet or the headline to a Google+ post on the new policy.

Getting your story heard above all the electronic cacophony—getting people to click on links to your story—is an art that must be honed through practice and studying how others do it right. It's not a talent hidden inside a formula such as the inverted pyramid. And getting people to actually read your story requires writing that is crisp. As William Strunk Jr. said, "Vigorous writing is concise. A sentence should contain no unnecessary words, a paragraph no unnecessary sentences, for the same reason that a drawing should have no unnecessary lines and a machine no unnecessary parts."

Slowing down improves stories. "Writers are often in a hurry to convey more information" and to do it quickly, especially in daily journalism.

Once you get the main information you need for your story when interviewing someone, try to connect and really converse. As journalists, we often put up a wall between us and the people we are interviewing, perhaps trying to remain objective. Tear down that wall, and try to connect. You can talk about anything, but let them drive the conversation.

Remember, a source is more than a source. It's a person, and the more we journalists can keep that in mind the more authentic our storytelling can be.

SOUL TRAIN ON MUTE

Michaella A. Thornton

The concerns of the world on the afternoon I found my landlords watching *Soul Train* on mute were these: the United States persuaded the European Union to delay billions of dollars in sanctions owed to the EU from a tax dispute, the Olympics neared an end in Sydney, Australia, and, in the United States, Nelly's "Country Grammar (Hot Shit)" hit number eight on the Billboard charts. Nelly was a rap artist my sixth grade North Carolina students knew. Nelly was proof that Missouri, my home state, existed. When I mentioned his name in my social studies class to contextualize where I was from, some students sang the lyrics in a startlingly good imitation: "Shimmy shimmy cocoa wha listen to it now / Light it up and take a puff, pass it to me now."

I was naïve enough to think many of my students didn't understand the words.

"Focus, class," I'd say. "Let's focus on the five themes of geography: location, place, human-environmental interactions, movement, and regions."

Eyes rolled and singing stopped as the themes were repeated.

"She don't know what she's talking about," an unidentified student whispered.

He was right, but the emotional and intellectual experiences of a place determine how we, as people, measure and value the distance between us.

This was my concern when I first arrived in Henderson, North Carolina: "One day, *all* children will have the opportunity to attain an excellent education." Teach For America, a two-year national service organization, had passed its mission onto me when I joined its "elite corps" of recent college graduates the summer of 2000. I decided to teach for two years after college because I'm from Italian-immigrant-grocer Kentuckians, Depression-era poor Missouri hillbillies, and my cinnamon-colored paternal grandmother's Creek lineage. I also liked being called "elite," especially since I come from people who ate spumoni and squirrel. I knew intimately what public education could do for poor children, my parents' parents, but I also craved the Ivy League prestige I could not afford. Finally, by joining Teach For America, I would work with graduates of the schools I had dreamed of attending: Harvard, Brown, Tulane, Yale, and Duke.

My rationale for choosing North Carolina as my placement region was less premeditated; I had heard the state was green, like my life experiences to date. Yet Henderson was far from green—the Piedmont region was a study in shades of brown with occasional hints of pine. No mountains, no quaint cabins and no mint juleps. I had these romantic, stereotypical notions of a Rockwell painting brought to life with a Southern drawl and a swig of sweet tea.

Since I have arrived in Henderson, many of the locals tell me to slow down and to repeat myself. I am ignorant of the customs and irritated that I have to adapt, especially on the highway. I've been pulled over twice for speeding and ticketed once; I am not a favorite pace around here. This methodical, Southern way of moving is not what I'm used to at age 22, but my students, their parents, this town and I are trying to calculate the distance between us. We're speeding up and slowing down. We're attempting to let each other over, to forgive lead feet and hearts, and to use our turn signals, even though we're often headed to and from different places.

Latitude: 36.329 North, Longitude: -78.399 West

On Saturday, Bill and Pattie watch *Soul Train* on mute in their wood-paneled kitchen while eating saltines with cheese food spread. I have lived here for 30 days and finally decided to stop by, something Bill and Pattie have encouraged me to do. "Here" is the Spring Valley Lake Apartments in Henderson, and, despite what the sienna sign with white lettering says, these rentals are not really apartments. They are one- and two-bedroom brick houses fashioned in Lego-block simplicity. They are drafty in the winter, ovens in the summer, and, therefore, affordable to renters like me, a first-year schoolteacher fresh from the Midwest. Field mice like these apartments. Lady bugs, too. Red-orange flecks litter the window ledges and fill the glass light fixtures when fall comes.

I live alone in the "apartment" detached from the others. Kudzu, soybeans and cornfields lead to Apartment 5, my new home. My closest neighbors are objects: the blackberry bushes, the small vineyard, the garden and the girl-next-door's trampoline. Bill leaves summer squash and zucchini in plastic bags on my front step; Pattie, a former registered nurse, advises me on how to cook these doorstep offerings. She shows me where to buy African violets and takes me to her parents' church to put silk flowers on their graves.

Bill and Pattie are not only my next-door neighbors, but also my landlords. They are modestly affluent, white Southerners. Bill does the building maintenance; Pattie collects the rent. They supplement their retirement by renting out seven brick apartments Bill built in the 1970s near Kerr Lake, one of the largest man-made lakes in the Southeast. Kerr is pronounced "car," yet I still say "cur," no matter how many times the locals correct me.

Pattie, in her late 70s and several years younger than her husband Bill, takes my check for October. She wears her hair in tight, white curls and is partial to floral prints. She's good at keeping her hands to herself. Bill is not. Bill keeps trying to get me to call him Dad. He tells me to think of him as "my daddy away from home." I have a father in Missouri, and he does not slap my ass as a way of greeting, which Bill sometimes does. I will not call Bill "Dad." He rides his lawn mower around the outer perimeter of my apartment at dusk. Bill doesn't go on his rounds for my physical safety. Bill performs these nightly patrols to uphold his Southern Baptist beliefs and our rental agreement, which specifically states, after the pet policy and accepted methods of payment, that:

> "At no times, if single, separated, divorced or widowed, will the opposite sex be an overnight guest in said premises. If so, lease will be terminated immediately."

Bill and Pattie are the second landlords I've had since arriving in Henderson. Henderson is a town where rentals like mine are found by word of mouth. In August, my first month of living in Henderson and teaching sixth grade, I was homeless. Regardless, I went to work at Eaton-Johnson

Middle School—cheerful 6th grade teacher by day, depressed transient insomniac by night. I spent a few days in a stranger's basement, a community member who took pity on me; a week in a disastrous rental house located on the appropriately named Bane Street, where the windows were nailed shut, no appliances were provided despite the ad's promise, and the doors had no locks; two weeks in my friends' doublewide trailer on a futon by an open suitcase and an alarm clock; and one week in a friend's living room on a cot. I found Bill and Pattie through a teacher at my school. I thanked my colleague profusely before I met them.

Bill had been expecting me when I pulled up to his tool shed.

After a brief tour, a couple of superficial questions and a deposit check later, I found out about Bill's "no-men overnight" policy. I was desperate, and I liked the apartment. At the time, I didn't have a boyfriend, and I knew I wouldn't if the local men were any indication.

The Local Men

1. A man, whose ash is longer than his cigarette, grins at me while we wait in line at a local hamburger joint. He is missing teeth. I look away.

2. The principal of my middle school tells me to keep my skirts short and the slits long. Janet, my assigned mentor teacher, says to ignore him. Instead, I buy more pants.

"Isn't that sexual harassment?" I ask.

"Oh, honey," Janet says. "He's just being a man. Don't take him so seriously. Lighten up."

3. Woody, the school's computer guy, asks Juanita, the media specialist, if I'm single. I cannot get over his name. He wants to be called Woody? Woody tries to ask me out in front of 30 sixth graders. Lena, a precocious and dramatic student, notices. It takes me the rest of the year to get Lena to forget Woody and to quit singing K-I-S-S-I-N-G whenever he approaches the classroom door.

Overnight loving isn't something I want to encourage here. Signing the rental agreement is easy because I cannot afford to be picky. It's the end of August. I'm tired of P.O. boxes and collect calls home from pay phones—a time period still removed from the ubiquitous cell phone or Facebook update. I want to move in, to establish a home away from home. I'm sure no-men-overnight is illegal, but I never ask. I just sign the contract. My guilt soars a week later after Janet, the person who recommended my new landlords, tells me what Bill said before I pulled up to his tool shed.

"He asked if you were 'dark-skinned,'" Janet said.

"What did you say?"

"I told him you were white."

That night I visit my neighbors. They too are white. In my haste for home, I've moved into a place where most of my students, colleagues and friends would not be, or feel, welcomed. Isolation lulls me to sleep. I feel trapped and indignant like the mice I keep setting traps for in the kitchen. In my unwitting compliance to Bill and Pattie's lust for silencing and segregating others for their viewing pleasure, I am guilty too. I know what they think, and I continue to smile and nod. Like the ladybugs on my window ledge, a part of me is dying from the shelter I have chosen.

The *Soul Train* episode Pattie and Bill watched was likely the one that featured Rachelle Ferrell, Changing Faces, Lil Bow Wow and Jermaine Dupree. I don't remember if those musicians were on stage or if Bill and Pattie simply stared at the *Soul Train* dancers, but I do remember the kitchen's 1970s-era floral orange sherbet and lemon wallpaper and wood paneling, the artificial orange of the cheese food and the hospitality my landlords extended when they offered crackers. I declined the offered crackers, but accepted the chair Bill pulled out for me. I slowly sat down to watch them watch younger, darker bodies dance in silent motion. I sat transfixed by their bizarre viewing habits until Bill pressed the power off. The screen of this memory blurs and then sharpens years later, when I acknowledge not only my landlords' racism, but also my part in it.

"Nothing will change until we demolish the 'we-and-they' mentality," Sam Hamill wrote in his essay "The Necessity to Speak." "We are human, and therefore all human concerns are ours. And those concerns are personal."

Human-Environmental Interaction

Joe, a fellow TFA member who teaches high school oceanography and biology and has only been to the ocean twice, tells me I should call my new landlords the Freshes.

Bill and Pattie's surname is exceptionally close to a popular brand for feminine wash. "Their last name," he says through a thick Southside Chicago accent in The Driveway, where many of the first-year teachers in our group go after school for cold beer, "makes them sound like douche bags." Joe laughs at his joke. Most of us do, myself included. We, the novice teachers of Henderson, gather at The Driveway for solace and comfort that we are not alone in our culture shock and classrooms in this new town. We circle near the steps of another first-year teacher's house, the easy entrance to the kitchen for beer, and tell stories about our schools and our ups and downs until it's time for dinner and grading papers.

The Driveway is not a bar; it is an actual driveway, where our unofficial leader Aaron, the homeowner, preaches novice teacher salvation by making mix CDs on the themes of Vance County: loneliness, friendship and ignorance. Aaron's refrigerator is stocked with domestic brew and screw-cap blackberry wine, which we drink in abundance as soon as we can reach the kitchen. One day, beer bottle in hand, I notice Aaron has crossed off each day on a refrigerator calendar with a thick, black marker. After this observation, I lingered at the calendar often, wondering when I wouldn't have to see it again, wondering what I had done with the time I had already spent.

Joe's laugh brings me back. I fuel the laughter with another story. Bill rides his lawn mower around the outer perimeter of my apartment in search of overnight guests and unfamiliar vehicles. "He's like a chastity belt powered by John Deere," I say. The Driveway goes wild. They cannot believe I've signed this no-men-overnight lease or that Bill actually has this nightly routine. In my driveway story they see a flash of green machine underneath a white old man.

I can laugh because I am now one of the bright and arrogant ones. We, of The Driveway ilk, teach the children of the people we make fun of, people a lot like my spumoni-and-squirrel grandparents. We are not bad people. We are here. There must be something redeeming about that, about spending two years to teach in places we've been told others don't or won't go to. But there's this: It is easier for me to laugh at my weird and racist landlords because *they're* weird and racist than to discuss my fears and insecurities: why I don't sleep well or often, how I worry not only about what I'm doing with my life, but also, more importantly, with other children's lives, or that I feel like I'm treading an insurmountable amount of water in my classroom. False bravado makes false judgment possible. Arrogance is often an unoriginal mask for fear. Most of us are drowning in our first-year classrooms. This is why we're gulping down failure and isolation. Most of us don't know what we're doing. Teaching is hard, and it is personal. Some of us stay and continue to teach in this town, but many of us don't.

Meanwhile, I don't tell The Driveway that I have grown to like Bill and Pattie despite, perhaps because of, their idiosyncrasies. I cannot explain this to Joe. He thinks they're douche bags.

Movement

After *Soul Train* and saltines, Bill and Pattie ask about my students, mostly out of politeness, and then abandon the ruse when they simply refer to my kids as "the black kids." I teach a continuum of colors and ethnicities, but, for Bill, life is black-and-white. Pattie usually mentions something her church is doing for the "needy" when I talk about the original movie script my students wrote and produced about Greek mythology ("Zeus Springer") or how most of my students can artfully analyze poems from *The New Yorker*. Bill shakes his head and says he doesn't know how I do it. I limit these conversations to no more than 30 minutes, usually less. Sometimes I can steer them onto the topic of their daughter, the one who met her pilot husband online. They show me pictures of their grandkids, and I tell them stories about my family, the ones I left 1,000 miles behind me.

Before I leave Bill and Pattie's kitchen, Bill asks if I would like to help him with his annual Halloween display. I look into his bespectacled blue eyes, see Pattie's beseeching look out of the corner of my eye, and I cannot, for the life of me, find an excuse, any excuse, to say no. "Annual Halloween display" ricochets inside my mind, but there's no loophole for escape, not even grading papers.

"Of course, I'll help you," I hear myself say.

The kitchen's wood paneling echoes my promise. My voice is clear, unmuted.

Bill and Pattie's front lawn is a faded green rectangle, like a weathered tennis court, adjacent to a brick, ranch-styled house. If lawns had soundtracks, Bill and Pattie's would hum like distant wind chimes or the filtered reverb of a car stereo at a clandestine party in the woods. Those real-life parties began around midnight, often on school nights, most likely the local teenagers having a little fun beyond the Wal-Mart parking lot. On those nights, I would lie in bed, stare at the wood paneling painted white, and wonder if I would ever fall asleep, knowing I had papers to grade, lessons to plan and mice to trap. But right now, the only sound I hear is the crunch of gravel under my tennis shoes. Thankfully, the dog that chases my truck in the morning is gone. I couldn't outrun him on foot; I realize this as I walk toward the ample yard that would comfortably welcome two of my apartments, maybe three. Instead of boxy, ill-insulated rentals, tall pines and oaks reach skyward as grass reaches outward, south toward the road and north toward the tool shed. This luxury of lawn is the turf where Bill and I build our Halloween display; this is our common ground.

Bill waves harder when he sees me walk up the drive, as if to will my feet to walk faster. I wave back and amble on, pace and enthusiasm unchanged, as I notice the bed of Bill's truck. It carries a six-foot-tall plywood witch and a three-foot-tall cat. The cat's back is arched, fur on end. There are also cornstalks, husks emptied, from the garden next to my apartment. Bill has gone to a lot of trouble for a scene relatively few will see. Our neighborhood is at the conclusion of a dead-end road. There's not much traffic. The irony, the simplicity of the cause that brings Bill and me together, is not lost on me as I transition my view to rectangular hay bales stacked by one of the pines. These bales are the building blocks of our diorama, where we'll place the light plum and peach-colored mums and prop the plywood witch and cat. Bill, clad in a long-sleeved checkered flannel and deep blue denim, the type of un-faded material older men and farmers wear, walks toward me with a perfect coil of orange extension cord. No hay clings to his crisp jeans.

My arrival signals Bill's commands: do this, move that, not here, there. I wonder if I am wanted for this task because of my willingness to do what he says, to reply "yes, sir" and mean it with the Midwestern manners my mama taught me, even if I grit my teeth and wonder why I'm doing this. But etiquette isn't the reason I'm here. Positioning plywood witches in my landlord's yard on a dead-end gravel road in Henderson, North Carolina goes beyond good manners. Saying no isn't that difficult either. What is difficult: explaining to The Driveway why I've volunteered to help Bill. Joe mentions douche bags. My friend Mike tells The Driveway about Bill's chastity-enforcing lawn mower. How can you help these people? My friends want to know.

This is what I've come up with so far: Since I arrived in Henderson, community is more about allowing an opening for unlikely yet necessary change and less about avoiding kitchen tables I would never before frequent. It's hard to tell The Driveway that a part of me is like Bill and Pattie in their black-and-white views. I don't share their thoughts on race, but I'm righteous in my ridicule of these ignorant Southerners. The Mason-Dixon Line of belief rests between us. They are wrong; I am right. Old-school bigotry vs. new-wave philanthropy. They are saved; I sin. No one wins or learns in this stalemate if no one moves. And so I sit at my racist landlords' kitchen table; I help Bill lug a plywood witch around for Halloween. I seek to understand people I'd rather not publicly admit to knowing, let alone liking, in the hope of better understanding how to change the status quo.

"Do you like my witch?" Bill asks in the middle of giving directions.

I nod yes. The sight of a six-foot witch in the middle of nowhere is well worth my reluctant participation.

"I made her and the cat in my tool shed," Bill says with pride.

I nod and laugh at his ingenuity.

Together, in silence, Bill and I arrange the bales of hay on which to place the pumpkins, band the corn stalks and stick them upright, and use the fruit-colored mums to fill in the gaps of space. Splinters of plywood and flecks of black spray paint come off in our ungloved hands as we lean the plywood witch against a tree. She stands upright with the help of wooden braces. Bill lets me pop in small red lights for her eyes as he finds the orange extension cord. The witch stirs her cauldron. The black cat, back arched, is not far from the witch, a little to the left. It is near dusk, and the lawn mower is finally put away. The display is done. I step back as Bill plugs in the lights.

The cat's eyes blink green, the witch's remain a steady, eerie red. Pattie stands behind the glass door, smiling. My contribution to this project is scant. I merely prop and position. Out of odds and ends, we have made a scene out of Bill's imagination.

Now, thirteen years later, I still see that stupid witch. I see her silhouette in the twilight; down a gravel road few will ever travel. Bill and Pattie died in 2012, Bill in August and Pattie in October. They had both lived over 90 years and had been married for over 70 years.

The summer following the witch, I left Spring Valley Lake Road for good. I was tired of living alone. I was tired of the no-men-overnight policy. I was also tired of the unspoken contract I had signed, the contract I subscribed to through silence because I was too tired or lazy or polite to say otherwise. To question why *Soul Train* would be muted, men disallowed and I held captive by Bill and Pattie's unquestioned beliefs. I answered this question by not asking it; I moved a few miles away to Spring Valley Road (no lake) and into a doublewide trailer with some friends from The Driveway. I considered this a step up even though my new neighbors were a new set of characters: goats, soybeans and a 40-something bachelor named Jim who still lived with his mother, Mrs. W, who bragged on Jim's favorite grade-school book, *Little Black Sambo*, to my roommates. My roommates told me the story, incredulous yet titillated. I would nod and laugh, out of earshot, just as I did with my old landlords. Then I told more stories about my *new* weird and racist neighbors to The Driveway, and I felt comforted that it wasn't me. It's them. I'm different. I'm better. I'm above *Little Black Sambo* and North Carolina crackers.

And when the past and present tense hit me, I look to the refrigerator door, not for bottles of beer or black Xs on a calendar, but to a photograph Bill and Pattie gave to me before I left Spring Valley Lake Road. In the middle of the photograph Bill hugs Pattie with one arm. Their Christmas outfits and smiles match.

This is a photograph I keep, and I don't know why exactly. Maybe it's because these imperfect people cared for me when I was first starting out in a new place, with a new job. Maybe it's because I wanted the people of Henderson to be so much more than a caricature of the South.

Maybe I want Bill and Pattie's story to remind me of why I still teach, why my students' success and well-being matters—that there are people who will shut you down, turn you off, and smile all the same while doing so. "This is how racism works," Nick Laird wrote in *The New York Review of Books*; "it blocks the possibility of living an undefended life." I am reminded of this infuriating reality on August 9, 2014, when Michael Brown Jr. was gunned down by a police officer 12 miles from where I live, where my community college students wonder if they are safe, if this event is an end, a beginning, or maybe both, if they can talk about Michael's death—and too many others—honestly and openly, and if those of us who make up our communities will ever admit our culpability and privilege and what we all can do to overcome institutionalized inequity.

Beyond Bill and Pattie, there are other, more treasured photographs I keep from my time in Henderson: the usually outgoing Lena, of the K-I-S-S-I-N-G fame, hiding from the camera behind her jean jacket; Roy, who hid behind a rack of clothes at Wal-Mart before I noticed him observing me, wanting to say hello, but not knowing how to say hello to his teacher outside of school; Raymond, who died too soon on the basketball court at Vance-Granville Community College, a boy so smart and creative he once told me he didn't have his homework ready one day because he had spent the night before on an "all-night humanitarian trip to Somalia" (a story, for sure—so alive in mystery and invention); Lenora, who went on to serve in the navy, a girl so bright and alive with curiosity she read Victor Hugo at age 11 and was a whiz in all subjects; Quincy, who I gave two detentions to for distracting others during class, but I later learned he simply needed help getting his binders and homework organized, extra attention and tutoring to help him succeed, and lots of encouragement; and Aaliyah, an incredibly quiet and hardworking student whose older brother died from an OxyContin overdose the summer before she started sixth grade, an awful fact I found out when I moonlighted as a reporter for the *Henderson Daily Dispatch*.

A profound sense of hope and fear lingers when I look into my students' faces.

May none of us put them on mute.

Michaella A. Thornton on objectivity and transparency

In the late 1980s, I spent a large portion of my childhood in an old dark-room. My maternal grandmother owned a small community newspaper, where my then-single mother also served as the vice president of the homegrown publication.

My sister and I spent hours in that darkroom coming up with story ideas and mocking up our own newspapers and ad campaigns with blue-gridded paper, rubber cement, clip art, and X-Acto knives. My first job at the paper included rolling newspapers until the palms of my hands were covered in ink. Later, when I was thirteen, my grandmother gave me my own editorial column, which was not only empowering but a gift that set my professional aspirations in motion.

Quite literally, I grew up in a newsroom, surrounded by my family, friends, and the pressman who routinely doled out butterscotch discs. As a result, I vividly remember the tangible nature of making print news, and I would be lying if I didn't admit I sometimes miss simpler, more tactile times in this digital age.

However, I know multimedia and social media gather wider, younger, more diverse audiences. Audiences we have a duty to better serve. But audiences always crave meaning-making and investigative reporting. The foundation of *which* photos, audio, and video we select or curate should reside firmly in the story itself. Attention to word choice, figurative language, and style helps viewers and readers process the world around them.

Given the popularity of audiences hungering for well-told true stories, it will be interesting to see if American journalists continue to explore, more and more, the role of objectivity in today's news. As the American Press Institute stated in its article "The Lost Meaning of 'Objectivity,'" journalism still hasn't developed a strong "system for testing the reliability of journalistic interpretation." This may be due to an overlap between creative nonfiction and literary journalism that is misunderstood. Creative nonfiction, according to Lee Gutkind, "can be an essay, a journal article, a research paper, a memoir, or a poem; it can be personal or not, or it can be all of these." Literary journalism is more selective about what constitutes the features of the genre, and I see it as a subgenre within creative nonfiction that often requires more research and reporting. For many in creative nonfiction, Emily Dickinson's "tell all the truth but tell it slant" serves as a rallying call.

Many journalists balk at this, but writers' cultures and backgrounds undoubtedly influence how we report and interpret events.

Writing "*Soul Train* on Mute" was challenging as I wanted to be mindful of my own relationship to objectivity and transparency in this personal essay, especially since I was reporting about race and racism in America. As a white, Native American, and midwestern woman, I think it was and is important for me to be forthright about my own ethnic, cultural and socioeconomic background, in addition to the privileges, power, and sometimes problematic thinking I brought with me to Henderson, North Carolina. I did not want to perpetuate yet another white-savior-teacher narrative, but instead I wanted to look within, to reveal the complicated and evolving reasons I became a teacher, and to be reflective and open about my own part in this uneasy story.

In terms of my writing and reporting process, I read and reread the words of Nikki Giovanni, Rebecca Walker, Jonathan Kozol, Sam Hamill, and many others. I wrote most of the essay from detailed notes I kept while teaching. Then I attended the Mid-Atlantic Creative Nonfiction Summer Writers' Conference, where the late Katherine Russell Rich, talented memoirist and reporter, shared many helpful notes with me. Around that same time I returned to the Missouri School of Journalism, where Mary Kay Blakely reminded me to delve deeper within this essay, to consider how to thoughtfully report on race, and provided writing and reading recommendations that made the essay stronger and more self-aware.

As someone who lives twelve miles from Ferguson, Missouri, and who cares deeply about working toward building a more equitable, less segregated world, I would love to see greater transparency about how we report on race, culture, gender, and class in the United States. As someone who found her voice in a community and family newspaper, I know we are up to the challenge.

1202 PARK AVENUE, 1999

Sona Pai

At 1202 Park Avenue, we marveled at the purple hyacinths in spring and the way they had just popped up without any doing of our own. We sat on the front porch in flip-flops and cut-offs, with Betsy in her funny housedress, navy blue with white flowers and handy pockets in the front. We wondered how long the fragrance of the hyacinths would last, and how long we should wait before clipping them, leaving those hollow green stems sticking up like fence posts in the flower bed that skirted our porch. That August, when Yasmin moved in, she hung gauzy white curtains on satin ribbons in the living room windows. They made the sunlight stream in like a dream.

It was our first real home. Not a dorm room, not an apartment, but a home. An old redbrick college rental with scratched wood floors, Rorschach water spots on the ceiling and a grumpy old furnace that refused to cooperate with Missouri's mood swings. When it wouldn't fire up during a cold snap, our landlord told us to turn the oven on and leave its door open a crack. When termites started weakening the floor beneath our feet—even beneath Lotus's tiny kitten feet—he covered the splintered boards with duct tape and called it good. Once a year, the sewer flooded, which we knew only because the guys who lived in the basement told us. The drain was right in the middle of their kitchen, which made us feel awful, but we were so glad we didn't have to deal with it.

We sat with our shoes on the couch and smoked cigarettes inside. Nat Shermans that were long and coffee-brown and left a hint of honey on our lips. We exhaled smoke away from the phone when our mothers called with gentle interrogations about when we would finally graduate, find a real job or think about marriage. "I'm not worried about it; it's fine," we would say, or, "Relax, Mom. I'm only 22."

At night, we drank spiced rum and Cokes and played Frisbee in the street or scribbled our names in the air with sparklers. We typed final papers and résumés in the living room, watching films like *Koyaanisqatsi* and *Baraka* and wishing we had more time to deconstruct the metanarratives.

Every day, for weeks at a time, we ate burritos with beans and cheese and fresh mango salsa when the mangoes were two for a dollar. Among the three of us, we could spend less than $15 and eat for a week, saving the rest of our money for a bottle of Bombay Sapphire gin and some goat cheese. We ate sticky sweets from our mothers, all sugar and love. Strawberry-rhubarb pie, baklava and warm gulab jamun dripping with rose-scented syrup. We savored them together, the three of us, conversing in mmmmms and smacking our lips, trying to imprint the flavors on our palates.

"I think I'll start wearing scarves," one of us would say, or lipstick, or headbands, wondering if we might be one of *those* girls who wear scarves and lipstick and headbands, and then deciding we were not. The calls from our mothers became more frequent, the questions less delicate. When are you going to start a career? What is your plan? When are you coming home next so you can meet our friend's son, the doctor? With the degrees we were about to receive in magazine journalism, photojournalism and art history, we'd soon be overqualified for our jobs at the health food store, the poinsettia nursery and the perfumy bath shop at the mall. But we needed time for our own projects.

Betsy documented people's love affairs with their cars and photographed Ricky, the transvestite with wiry red hair, great legs and a closet full of Kotex he would never need. Yasmin designed lamps of reed and colored rice paper and made woodcut prints of a woman in a flowing veil smiling as she freed a bird from its cage. I wrote essays that I read aloud in the living room and then stacked in a pile, where they waited for the perfect sentence or image or title that would make them publishable.

We felt productive. Besides, our jobs were fun and easy, and the people were so nice. We could leave in a heartbeat, and they would still give us goodbye parties and presents and discounts. One day, we read a newspaper article about retired people learning to appreciate the little things—the little things they were just beginning to enjoy again after years of working too hard and too much. We would never forget those little things, we swore. We would never groan about the grind. When Yasmin asked, "Are we slackers?" I responded quickly. "No way. Slackers waste time."

It took less than a year for us to get tired. Tired of being on our feet all day. Tired of making just above minimum wage. Tired of coming home too exhausted to do anything but have a beer and take a nap. The living room at 1202 cluttered up with dirty dishes and unfinished projects, scraps of reed and rice paper, drafts in need of revision, undeveloped rolls of film. We forgot to collect the hyacinths, and they wilted and fell apart, leaving dried up bits of purple in the flower bed that hemmed us in.

Betsy was the first to say it out loud. She came home one afternoon, muscles aching from hauling poinsettias all day, and said, "I have got to get out of here." She hunched her shoulders up when she said it and scrunched her nose. She said she was feeling cagey, but she meant she was feeling trapped. I started downloading grad school applications, and Yasmin began studying a map.

In no time, it seemed, Betsy scored a job at a stock photo agency in Maine, where she had interned a few years before. I picked a grad school in Oregon, where I'd find the guts to let other people read my work. Yasmin decided to check out resort life in Colorado, the pit stop for the young and employable on the way to figuring things out.

We packed what we could of 1202 into our cars and gave the rest away. Our mothers stopped asking questions—for a while, at least. We cried and squeezed hands. We assured each other we'd never have to settle or sell out, that we could live our lives in transit, that we would live together again. When Yasmin took down the dreamy white curtains, the glare from outside was harsh, almost overwhelming. 🖾

Sona Pai on the power of the personal essay

Every writer today has heard it: people don't read anymore.

They'll watch videos. They'll scroll through mind-numbing social media feeds. They'll shoot their way through hours of online gaming.

But they won't read. Unless it's all bullet points and buttons. Benefit statements and calls to action. Exactly what they want to know. Precisely when they want to know it.

To be a writer today—and tomorrow—you have to believe that's completely false. Seriously. You have to reject the conventional wisdom outright. You have to believe that people care about more than diversion, distraction, and definitive answers.

You have to count on humans being humans.

Look around, and you'll see people scrolling line-by-line through entire novels on their iPhones. You'll see coffeeshop laptop jockeys with eight different browser tabs open, clicking between email, Tumblr, their latest job search, the website they're working on, and an essay on Medium, Longreads, or Grantland.

Reading isn't dead. And no new medium will ever kill it.

We might skim and scan. We might skip to the end. We might get distracted and have to come back later. But we will always read. We will always crave the satisfaction of assembling meaning from letters, words, sentences, and paragraphs. Of constructing someone else's experience in our own minds and connecting to it in our own way. Of getting pulled into a story even when we don't have time for it. Of having to work for the payoff.

In the work I do for a living—writing on behalf of brands—the question everyone keeps asking is: how should we write? In other words, how do you tell a story that cuts through the clutter of the digital age?

Research gives us mixed messages. We hear that online readers are lazy and overstimulated. They need boldface, bullets, images, video, and 360-degree, immersive experiences. They'll bounce out in the first six seconds. Writing in the first person is suspect; it has to be all about *you*. Which means it has to be all about *them*.

On the other hand, we hear that longer blog posts outperform shorter ones. Narratives are more memorable than transactions. Content is king. Connection is currency. Advertising can't just capture eyeballs by being loud and flashy. It has to be as informative, entertaining, and useful as the independent content around it. It has to sing for its dinner.

When the captive audience no longer exists, the only way to win is to be captivating. I think we should be asking a different question. It's not just about *how* we write. It's about *why* we write.

As a journalist who's been making a living in marketing for the past decade, I spend a lot of time picking apart stories, figuring out how they work, constructing new ones, and persuading people that they matter. Writing personal essays on the side is like a guilty pleasure.

I wrote an early draft of the essay I submitted to this anthology in 2000, when I was in graduate school at the University of Oregon. I remember how difficult it was to pitch. I couldn't articulate what the story was about or why it would be important to anyone. I couldn't boil it down to a nut paragraph.

I just knew that I needed to tell it. That I had to pinpoint a specific time and place before it faded away, and writing was the best way to do it.

I felt (and still feel) a little sheepish about submitting this essay—it obviously doesn't have the gravitas of most of the pieces around it. But of everything I've ever written, this story has made the most lasting impression on me as a writer. It doesn't educate anyone, inform them, motivate them, or make their life easier. But when people read it, they tell me it reminds them of a time and place in their own lives. Even though the details are not the same. There's just a feeling. The story presents something we have in common. It draws us closer.

That makes me optimistic about the future of the personal essay, even in a world that screams for click-bait headlines, "infographics," and seven easy ways to do everything.

Despite all the "best practices," foolproof strategies, and proven tactics, there is still room for a story that isn't trying to make anyone understand or believe or do or buy anything. You can still lead readers down a path without giving everything away in the lead. They will go along with you.

They will go along with you because a personal essay gives readers a moment to escape from tiny screens, busy lives, and the daily deluge of information. A personal essay gives readers a chance to be curious about someone else and to find a way to relate to them. It gives readers—and writers—the gift of human connection. And we will always need more of that.

AFTERWORD
Defeating That Crippling Sense of Inadequacy

Ginger Hervey

For two years, I helped edit and compile this anthology of stories and postscripts by twenty-six talented Missouri School of Journalism graduates, a process that taught me more than I thought I wanted to know about journalism.

Throughout high school, I planned to someday go to law school. Journalism was an afterthought, and attending the University of Missouri was a way to get out of Texas, where I grew up.

Mary Kay Blakely, chief mastermind and unstoppable force behind this anthology, was one of the first people I met in Columbia at the Missouri School of Journalism, when I was chosen to help her with her research. In August 2013 she and I lunched together, and from the corner of an otherwise empty restaurant whose name I have forgotten she painted her plans for this anthology. She told me about all the world-class writers that the journalism school had produced, and how no one knew many of their best stories, much less all of them. Swept up by her passion, I left that lunch with no doubts. It didn't matter that I had no knowledge of long-form journalism and planned to study strategic communications. I was in.

Hours of work and hundreds of emails later, we had compiled shining examples of the best journalism of our day. None of the stories were alike—they varied radically, like the writers who penned them—but they contained adventure and wit, love and loss, and the inviolable truth that is inherent in real storytelling. I admired the writers who could drag me headfirst into someone else's world as convincingly as an omniscient fiction writer.

317

To me the stories seemed polished and untouchable. Reading them, I was an aspiring painter looking at her first Monet and sheepishly realizing she had been using only black and white paint for her entire life. How someone could tell another person's story with such detail and truth, and still be in the realm of nonfiction journalism, was something I had never considered. I reread stories I had written for my high school newspaper and cringed at the work I had once been proud of.

I was in a stage of shy admiration, experiencing Ira Glass's "good taste" gap: I knew great writing when I read it, but trying to create it was as futile as trying to paint Monet's lilies in black and white.

For me this collection did what journalism schools are very good at doing for their students: Forcing them to compare their work with the work of others. Honing good taste and not necessarily showing the process behind the product. Reading great writing is inspiring, but sometimes what it inspires most is a crippling sense of inadequacy. Recognizing this, Mary Kay decided that the anthology needed to help students learn to tell these stories. It needed postscripts.

Of the many learning experiences I had during my two years working on this book, the most valuable was reading the contributors' postscripts, which I found to be funny, informative, and—most significant—humanizing. Reading the postscripts I could reassure myself that even though my high school newspaper articles weren't *New York Times* quality, I could still learn. I hope other readers will be reassured in the same way, that when they doubt themselves they can read these postscripts and see that Doug Meigs writes first drafts so shitty that he has an acronym for them. That Pate McMichael doesn't think he's written a truly great story yet. That Jason Effmann characterizes not just his college years but the four years after them as a time of making "foolish mistakes at a thousand miles an hour."

As this anthology took shape, it went from a coffee-table token of school pride to a textbook that I imagine will be dog-eared, fallen asleep on top of, highlighted, coffee-stained, and tossed haphazardly into backpacks. Some will read and reread it until the cover falls off, and some will shirk and not open it at all. I hope that it will inspire, encourage, and change the way that someone sees journalism. For me it already has.

LAST WORDS

Mary Kay Blakely

Although this book offers twenty-six examples of great writing, I also want to share some great advice from nine other graduates of the Missouri School of Journalism now working nationally as editors, authors, and free-lancers. These nine have experienced just about every stage—and every drama—on the way to becoming successful writers. Below, Tracy Barnett, Matt Davis, Dawn Fallik, Ann Friedman, Kristen Hare, Eve Kidd Craw-ford Peyton, Jessica Royer-Ocken, Mitch Ryals and Robert Skole they share learning experiences, helpful tips and techniques, and anecdotes that may be useful to beginning writers.

"Do you think I should be a writer?" students would ask author Annie Dillard when she visited university campuses on book tours.

"I don't know," she'd reply. "Do you like sentences?" You have to like sentences if you want to be a writer. And paragraphs. And poems, essays, novels, newspapers. You have to *love* reading, she would tell them.

Dawn Fallik, a longtime writer at the *Wall Street Journal* who taught at the University of Delaware, met students who thought they were already great writers before the first day of class. "Overwhelmingly, they were pretty terrible writers," she says. "They haven't read nearly—*nearly*—enough." Writer and photographer Jessica Royer-Ocken discovered that her own writing improved dramatically when she made time to read. "Nothing jolts me out of a rut in my work like reading a fabulous turn of phrase or particularly insightful description. It's not always a matter of emulation but

319

inspiration for sure." Even reading brief quotations from classic works of literature on tea-bag tags can provide inspiration.

It can be ego-crushing to recognize a favorite writer's voice embedded in your own, but that doesn't mean you lack originality and style. More likely it means you've found a writer who uses words and language to do exactly what you're striving to do. Writers who persevere will discover their own voice and style and eventually be grateful for wordsmiths who served as early influences on their work. "Bob Levey at the *Washington Post* taught me how to hear a good quote," Fallik says, and she identifies other writers whose work taught her what she needed to learn: "Anne Lamott is all personal style and humor. Gene Weingarten magically finds ways to write about the human struggle—beauty, dignity, grief—without getting all pompous."

Matt Davis, author of *When Things Get Dark*—a memoir of his Peace Corps years in Mongolia—learned a lot by reading author Peter Hessler, who expertly "reports on an individual to get at larger themes about a country or culture." Davis also studies the elegant narrative reporting of Katherine Boo and novelist Michael Ondaatje, who can "take immense amounts of research and distill it into beautiful prose. Read the sections of Kip, the sapper in *The English Patient*—sheer brilliance."

Longtime journalist Robert Skole says, "Like every reporter of my generation, a tip of the hat to Hemingway." For writers, reading isn't only a pleasant pastime. It's essential for their ongoing education.

Revered writer William Zinsser, author of eighteen books including the classic *On Writing Well*, spoke to a Connecticut conference about writing as a vocation, and he was joined by another speaker, a surgeon who had sold a few magazine stories, who talked about writing as an avocation. Zinsser observed that the surgeon was "dressed in a bright red jacket, looking vaguely bohemian, as authors are supposed to look," and had upbeat answers for every question. The doctor told the audience that writing "was tremendous fun" and "a great way to relieve tensions after a difficult day. The words just flowed. It was easy." Zinsser said his own writing was never easy or fun. "It was hard and lonely, and the words seldom flowed." Each man found the other enormously interesting. It had never occurred to the doctor that writing could be hard. Zinsser never thought it could be easy, and he concluded at the end of the conference: "Maybe I should take up surgery on the side."

I've had identical exchanges with almost every airplane seatmate who's asked me what I do for a living. I no longer admit I'm a published writer, because the reaction is almost always unnerving: "Oh! I'm going to write a book someday too!" I don't believe any of my seatmates were deliberately lying—all of them had important stories they needed to tell. (I've heard many of them at very high altitudes.) But I suspect none of them will actually write a book. Most people think writing is easy until they start doing it. Most of my writer friends don't like to write, either—as they say, they like having written.

If writing is difficult and almost all full-time writers are happiest when it's over, why do people keep doing it? In Virginia Woolf's essay "A Moment of Being," she asserts that her "shock-receiving capacity" is what compelled her to become a writer. Writing, though enormously difficult, was the most reliable way she had to find answers to confounding questions about her personal life as well as her social and political life. "I hazard the explanation that a shock is at once in my case followed by the desire to explain it. I feel that I've had a blow; but it is not, as I thought as a child, simply a blow from an enemy hidden behind the cotton wool of daily life; it is or will become a revelation of some order; it is a token of some real thing behind appearances; and I make it real by putting it into words. It is only by putting it into words that I make it whole; this wholeness means that it has lost its power to hurt me."

Peyton has had similar experiences:

> Writing is how I process the world around me, and even if I don't actually typeset it, I am writing a narrative in my brain pretty much all the time. And the significant events, especially the tragic ones, well, I write about those the most because I need to make sense of them the most. If you met me casually, at a party or a PTA meeting, I wouldn't mention my dead siblings or my miscarriage or my divorce. I would tell you that I was an only child (because I really was raised that way), that I have two incredible

daughters and a terrific stepson (because I do), that my husband is great and my ex-husband and I are friendly (because he is and we are). I wouldn't lie, in other words, but I would give you the easy-listening version of the truth.

Peyton's easy-listening truths become much more powerful and memorable whenever she writes about the not-so-easy truths beneath them.

In a college composition class, she says, "I wrote something about my brother's death, and the professor made a big deal about how good it was, how brave, how honest. As we walked out of the classroom, my biggest rival muttered just loud enough for me to hear, 'Ugh, I wish I had a dead brother.' I felt stung, largely because she was right. Writing about my brother's death was necessary for me; it was therapeutic; but it was also, at times, just so easy. It was rich material, and I just kept going back to the well." Since then, she's become much more discerning about "trotting out my 'dead brother,' and now my dead sister, whenever I need something to write about. I still write about it—because I have to—but I try not to do it in really attenuated ways. Just as gifted actors can take even the smallest roles and make them their own, good writers need to be able to write about the mundane in exciting ways. You make the stories; you don't let the stories make you. I agree with that. I try to live up to it."

Royer-Ocken, who recently added motherhood to her professional work, also believes that despite the difficulties she'll always keep writing. She readily admits that she doesn't love that "blank screen moment when I have a pile of notes and need to make sense of them on a deadline . . . but once I find a way into the story, I feel in control and creative in a way nothing else provides. It's a bit like solving a puzzle or translating a code. I sort through the information I've accumulated, decide what's most relevant, and find a clear, engaging way to present it." She enjoys "making sense of things, imbuing facts with meaning and emotion" and has discovered again and again that writing leads to greater self-awareness: "Sometimes I don't know what I think or feel until I write it down. That's the way I make sense of the world, that's how I find meaning in life, both personally and professionally."

Fallik became a dedicated journalist not only to make sense of the world, but also to satisfy an endless curiosity. "Being a reporter allows me to question authority and talk to people about their lives and see through their eyes," she says. "Once in a while, you get to change a life. As a reporter, you have great power and great responsibility. I like both." Mitch Ryals, another successful journalist, also has a large curiosity but acknowledges, "I've always been an introvert, so meeting new people is a bit nerve-wracking. But I usually end up enjoying the people I meet. Most of the time a source will clarify something in my own life, and that's really cool. Beyond the personal gains, writing about someone is an awesome privilege, and I'm humbled whenever a person who was a complete stranger trusts me enough to tell their story." As longtime journalist Bob Skole described his commitment after nearly half a century: "I write, therefore I am. Old reporters never die, we just write away."

Writing with the intention of publishing is very different from writing in a diary or journal—where, indeed, the words often "just flow." Unedited rivers of prose are often repetitive, narcissistic, and not entirely cogent. It is another kind of work entirely when you are communicating with an audience—even if only a small one. When publication is the goal, it is critically important to read the magazine, newspaper, or website before submitting anything to the editors, not only to learn what issues have already been covered but also to know what they expect. Davis became a successful freelancer after he learned how much treatment of the same topic could vary from publication to publication. "Let's say you're writing a sports story with social dynamic implications. Let's keep it realer and say you're writing about Michael Sam," he says, referring to the gay football player who came out just before the NFL draft in 2013. "The kind of story you would write for *Sports Illustrated* is different from the kind of story you would write for *Harper's* or *Mother Jones* or the *Nation*. They could all be great stories, but different venues require different themes and structures."

Writing a query letter to pitch the story can be as hard—or even harder—than writing the story itself. "Pitching takes far more effort than people realize," Fallik says. "Mostly, my editors want to know who I'll be interviewing, why the story is timely, and whether I have any studies or numbers to back up whatever I'm writing about. They all want to know if I can get it done tomorrow, so I try to finish a lot of reporting before pitching." Skole observes that "there are stories everywhere, and there is always a home for them. There is no such thing as a dull story, only a dull reporter." Because most newspapers and magazines have many talented writers on their staffs, freelancers need to offer insights or points of view not readily available to these publications. It's very difficult to persuade editors that you can write about a topic in a way that no one on the staff could. Perseverance matters, because rejection is ubiquitous. Skole remembers receiving "a polite rejection from an *Esquire* editor who said the story I pitched sounded like one that would put him to sleep. Later I pitched that same editor a story idea he liked." After the story was published, it became one of Skole's favorites.

Ryals says it's also important for freelancers to help their editors with their job. "You can't just say 'I want to write about suicide' or 'the homeless' or 'police brutality.' Do some reporting. Find people who are interesting. . . . give the editor a headline and then expand on the main characters." Ryals knows too that he has little time to impress each editor with his ideas—every editor's desk is piled with manuscripts to read and decisions to make. He allows himself one typed page for each story pitch. Brevity is extremely important but very difficult given how much information the query has to include: who you are as a writer, why you're terrifically qualified to cover this subject, what sources you have access to, when you can turn it in, how long it will be, and how much it will cost. It is hard to do in one page. As Blaise Pascal wrote in a letter to a close friend, dated 4 December 1656: "*Je n'ai fait celle-ci plus longue que parce que je n'ai pas eu le loisir de la faire plus courte.*" ("I would have written a shorter letter, but I didn't have the time.")

All of these writers had different ideas about what turned a good story into a great one, depending largely on the kind of writing they did. Reporters and journalists like Skole defined a great story as one that had an impact. He remembers a story he wrote for *Esquire* in 1969 "that upset a lot of people in Washington"—a high achievement for a journalist then, akin to going viral today. "It resulted in arms merchants and the military sobering up at trade shows, at a time when GIs were getting killed and wounded in Vietnam. The story was headlined, 'At Play with the Military-Industrial Complex.'"

Including numbers and details can add color and significance, Fallik teaches her students. "Did the girl die or did she die ten steps from her front door? The great crime reporter Edna Buchanan always asked police what was in the victim's pockets. The danger here, of course, is going overboard. The details have to matter," she says. "Don't tell us that the next door neighbor's dog panted wearily just because you happened to notice the dog." She says that unnecessary details can make stories "groan under the weight of useless dreckitude. Yes, it's good that you noticed she wore ruby red lipstick that reminded you of Marilyn Monroe in that film you once saw, but why is this important? What does it tell us about her? And why are you in this story at all?"

Royer-Ocken agrees that objectivity sometimes requires writers to remain entirely outside their stories, but in others "being willing to share some of yourself can illuminate your point and connect with readers better than anything else." She strongly prefers clean and simple language, but also thinks "a touch of alliteration can add some fun and refreshment to even the driest stories." It's critical to notice repetitious phrases and words—especially when synonyms do not readily come to mind. Clunky or repetitive language is often the sign of rushed communication: "Collecting weekly garbage, a garbage man has to be wary of sharp objects in garbage bags." Better: "Collecting weekly garbage, sanitation workers have to be wary of sharp objects in trash bags."

Skole learned a great deal about using creative language at his first reporting job at a weekly Boston newspaper "famous for its irreverent, imaginative writing style. The publisher-editor insisted he wrote in pure Dickensian. Bums were gentlemen down on their luck, hookers were ladies of the night, police were untouchable sleuths, bookies were social workers, defense lawyers were champions of justice, and nothing was sacred. By the time Skole moved on to his next job, he could boast, "I never got sued or shot."

While advice from experienced writers can be useful, it is also important to apply it sparingly. Times change, if sometimes imperceptibly. Journalism professor Samir Husni at the University of Mississippi—known sometimes as "Mr. Magazine"—has lectured to magazine staffs from coast to coast and persuaded them to include numbers in cover lines to help to sell magazines, with decades of scholarly studies to prove that it works. But the numbers keep getting bigger and bigger, and the practice is so overdone by now that grabbing readers' attention with "376 Ways to Be Sexy in Bed!"

may in fact be depriving readers of sleep. Husni's studies about cover lines may be valid, but most of the numbered stories inside the magazines now seem like a stretch.

Journalist and travel writer Tracy Barnett says the single most important goal for a writer is to write from the heart, which sounds much easier to say than to do. "To reach that level of clarity, one must truly know one's own heart. Sometimes it takes a long time to get there, but keep trying," she says. "Especially when the truths that emerge are not convenient and take you down a far different path from the one you expected. They might not lead to the professional and public recognition you hope for, but it's important nonetheless to write them. Therein lies one's integrity as a writer." When I began writing a newspaper column in the *Fort Wayne Journal Gazette* in 1976, I was terrified of being perceived as a "man-hater"—as most feminists of the seventies were invariably called.

But as Barnett speculates, the difficult truths I revealed didn't offend readers as the editors assumed they would, being cautious about presenting unwelcome news to the paper's conservative, midwestern audience. Instead, these unspoken realities confirmed readers' own experiences, and many letters to the editor expressed gratitude for validating them. Years later, when Fort Wayne readers followed my byline to the national press, they wrote to ask how in the world I was permitted to address verboten topics like pay discrimination and sexual harassment in monthly women's magazines, which aggressively avoided controversy to court more advertisers. I could honestly reply: "Reader mail saves me every month." Turns out, readers' opinions mattered more than money.

As Fallik reminds her students, "Being a writer requires an odd balance of massive ego and great humility." You need to believe you have "asked the right questions and reflected others accurately." But you must also bravely or foolishly "put your voice, your words, and your reporting out there for others to slash and burn." You need to be both brave and humble, because half the time, if not more, you're not as good as you think you are. "If you finish something and think 'that's perfect' and prance on, all happy, that's not writing. It's probably the drugs talking. The truth is that nothing will ever be good enough. It can always use tweaking and editing and rewriting," Fallik says. "If you forget that, don't worry. That's why editors exist. They will dash your darlings and insert semicolons even though you hate semicolons. There will be sobbing over your lost paragraphs. Hence the ego aspect must arise again so you don't crumble into a small heap of despair and a bucket of mashed potatoes. Or vodka. Your choice." (Fallik doesn't recommend vodka or other mind-altering substances. Neither do I. It's much easier to revive flattened egos after consuming those buckets of mashed potatoes.)

Tedious though it may be, the critical need for rewriting cannot be underestimated. For Ryals, "rewriting is the most painful but most necessary step of the whole process. Sometimes I would rather stick my head in a toilet than reread a draft I've just written, but I have found it has immensely improved the clarity of my writing. I try to set a personal deadline one or two days before the editor's deadline for a first draft, so I can rewrite before I send it in." Davis thinks revision is "the most important part of writing. It's a rare case when you write well on a first shot. You're lucky if you get that three times in a career." It usually takes him several rewrites before he turns anything in to an editor. "At that stage, it becomes collaborative. But if you're looking for an editor or a publication to help you with your rewrites, you've lost."

Zinsser not only rewrote over and over, he often rewrote "what I had just rewritten." His Connecticut conference co-panelist said he never rewrote, and advised the audience to "let it all hang out." Whenever the hobby writer had trouble, he put it aside until it got easier, which it invariably did. When Zinsser had trouble, he did what every professional writer has to do: he stuck to his schedule, stayed in his chair, and slogged through it.

Whenever my students got stuck on an assignment (like almost every writer does), it wasn't usually helpful to be sympathetic and grant an extension. They'd invariably get stuck again. They needed to find their own unique way of resolving it. These routine stoppages are called "writer's block," but the problem is rarely that writers have forgotten how to write. The problem is usually that they haven't finished the necessary thinking before the writing begins. They still have decisions to make about structure, themes, audience, content, voice, and style—that is, they don't yet know what kind of skeleton to build that will hold all their words and keep their ideas functioning together.

It's sometimes possible to avoid writer's block by owning your eccentricities and satisfying them in advance. If you believe you can only write a first draft with a number 2 lead pencil, then have plenty of them sharpened and in your desk drawer. If you can't compose when you see dust on the floor, apply the mop before you sit down. It may well be that you need to sharpen some pencils or vacuum a rug to finish thinking about what you're trying to write.

When that fails, seasoned writers often invent odd ways to get back in the saddle and start making progress again. Ann Friedman—former editor of *Good* magazine who now writes a highly successful blog, the *Ann Friedman Weekly*—says, "When I'm feeling uninspired but a deadline demands that I start producing words, I do a thing that I call 'busy fingers.' I set a 10-minute timer and make myself type continually for ten minutes. It's pretty rocky at first. But by the end of the ten minutes, I'm usually out of my wasting-time-on-the-Internet mode and into a writing mode."

A few decades ago, I was seriously stuck on a deadline for editor Julia Kagan at *Working Woman* magazine, who advised me to try "bicycling downhill." What? "Just start retyping what you've already written and when you get to the end of your last page, just keep typing." She introduced me to what I now think of as "the momentum theory of composition." Retyping what I'd already written was hardly exacting, but it did put me in the frame of mind I'd been in before I stopped and got stuck. By the time I reached the last sentence, I had the next thought it was leading to and could continue. Bicycling downhill didn't always work, but it sure did sometimes. Another editor suggested I lacked confidence in my own thinking and flatly told me to "stop quoting so many 'experts' and just make your point. What do *you* think?" (You mean I can think too? And what *do* I think, anyway? Whoa. That was a new one.)

Barnett, along with other writers I've talked with about writer's block, believes that separating yourself from your computer can help. "Go for a hike, water the garden, plant some seeds, take a yoga break, play your guitar. Even a nap can help—anything to open a new track in your mind so that you can start fresh from a different angle." Barnett suggests teaming up "with a fellow writer to jump-start your thinking, share updates and reports. Writing is such a lonely enterprise, it's necessary sometimes to have someone who understands, who can hear your agony and reflect back the reality that you *will* get through this, you *will* write the piece, and it *will* be good."

"The important thing to remember is you're not a writer if you don't write," says Friedman, who's coached many writers through difficult assignments when she was editor at *Good*.

> Make yourself just start doing it. Block it out the way you block out, say, time to exercise. If you want to write for consumer magazines and websites, you're going to have to have lots of great ideas. So give yourself a challenge: Write 500 words every day. Could be about an issue in your life, something you and your friends keep talking about. Something you read in the news that made you angry or whatever. It might help keep you accountable if you put your writing up on a personal website . . . or a tumblr blog. The great thing about being a writer in the modern era is that you don't need anyone's permission to publish. You can put your work into the world whenever, and however, you want.

A main worry of one of my journalism students was whether she could write full time and still have a life. Before my students had family responsibilities they were already distressed about compromising either their loved ones or the quality of their writing. Of course, it's true: the way both families and jobs are presently structured, it's nearly impossible to do both without feeling compromised. But what's the alternative? I remember the struggles of being a full-time writer and single mother. Since I worked mainly at home, I congratulated myself for being mostly *there* for my two young sons, even though my office door was closed most of the time. They knew not to disturb me when the door was closed, "except for emergencies." I instructed them many times on the meaning of "emergency"—which is very different for a six-year-old needing a treat and a writer working on deadline: "'Can I have a Popsicle, Mom?' isn't an emergency, even though it might feel like one. Emergencies require a show of blood."

As my sons were entering double digits, I was leaving notes on the bathroom mirror to keep them abreast of domestic conditions. I still thought of myself as a good mother because we had a lot of quality time, if often at weird hours, until I heard a friend of my youngest son read one of my notes on the bathroom mirror and ask, "'Deadline Day'—what does *that* mean?" Darren replied flatly, "It means be quiet or die." So much for "good mother."

My backward-looking notion these days is that you *can't* be much of a writer unless you also have a life, staying connected to other people, family, and social and political issues—which we care about so deeply because every social issue affects somebody we love, no?

"It's okay to live your life," says journalist Kristen Hare, a reporter for the Poynter Institute and former Peace Corps volunteer who has wrestled with this dilemma for almost two decades. After graduating from the Missouri School of Journalism, she says,

> someone asked me why I was joining the Peace Corps instead of going straight into a newsroom. My answer then: I want to have some stories of my own before I spend the rest of my life telling other people's. Fifteen years later, I think that was pretty naive. Of course I've continued having my own stories, and I think each of them has made me a better journalist. Each experience— living in another country, being a minority, marrying someone from another culture, becoming a mother, watching a parent die, moving across the country—has given me more ways to connect with people and, I hope, tell better stories.

Fallik says her best advice to beginning writers is to consider accounting instead: "It's way safer, offers better hours and money, and you can still wear the cardigans with the elbow patches. If you must write, prepare yourself for many, many first dates in which the other person will tell you 'I always thought of myself as a writer.' Try not to stab them. Because if they were a writer, they would write. You have no other choice."

Of course, you do have other choices. Lots of them. But if you do continue writing, full or part time, you will become accustomed to that "shock-receiving capacity." You will perhaps even welcome it, because it ignites the need to know what and why and how the world works—or doesn't work.

Ignorance is no longer bliss, if it ever was. While writing is certainly frustrating at times, especially when you've landed in a thorny patch of more questions than answers, I know of no greater human satisfaction than the peace that comes with understanding. And the incomparable joy of having written.

To learn more about the writers interviewed for
"Last Words," see "Contributor Biographies."

CONTRIBUTOR BIOGRAPHIES

Bryan Burrough is a special correspondent at *Vanity Fair* magazine and has written six books, including the number-one *New York Times* bestseller *Barbarians at the Gate*. A three-time winner of the Gerald Loeb Award for Excellence in Financial Journalism, his reporting has taken him all over the world from Hollywood to Moscow. The Temple, Texas, native graduated from the University of Missouri School of Journalism in 1983, when he became a reporter for the *Wall Street Journal*. Since 1992 he has been a contributor to *Vanity Fair*. His latest book, *Days of Rage*, details the 1970s battles between homegrown revolutionary terrorists and the FBI.

Melanie Coffee knew when she was still in high school that she wanted to be a journalist. She saw it as her way to give a voice to the voiceless. After graduating from the University of Missouri in 1999, she started working for the Associated Press as a reporter in Missouri and Kansas. She later moved to Chicago, where she was an AP reporter and then editor who shaped many of the nation's biggest news stories. After having two energetic sons, she left the AP for the flexibility of working as a freelance journalist. While freelancing for publications such as *Crain's Chicago Business*, she also was the web editor for the *Chicago Reporter*, an investigative magazine. She now lives in Portland, Oregon, has an award-winning blog (*She's Write*), and is a regular contributor to the *Huffington Post*. She's still passionate about meeting people who have overcome tremendous challenges and sharing their stories.

After obtaining his degree in international affairs from the Paris Institute of Political Studies, **Kevin Dubouis** moved to America's heartland to learn how to conduct interviews, write, and report. In 2013 he moved to Mumbai, India, and wrote for *Daily News and Analysis*, one of India's largest English-language newspapers. By the time he earned his master's degree in international reporting in 2014, he discovered the power of storytelling and got hooked on journalism. Persuaded that stories can change minds and capture hearts, he wants to travel the world and find the unheard voices. He joined the international news network Al Jazeera in January 2014.

After graduating from the University of Missouri's School of Journalism in 1998, **Jason Effmann** spent four years writing at now-defunct newspapers and magazines in Chicago before packing up for a copywriting job at a company in the Pacific Northwest. Effmann now lives in Portland, Oregon, with his wife, Heidi, and their four kids. He is busy working on a memoir about love and step-parenting, because what the world really needs right now is another memoir. The editors of this anthology told him he could fill the remainder of this space however he likes, so here's a list of things he's afraid of: Heights. Depths. Slippery slopes. Total eclipses of the heart. Any animal with eight or more legs. Russian nesting dolls. Raccoons. Romantic comedies. Pizzas featuring seafood as a topping. Middle school band concerts. Conclusions.

Shane Epping received a camera at his high school graduation and a set of golf clubs when he graduated from college at the University of Chicago in 1995. He still owns both gifts but only uses the former. After earning a master's degree from Washington University in St. Louis, he continued his career as a high school teacher and wrestling coach. A passion for photography and writing led him to the University of Missouri, where he earned a second master's in 2008. He ended up staying at Mizzou, where he has worked as a photographer, writer, and adjunct faculty member for seven years. His photos have been published by ESPN/ABC, CBS Sports, AP, Fox Sports, Huffington Post, NFL.com, NBC Nightly News, and *Runner's World*.

Ken Fuson began working in newspapers when he was a sophomore in high school, covering sports for the *Woodward (Iowa) Enterprise*. Set to enter the University of Iowa, his high school journalism teacher said, "Why don't you go to the University of Missouri? It's the best journalism school in the country," a claim he confirmed between 1974 and 1978. Funny story about graduating: he didn't, skipping finals to cover a speech for the *Columbia Daily Tribune*, where he began his professional career. He's still waiting for an honorary degree. In the meantime, he worked twenty-four years at the *Des Moines Register* and three years at the *Baltimore Sun*, winning the ASNE Distinguished Writing Award, Ernie Pyle feature-writing award, Penney-Missouri Award, National Headliner Award, and several Distinguished Achievement in Writing awards in the annual Best of Gannett contest. He left newspapers in 2008 and now works in the marketing department at Simpson College in Indianola, Iowa. Simpson doesn't show much inclination to award him an honorary degree either.

Jessi Hamilton graduated from the Missouri School of Journalism in 2002. She spent several years not selling out until she broke on through to the other side to become an advertising copywriter. Since then she's won numerous awards, learned finally to drink free beer, and has fine-tuned the art of practicing comedic timing on unsuspecting suits. Her clients include Burger King, Sonic, Trump Hotels, Taylor Guitars, and Asics. Jessi currently lives in San Diego, where she is a senior copywriter. Her creative outlet is from-the-gut storytelling in the form of poetry and personal essays that make her mom cry.

Walt Harrington was a longtime staff writer for the *Washington Post Magazine*, where he wrote numerous benchmark profiles of notables such as George H. W. Bush, Jesse Jackson, Jerry Falwell, and Carl Bernstein, as well as scores of in-depth stories on ordinary people. His work has won numerous journalism awards. His book *The Everlasting Stream: A True Story of Rabbits, Guns, Friendship, and Family* became an Emmy-winning PBS documentary film. His book *Crossings: A White Man's Journey into Black America* won the Gustavus Myers Award for the Study of Human Rights in the United States and was declared a "vital" book on race in America by the *New York Times*. He is the author or editor of seven other nonfiction books, including *Acts of Creation*, *Next Wave*, *American Profiles*, *At the Heart of It*, *The Beholder's Eye*, and *Intimate Journalism*. He holds master's degrees in sociology and journalism from the University of Missouri and is a journalism professor at the University of Illinois at Urbana-Champaign, where he teaches literary feature writing. His website is waltharrington.com.

Justin Heckert, a 2002 graduate of the Missouri Journalism School, is a native of Cape Girardeau, Missouri, and now lives and writes in Indianapolis. His first job in journalism was at *Atlanta* magazine, writing long-form stories about the people and issues of Georgia, including its LGBT community, participation in the national spelling bee, the science of neuromarketing at Emory University, and the making of an Adult Swim show on Cartoon Network. Heckert was twice named writer of the year by the City and Regional Magazine Association. He was hired in 2005 by *ESPN* magazine, where (among other stories) he wrote about a famous NFL player, tracked down a Pittsburgh Steelers imposter, lifted one thousand pounds with the help of a Russian weight trainer, rediscovered an abandoned racetrack buried beneath the biggest lake in Georgia, and went to the Egg Bowl with a homeless poet named Chico in Oxford, Mississippi. Heckert has also written for *Esquire, Grantland*, the *New York Times Magazine, Sports Illustrated, Men's Journal*, the *Oxford American*, and *Indianapolis Monthly*, among others. His story about a father and son swept out into the ocean was recently anthologized in the collection *Next Wave: America's New Generation of Great Literary Journalists*.

Jane Gordon Julien is an award-winning storyteller who is a regular contributor to the Sunday Styles section of the *New York Times*, where her work on the popular "Vows" and "State of the Unions" features has won acclaim. She has also written for the paper's Metropolitan, Education, and Business sections, the Associated Press and NBC/Today, and numerous publications in Connecticut, including the state's largest newspaper, the *Hartford Courant*, where she was a writer and editor for many years. After graduating from the University of Missouri School of Journalism she began her career writing for the *Independence Examiner* in Harry Truman's hometown of Independence, Missouri, before becoming the first female editor ever to work on the Metropolitan Desk at the *Birmingham Post-Herald* in Alabama. She has served as an adjunct lecturer in journalism at the University of Alabama-Birmingham and has been a guest lecturer at the University of Connecticut. She lives in Glastonbury, Connecticut, with her husband, Andrew Julien, the editor of the *Hartford Courant*, and their four children.

Robert Langellier graduated from the University of Missouri studying French and journalism in 2014. He's never had a real internship or job in media, but surely he will soon. He has freelanced for the *Kansas City Star* on invasive beetles, for *Belt Magazine* on a city's relationship with its slumlords, and for *Vox Magazine* on hitchhiking. Most recently he took a year-long journey on the road as a long-haul trucker. That story is still in editing, but at least his student debts are paid. At publication, he will be living in temporary housing.

Besa Luci is the cofounder and editor-in-chief of *Kosovo 2.0*, an independent media endeavor that engages society in insightful debate through its multimedia website, print magazine, and public debate events. Besa began her journalism studies at the American University in Bulgaria (2002–2006), and in her senior year became chief editor and reinvented the university's only print magazine, *Verve*. She continued her studies at Mizzou, graduating with a master's degree in 2008. During her time in the United States, she was an editorial intern for *Gotham Gazette*, *Women's eNews*, and *New York* magazine. Upon her return to Kosovo in 2008, Besa worked as a policy researcher for such acclaimed think tanks as the Foreign Policy Club and Youth Initiative for Human Rights. Critical of media practices in the western Balkans, Besa launched the *Kosovo 2.0*, which to date is the only media venue in the western Balkans that operates in three languages: English, Albanian, and Serbian. *Kosovo 2.0* gathers around one hundred thousand readers a year and provokes and challenges public debate through its biannual themed print magazine, examining topics such as corruption, religion, sex, public space, and migration.

Sean McLachlan worked for many years as an archaeologist on excavations in the Middle East, Europe, and the United States. Turning to writing full time after getting a master's degree in journalism from Mizzou in 2005, he specializes in history and travel. For his travel writing, he focuses on historical destinations and adventure travel. The piece published here won the Gold Award in the Personal Comment category in the 2013 Lowell

Thomas Travel Journalism Awards. He is also the author of *A Fine Likeness*, a historical novel set in Civil War Missouri, as well as several other works of fiction. Sean spends much of his time on the road, researching and writing. He has traveled to more than thirty countries, interviewing nomads in Somaliland, climbing to cliff-top monasteries in Ethiopia, studying Crusader castles in Syria, and exploring caves in his favorite state, Missouri. He can be found online at midlistwriter.blogspot.com.

Pate McMichael ran out of money. Sadly for him, that meant graduating from Mizzou in 2005—way too early. His narrative journalism has been published in award-winning magazines like *Atlanta* and *St. Louis*, as well as national websites like Zocalo. In 2008, Pate was named a finalist for the Livingston Awards for Young Journalists. His first book, a narrative examination of the King assassination, is currently under contract with the Chicago Review Press. At Georgia College, a public liberal arts university, he teaches journalism and media law at the rank of senior lecturer.

Mary McNamara is a television critic and senior culture editor for the *Los Angeles Times*. A Pulitzer Prize winner in 2015 and two-time Pulitzer Prize finalist for criticism (2013, 2014), she has won various awards for criticism and feature writing. She is the author of the Hollywood mysteries *Oscar Season* and *The Starlet* (Simon and Schuster.) She lives in La Crescenta with her husband, three children, two dogs, and a hamster named Toastie. You can follow her on Twitter: @MarymacTV.

Doug Meigs has dived with sharks for the *Wall Street Journal*, collected wild mushrooms in China's Yunnan Province for CNN, profiled fishers recovering from the Tōhoku earthquake for Japanese broadcaster NHK, and investigated woolly mammoth ivory dealers for *China Daily*. The native Nebraskan has worked stints at the *Omaha World-Herald*, graduated from the Missouri School of Journalism in 2007, and received the school's O. O. McIntyre Postgraduate Writing Fellowship. He recently returned to Omaha after five years working in Asia.

Simina Mistreanu, Missouri School of Journalism 2013 master's recipient, loves narrative journalism so much that she moved from Romania to the United States to learn more about it. While on this continent, she has been published in the *Columbia Missourian*, the *Wichita Eagle*, and the *Oregonian*, where she has covered everything from breaking news to local politics. The story about the West Plains girls remains one of the most important to her because it offered her the opportunity to help readers meet and understand a group of people who merited their attention but might have been brushed off because of their age and their behavior. Plus, one of Simina's favorite people in the world, Jacqui Banaszynski, edited it.

Sona Pai is editorial director at AHA!, a strategic communications agency just outside of Portland, Oregon. Her work has been published in the anthologies *Best Food Writing 2008* and *Waking up American: Coming of Age Biculturally*, and publications including *Culinate, Oregon Humanities*, and *MIZZOU*. An earlier version of this essay was published in the 2007 volume of *Praxis*, AHA!'s annual publication of employees' creative work. Sona graduated from the Missouri School of Journalism in 1999 with a bachelor's degree in magazine journalism. She has a master's degree in literary nonfiction writing from the University of Oregon School of Journalism and Communication.

A first-generation Chinese born and raised in Panama, **Suan Pineda** has left the mellow Central American Pacific coast for a series of landlocked places: Columbia, Missouri; Madrid; San Antonio, and Salt Lake City. Her work has appeared in magazines in Latin America, *The World and I* and *In the Fray* magazines, and the *Salt Lake Tribune*. She received a bachelor's degree in journalism in 2004 from the University of Missouri and holds a master's degree in Spanish literature from the University of Utah. She is the cofounder and editor-in-chief of the translingual cultural magazine *Entremares*. She currently works as an editor for CNET in San Francisco.

Lois Raimondo got hooked on journalism translating for CBS News during President Reagan's 1984 trip to China. At the time, she was living in a small Chinese village and riding a Flying Pigeon bicycle through the countryside, collecting folktales for a master's project in comparative literature. As the presidential trip concluded, a CBS editor (and Moberly, Missouri native) suggested she pursue her passion for story from the street by doing journalism—starting with study at the University of Missouri. Completing that degree in 1988, Raimondo immediately took off for Tibet under martial law and stayed in Asia for ten years, reporting primarily for magazines in China, India, Vietnam, and Thailand. Eventually returning to the United States, she joined the *Washington Post* for ten years and turned her attention to conflict in the Middle East. Her front-line reporting from the war in Afghanistan was recognized with the Edward Weintal Prize for Diplomatic Reporting. She is currently writing a set of essays based on her time living between the lines in Asia. In 2005, Raimondo was a recipient of the Alicia Patterson Journalism Fellowship. She spent the fellowship year in Pakistan working on stories related to women's jails and the rise of Islamic fundamentalism.

Randall Roberts is an award-winning writer and journalist and currently the pop music critic for the *Los Angeles Times*. Over his career he's floated the Mississippi River in a working towboat to better understand the country's barge industry, traveled to Myanmar to report on the U.S. State Department's work at cultural outreach, competed in a demolition derby, covered the ascent of Midwest hip-hop, and documented the rise of EDM culture in Southern California. He's interviewed Brian Eno, Mick Jagger, PJ Harvey, Outkast, Trent Reznor, Elton John, Earl Sweatshirt, and many others. Before becoming an *LA Times* critic, he was the newspaper's pop music editor, a role he has also served for *LA Weekly* and for the *Riverfront Times* in St. Louis. At Mizzou, before graduating in 1988, Roberts prepared for his future by taking writing, folklore, and filmmaking classes and working as program director at 88.1 FM KCOU, doorman at the Blue Note, and vinyl slinger at Streetside Records. Follow him on Twitter: @liledit.

Robert Sanchez is the senior staff writer for *5280* magazine, in Denver. A former staff writer for the Associated Press, *Denver Post*, *Philadelphia Inquirer* and *Rocky Mountain News*, Sanchez is a four-time finalist for the City and Regional Magazine Association's writer-of-the-year award and a three-time finalist for the Livingston Awards for Young Journalists. His work has been anthologized twice in the Best American Sports Writing series, and one of his stories is included in *Next Wave: America's New Generation of Great Literary Journalists*. He often contributes stories to *ESPN* magazine and has been published in *Esquire*. Sanchez graduated with honors from the University of Missouri School of Journalism in 1999 with an emphasis on news-editorial. He is married to his high school sweetheart, Kristen. The two have a daughter, Alexandra, and a son, Michael.

Sara Shahriari is a print and radio journalist based in Bolivia. Her reporting often focuses on social justice, politics, and the environment, and her stories are regularly published in the *Christian Science Monitor* and the *Guardian*, among others. Sara holds a BA from the University of Pennsylvania and an MA from the Missouri School of Journalism (2009). Before beginning her career as a journalist Sara worked in legal aid, wrote for magazines for children, and taught English in the Marshall Islands and Ecuador. In her free time Sara hikes the Andes, horseback rides, and lounges on the sofa watching all sorts of unremarkable television.

Mississippi native **Wright Thompson** began writing about sports at the University of Missouri while working as a sports columnist for the *Columbia Missourian*. From there he moved to the *Times-Picayune* in New Orleans, where he became the LSU beat writer, and the *Kansas City Star*. In 2006 he became a staff writer for ESPN and *ESPN* magazine. His "Ghosts of Mississippi" article about the 1962 football team's perfect season and the violent reactions to integration that followed became a *30 for 30* series documentary film. He continues writing for ESPN on everything from football and soccer to auto racing and cricket.

In 2007 **Michaella A. Thornton** returned to Henderson, North Carolina, to see many of her former students graduate from high school. Her experiences teaching and living in the rural South changed her life's work and deepened her understanding of social inequalities and the challenges inherent in short-term educational reform. Michaella has served as a nonfiction editor of the *Sonora Review*, and her writing has appeared in *Creative Nonfiction, Kairos: A Journal of Rhetoric, Technology, and Pedagogy*, National Public Radio, *Sauce Magazine, Tucson Weekly*, and elsewhere. She graduated from the Missouri School of Journalism in 2000, received an O. O. McIntyre Fellowship upon graduation, and gained her MFA in creative nonfiction from the University of Arizona (2006). As the first woman in her family to earn an advanced degree (and as a second-generation college graduate), she is committed to empowering the students she teaches at St. Louis Community College to find their voices and stories.

Seth Wickersham is a senior writer at *ESPN The Magazine*, where he's written since graduating from the University of Missouri in 2000. Although he primarily covers the NFL—profiling the likes of Peyton and Eli Manning, Tom Brady, and Michael Vick, and co-authoring a much-discussed investigative piece about the relationship between Roger Goodell and the Patriots—Wickersham has also written about gay rugby, the plight of a fired college basketball coach, suicidal Kenyan runners in Alaska, and racehorse euthanasia. He also suffered the laborious task of traveling to London to interview legendary Queen guitarist Brian May about "We Will Rock You," the most-played stadium anthem ever. Wickersham's work has been anthologized in *The Best American Sportswriting* and in *Next Wave: America's New Generation of Great Literary Journalists*, and he's won several awards from the Pro Football Writers Association. He's part of a staff at ESPN that twice won the National Magazine Award for General Excellence. Born in Boulder, Colorado, raised in Anchorage, Alaska, and currently living in West Hartford, Connecticut, Wickersham enjoys heli-skiing, Springsteen concerts, guitars, Moose's Tooth pizza, and hanging out with his wife, Alison Overholt, and daughter, Maddie.

Writers Interviewed for "Last Words"

Tracy L. Barnett began her writing career at thirteen with the creation of a children's magazine for her many siblings and neighbor children. She dreamed of becoming a novelist but finding herself at twenty-one the divorced mother of a small daughter realized she'd have to find a quicker way to put food on the table—hence journalism. She has written and edited for newspapers in Missouri, California, Illinois, and Texas, taught at MU for eleven years, cofounded two Spanish-language newspaper initiatives, and served as travel editor for the *San Antonio Express-News* and the *Houston Chronicle*, where she won various awards from all three major travel writing associations, including a couple of Lowell Thomases. In 2010 she backpacked through Latin America collecting stories on innovative environmental initiatives. She currently lives near Guadalajara, Mexico, freelancing for various publications, and is working on a book about her journey.

Matthew Davis graduated from Missouri in December 1999. Six months after graduation, he moved to Mongolia as a Peace Corps volunteer. His time there inspired his first book, *When Things Get Dark: A Mongolian Winter's Tale,* published in 2010 by St. Martin's Press. He holds an MFA in nonfiction writing from the University of Iowa and an MA in International Relations from The Johns Hopkins School of Advanced International Studies. He was a Fulbright Fellow to Syria and Jordan during 2010–2011 and is currently a Tom and Mary Gallagher Fellow at the Black Mountain Institute at the University of Nevada, Las Vegas, where he is completing a novel. His work has won many awards, including ones from the *Atlantic, The Best American Travel Writing,* and Peace Corps Writers. He is forever grateful to Mizzou for giving him the tools and confidence to pursue his dream of becoming a writer.

Dawn Fallik became a journalist because she was failing Japanese at the University of Wisconsin—Madison. She discovered she could hang out with the Indigo Girls if she wrote for the paper. She bullied/begged her way onto the *Troy (N.Y.) Record.* After a series about non-bid asbestos work at the schools, the owner of the asbestos company took out thirteen neon-yellow billboards saying she was fat and her editor was a dog. It was the best day ever. After five years at the Associated Press, she got her M.A. at Mizzou specializing in computer-assisted reporting. She then moved to *the St. Louis Post-Dispatch* and then the *Philadelphia Inquirer* as a medical reporter. She joined the faculty of the University of Delaware in 2007. Students describe her as a "life-changing motivational force" or say that if "she was dying of thirst in the street I wouldn't spit in her mouth." She continues to write for the *Wall Street Journal,* the *New Republic,* and *Neurology Today.*

Ann Friedman is a columnist for *New York* magazine's website and for the *Columbia Journalism Review.* She also makes pie charts for the *Hairpin* and *Los Angeles* magazine. Her work appears in *ELLE, Esquire, Newsweek,* the

Observer, the *Washington Post,* the *Los Angeles Times,* and many other outlets. She lives in Los Angeles, where she is a writer, editor, and speaker for hire. Read her work at www.annfriedman.com.

Kristen Hare hoped to write for magazines after college, but after a semester at the *Missourian,* she swerved happily into newspapers. Hare graduated from MU in 2000. She left one month later for Guyana, South America, where she spent two years in the Peace Corps, fell for a young man in her village, and taught sex ed to wide-eyed high schoolers. After returning to the U.S., she married Jailall, the young man from her village. Hare spent five years as a features writer and assistant features editor at the *St. Joseph News-Press* in St. Joseph, Missouri, and five years as a staff writer for the *St. Louis Beacon* in St. Louis, Missouri. She's currently a media reporter for the Poynter Institute for Media Studies in St. Petersburg, Florida, and the author of the book *100 Things to Do in Tampa Bay Before You Die.* She's also the mom of Max and Leela, seven and three, who think her job is pretty cool because she gets to talk to strangers.

Jessica Royer Ocken enjoyed an array of unpaid internships before landing in journalism school. She completed a masters degree in magazine journalism at MU in 1999, and her first full-time employment in the field— as a staff writer with Sun Publications in Chicago's suburbs—lasted six months. She left to write for CITY 2000, a documentary project about Chicago at the turn of the millennium. Since this taste of collaboration, she's worked almost entirely as a freelancer: writing, editing, and contributing to projects on subjects from technology to teenagers, fashion to fine arts, and healthcare to popular culture. Her work has been published in *The Court That Tamed the West* (2013), *McDonald's @ 50* (2005), and *Fantasy Girls: Navigating the New Universe of Science Fiction and Fantasy Television* (2000), as well as the *Chicago Tribune* and *Tribune Magazine,* and through the syndication services of Content That Works. She has also collaborated on a wonderful family and very happy life with photographer Chris Ocken.

Eve Kidd Crawford Peyton, B.J. '02, M.A. '04, grew up in New Orleans, lived in the Midwest for a decade, and returned home in 2008. She served as the editor/managing editor of New Orleans Homes & Lifestyles, Louisiana

Life, Acadiana Profile, and Gulf Coast Wine + Dine magazines from 2008 until 2013 when she accepted the position of director of editorial services at Loyola University New Orleans. She has won awards from the Press Club of New Orleans and the Society of Professional Journalists. Her blog, "Joie d'Eve," runs every Friday on MyNewOrleans.com and is excerpted monthly in *New Orleans Magazine*. She lives with her husband, Robert, her two daughters, Ruby and Georgia, and her stepson, Elliot, in a house she would like to characterize as "charmingly messy." She loves grammar, lunchtime cocktails, oversharing on Facebook, and Southern Gothic chaos; she is active in the PTA of her older daughter's school, which is a sentence she never thought she'd type; and she is especially proud of her semicolon tattoo and the elaborate baked goods she sends to school bake sales.

Mitch Ryals graduated with degrees in journalism and English in 2012 and a master's degree from MU in 2014. His work has appeared in *Vox* magazine, the *Columbia Missourian* and *Inside Columbia* magazine. His curiosity of different people and places found an outlet on MU's diversity website as he is currently writing about diverse students and faculty at Mizzou. On days when long-held literary aspirations seem unattainable, Ray Bradbury provides inspiration. In bouts of extreme writer's block, he'll ride his bike or whack the crap out of some golf balls. His favorite Ninja Turtle is Leonardo, and he prefers newspapers and paperbacks to tablets and e-books.

Robert Skole began his journalism career at age eighteen, editing the "8th Cavalry Regiment" newsletter in Tokyo after World War II. After receiving a BJ at MU in 1952, he worked as a reporter and editor in Boston, Florida, The Bahamas, Tokyo, and Washington. For some twenty-five years, he was chief correspondent in Stockholm for McGraw-Hill World News, reporting for *Business Week* and McGraw-Hill trade magazines. He has written or edited a dozen books published in Stockholm, mainly about Swedish business. Among his books published in America and coauthored with Paul Dickson are *The Volvo Guide to Halls of Fame* and *Journalese—A Dictionary for Deciphering the News* (2013). His only novel is *Jumpin' Jimminy—A World War II Baseball Saga—American Flyboys and Japanese Submariners Battle It Out in a Swedish World Series*. He and wife Monika live in Boston and Stockholm.